GLOBAL GOVERNANCE AND BIOPOLITICS

Regulating human security

David Roberts

D1570674

Zed Books

LONDON | NEW YORK

Global Governance and Biopolitics: Regulating Human Security was first published in 2010 by Zed Books Ltd, 7 Cynthia Street, London N1 9JF, UK and Room 400, 175 Fifth Avenue, New York, NY 10010, USA

www.zedbooks.co.uk

Set in Monotype Plantin and Gill Sans by Ewan Smith, London
Cover designed by View Design Studio
Printed and bound in Great Britain by the MPG Books Group

Distributed in the USA exclusively by Palgrave Macmillan, a division of St Martin's Press, LLC, 175 Fifth Avenue, New York, NY 10010, USA

A catalogue record for this book is available from the British Library
Library of Congress Cataloguing in Publication Data available

ISBN 978 1 84813 216 0 hb
ISBN 978 1 84813 217 7 pb
ISBN 978 1 84813 218 4 eb

ABOUT THE AUTHOR

David Roberts is senior lecturer in international politics at the University of Ulster. He is the convenor and chair of the British International Studies Association Human Security Working Group, external examiner with the Royal University of Phnom Penh and the University of Coventry, and visiting research fellow at the Centre for Governance and International Affairs, University of Bristol. He has published a previous monograph on human insecurity (Zed Books 2008) and another on post-conflict democratization in Cambodia, and in 2010 will publish a monograph critiquing liberal peacebuilding in developing societies. He has published more than thirty other chapters and articles in peer-reviewed outlets on human security and peacebuilding.

CONTENTS

TABLE AND FIGURES

ACKNOWLEDGEMENTS

I am indebted to many people who have contributed in many different ways to this work, providing intellectual guidance and personal support in abundance. I would like specifically to thank Alessandra Asteriti, David Chandler, Ryerson Christie, Gustavo Fernandez (MD), Chris Gilligan (again), Sir Richard Jolly, Robin Luckham, Emma McClean, Malcolm McIntosh, Kerstin Mechlem, Lilian Moncrieff, Rachel Naylor, Jack Piachaud, Graham Shaw, Mark Shevlin, Anne Smith and Nadine Voelkner, all of whom contributed, sometimes knowingly and sometimes unwittingly, to the completion of this work. Many others have contributed over a much longer period of time to the ideas and beliefs that underpin this work, few more than Stephen Riley.

The inevitable mistakes are all my own.

ABBREVIATIONS

BMA	British Medical Association
CBO	community-based organization
CSP	common social patronage
DfID	Department for International Development (UK)
FoI	Freedom of Information Act
IFI	international financial institution
IMF	International Monetary Fund
IPE	international political economy
IR	international relations
LIP	Local Initiatives Projects
MSC	most significant change
NGO	non-governmental organization
PRSP	Poverty Reduction Strategy Papers
PWC	Post-Washington Consensus
RBM	Roll Back Malaria
TNC	transnational corporation
U5MR	under-five mortality rate
UN	United Nations
UNDAF	United Nations Development Assistance Framework
UNDP	United Nations Development Programme
UNRISD	United Nations Research Institute for Social Development
WB	World Bank
WHO	World Health Organization
WTO	World Trade Organization

'The universe is change; our life is what our thoughts make it'. Marcus Aurelius

'Anything one man can imagine, other men can make real'. Jules Verne

For Karen and Emma,
my sister and my amazing niece;
for Squadron Leader Norman Rose (ret'd),
who had faith in me long before I did;
and for 'Ripley', who saved the day.

INTRODUCTION

This book examines how global governance regulates human life and death in a socially constructed world. It is the first full-length work to relate the human security debate to the ways in which international architectures of power undermine the broader security of humans but, at the same time, to suggest that those architectures contain unrealized potential for substantially enhancing human security. The book draws attention to the institutions and values of global governance in the determinism of human security; proposes their limited reformation and reconstruction; and identifies how this may be achieved. It argues that the condition of the world 'is a political choice' (Gordon 2007: 251) open to frequent reformation. Understanding our world as deliberately and consciously organized by political choices, rather than it being the result of a convenient Darwinist fatalism over which we have no control, presents opportunities to engineer change: there are many different forms our world can take, and its conditions are manageable not necessarily with radical revolution or the disinvention or disaggregation of the present world system, but with relatively minor tweaking of global governance authority and functions. By tweaking rather than transforming, refining rather than revolutionizing, broad human security can be substantially improved. This book is a bottom-up approach to thinking about human security, starting with the most vulnerable humans and their incontestable physiological needs, none of which is considered urgently or met by current security thinking in either the mainstream or the human security debate. It argues that this matter, of the preventable termination of millions of everyday lives, cannot be properly understood unless it is considered in relation to power and global governance, which regulates human security arbitrarily.

The objective of improving the dreadful life conditions faced by more than a third of humanity has been castigated unreasonably as utopian, in a world where identifying anything as utopian risks discrediting it. But the notion of improving life and changing worlds can be thought of as a 'realistic utopia ... perhaps more modest than those offered by both utopians and dystopians alike'. George Lawson suggests that the belief that human conditions can and should be improved requires 'an attempt to steer, nudge and guide world historical processes rather than transform them from some kind of *tabula rasa*' (2008: 2). Lawson wisely suggests that the era of uncertainty that has followed the end of the old world order in the late 1980s may be a period in which, instead of struggling inadequately to explain a dysfunctional system, we may be able to think about how we can leave that disorder behind and make substantial human progress, as long as we realize we are able to extricate ourselves from the ways of thinking that sustain the present dystopia. To paraphrase Voltaire, as long as people believe the absurd claim that we cannot change the world, it will continue to be an atrocious place for millions of people. This myth of immutability – 'it's just the way of the world' – is maintained in the face of overwhelming evidence to the contrary by the process of adiaphorization, or the indifferent excusing of a shocking and morally unacceptable condition by the 'scientifically' authenticated claim that the condition is inevitable and can't, therefore, be fixed.

Encouragingly, Immanuel Wallerstein also saw opportunity for positive transformation amid confusion and uncertainty. He predicted that 'the first half of the twenty-first century will be far more difficult, more unsettling, and yet more open [to change] than anything we have known in the twentieth century' (1997). To embrace and imagine change, we must think 'outside the box' and not be constrained by the limits of our pasts in order to imagine a different future. This future, Lawson proposes, 'tends to generate ... images that lie outside, beyond or on top of [our] history rather than visions which take their roots from what is immanent in history' (2008: 2). With different thinking, then, the future could be changed to look substantially different from the past and the presents (since there are many different 'presents' depending on who you are and where you live). The challenge becomes to move beyond temerity to imagine and construct a different world not rooted in the beliefs, attitude, values and, importantly, expectations that created our pasts and the associated rules that maintain our present. Our imaginings and preparations for the future – the way we think about what we would like to happen and what we can be – should not be constrained by the unenlightened and orthodox thinking that shaped our dystopian past and maintains our violent present.

This book stems from the lack of urgency attached to systemic and material change, and from the belief that our past world and its present component functions are socially constructed from ideas and thoughts that can be unpicked and reorganized in a form more beneficial to a larger number of human beings. Robert Jackson and George Sorenson wrote that:

> The international system is not something 'out there' like the solar system. It does not exist on its own. It exists only as an intersubjective [shared] awareness among people; in that sense the system is constituted by ideas, not by material forces. It is a human invention or creation not of a physical or material kind but of a purely intellectual and ideational kind. It is a set of ideas, a body of thought, a system of norms, which has been arranged by certain people at a particular time and place. (2007: 162)

Although this does not capture the full richness of constructivist thought – much of which emphasizes material force in addition to ideational direction – it conveys the notion that we have created the world in its present shape, and accordingly, we may reshape it in different form.

The book will argue that our political world's present trajectory and potential are currently dominated by (mainly) man-made ideas, values and priorities that are lethal for millions of people annually; that this ideational hegemony can be changed with human intervention; and that such intervention is already under way. It reflects the notion that 'if the thoughts and ideas that enter into the existence of international relations change, then the system itself will change as well. That is because the system consists in thought and ideas ... Everything involved in the social world of men and women is made by them' (ibid.: 162, 165). This concept has substantial intellectual pedigree. Writing in 1936, the economist John Maynard Keynes noted that 'the world is ruled by little else' other than ideas (1936: 383). The book takes the view that what we perceive as 'common sense' is only a reflection of prejudices developed early in life; that such prejudices are embedded in and concealed by our uncritical take on normality, in a process that can be both empowering for many but also brutally destructive for many more; and that because these are human ideas and beliefs, they can be adjusted without recourse to global revolution. It proceeds in the belief that ideas can only ever be subjective and they can never be value free and, as a result, they reflect our preferences and prejudices.

It rejects the notion that our social behaviour is enslaved to our biological origin, and it rejects the notion that some form of fatalistic, supernatural force or natural law underlies, organizes or can be held responsible for our actions and conditions. This is facile and convenient, especially with regard to the proclaimed universality of human nature and an underlying Grand Theory that might explain everything as long as we keep pursuing this imagining of Shangri-La with positivist tools. Beyond realism, 'the vogue for Grand Theory faded a generation ago not because its foundations were seen to be insecure but because no foundations were found' (Watson 2009: 44). This work rejects the notion of any absolutism and Grand Theory in social behaviour, in no small part because human nature exists in no biology book and has never been scientifically identified, even with advancements in DNA sciences. The idea that there is a universal human nature is scientifically falsifiable, since we are all different and demonstrably able to fight or cooperate (for example) in response to differing socially constructed and environmentally influenced circumstances. Correspondingly, this book rejects the idea that we are stuck with a rotten borough of a world which cannot be changed.

But it also challenges the cosmopolitan view evolving from the other end of the international relations (IR) spectrum, of a universal peace achieved through democracy and liberal economics. There are two reasons for this second position. First, if such a vision is achievable or desirable, it probably lies far ahead in the future, a result of a gradually evolving, rather than revolutionary, paradigm shift. The need for broader human security is too urgent to wait for the evolution of such a system by existing means and priorities. Second, the cosmopolitan future involves liberal assimilation and the inevitable abnegation of diversity by design. Although its proponents claim otherwise, neoliberal economics, embedded or raw, convert planetary resources to saleable commodities with scant regard for the inevitable unsustainability of equitable growth; it brands and rebrands the unnecessary to make it consumable and profitable; and it submits humanity to the service of profit, without which the neoliberal model cannot function. A cosmopolitan liberal future perpetuates the subjugation of humanity to a variant of neoliberalism and the explicit hierarchies of power and advantage required to maintain a competitive economic model, as a universal ideal. Even if social safety nets are created, this does nothing to remove the structural inequality embedded in neoliberal rules that sanction competition for resources among differently advantaged groups of people, the weaker of which are disenfranchised by the very system in whose participation they are told their salvation lies, and which imagines a world of equality without considering the resource consequences of a widely wealthy 'cosmopolitan' world of inevitable illiberalism. In the *Cosmopolis* (Gills 2007), people will become liberal, whether they like it or not, want it or not, or benefit from it or not.

In a sense, it is reminiscent of the social prescription of 'Big Brother' (Orwell 1950) and *Brave New World* (Huxley 1977).

This book therefore proposes a middle path between those who believe little if anything can be changed, on the one hand, and, on the other, those who, equally problematically, propose cosmopolitan reform to achieve global peace and prosperity. It proceeds with the intellectual rationale that human security debates must engage with matters of power in global governance, and that global governance scholarship should consider more openly power and causation in the international system (amid signs that some scholars, to whom I shall turn in following chapters, have taken up this debate). Broad human security is analytically and intellectually indivisible from some of the biggest debates of the day, and is a window into the nature of the international system itself. And this work also proceeds with the rationale that, for the most vulnerable children in the world, who, quite preventably, die before their fifth birthday in their tens of millions, there isn't time to engage with a grand cosmopolitan strategy of gradual global democratization or embedded liberalization, whether or not one views such an ambitious project as feasible, desirable or otherwise. This is too important an issue to be left behind by abstract or theoretical debate conducted leisurely in comfortable offices and conference suites. That it remains relegated to the corners of debate and has such a lowly status is a reflection of the lack of value mainstream IR places on human life. It is 'for that reason morally urgent' (Buchanan and Decamp 2007: 511). In this respect, the work takes the position that neoliberalism as the means advanced for growth and development is brutally unfair to billions but presently irrevocable in any meaningful sense that will either adjust inequitable development or reroute climate change. It assumes a prolongation of neoliberalism, which in its essence underscores most global problems because of its individualist emphasis in a world whose survival depends upon pan-national communal cooperation. Insofar as the human population is hamstrung by this paradox, the most that can be hoped for is a decrease in structural inequality. This does not, however, sanction the neoliberal project as a viable means for sustainable, equitable and reasonable human evolution. Within that core caveat, however, neoliberalism's social construction and its susceptibility to change provide the avenue through which its worst practices and consequences may be restrained and refocused to make it the least worst scenario. The work takes the position that this is the best that can be achieved until more profound changes evolve. It does not accept neoliberalism as a valid form of socio-planetary organization.

This middle path revolves around institutionally caused civilian mortality to distinguish it from random death and military casualties. It is advanced to accelerate the securing of tens of millions of human lives in ways that no conventional security paradigm will consider. It could readily be put into practice by challenging basic ideas that we widely, and understandably, perceive as reasonable when they are distinctly not. Although we may often find ourselves uneasily succumbing to the claim that There Is No Alternative (TINA) to the present system, this book argues that there are other ways that are less uncompromising. This critical eye emerges from SHIVA, or Scholarly Inquiry into Viable Alternatives. It will argue that there are various alternatives requiring only limited scaling back and retraction of some of the most problematic policies, not because they are consciously violent, but because they have become the hegemonic norm. Thomas Pogge puts it well when he writes that these conditions are 'not bad luck but bad organization' (2008: 531). In other words, this work begins with the view that child mortality is the consequence of conscious policy: it is a socially constructed consequence of *biopoverty*, upon which I shall elaborate in later chapters. It regards national and supranational public policy as the basis of the under-five mortality rate (U5MR), because national and international policy prevents human beings in their millions from accessing those things they need to keep children living. It keeps water and sanitation, literally and financially, far from people who need them; it puts cheap and reliable vaccinations beyond reach; and as a result, it exposes children (and adults) to preventable and curable diseases. These policy outcomes are readily fixable with relatively small changes in policy thinking. As Gordon puts it, 'there is no need for any person in the twenty-first century, anywhere, to starve, go without clean drinking water, toilets or access to basic healthcare and education', adding that 'providing poor people with all these things would not have any significant (or even noticeable) impact on [Western] lifestyles' (2007: 251).

This work focuses on global governance and the U5MR as a matter of human security. It examines how the relegation of avoidable multimillion child deaths to the periphery of the security debate (and into the field of 'development' or 'human rights', which are not prioritized for state policy interventions) leaves the causative power structures and institutions behind this problem out of the equation. It views this aspect of human security as determined by systems – in this case, the system is global governance, which, as well as being responsible for broad but unequal wealth in the mature democracies, also sanctions and projects institutions and priorities that deny resources for the sustenance of life on a quite epic scale. Rethinking the U5M figures as a human *and* security priority (instead of something that might slowly be treated over the next few decades as a development concern) has already allowed us to trace causation methodically to its roots in present global governance ideas and the priorities that derive from them (Roberts 2008a). This book builds on that analysis and identifies how, in addition to the oft-cited examples of international civic challenge to neoliberalism, there is also an expanding counter-hegemonic epistemic community – what Upendra Baxi calls a 'discursive insurrection' that challenges dominant norms in response to the severity of the market and the priorities and values of economic global governance in relation to human security (1998: 129). The intellectual endeavours of this disparate but converging constellation of forces, or 'nebuleuse', provide epistemological substance to the study of *humane* security; describe how the social construction of neoliberalism is susceptible to pressure from those who present alternative norms of organization as feasible; and demonstrate the means by which harsh neoliberal rules can be adjusted without demanding the dismantling of the system, whether this is desirable or otherwise. In short, the scholarship of this evolving nebuleuse affirms the fluid, transformable social construction of global governance and its inherent power structures, rather than accepting the immutably fatalistic determinism of its partisan nature and discriminatory procedures. It offers both critique and solution, but not resolution. That is, while critically engaged with and critical of neoliberalism, it does not attempt to subvert neoliberal practices and offer an alternative, but seeks instead to minimize the damage done by the worst excesses of the system described by Stephen Gill as 'ahistorical, economistic, materialistic, "me-orientated", short-termist and ecologically-myopic' (1995: 399). Ultimately, such a reconfiguring approach allows for human security to be improved within the constraints on the achievement of human security imposed by neoliberal processes and Enlightenment positivism.

In 1991, Samuel Huntington invoked a divisive and ultimately destructive debate on civilization, arguing that it was geographically defined as the 'West' versus Islam. Not only was this damaging, but it also distracted attention from more profound representations of civilization as the progressive evolution of collective human behaviour. Dostoevsky famously declared that the level of civilization of a society could be judged by looking in its prisons. Others have argued that the treatment of animals is a guide to civilizational development. What such views have in common is that they are comments on power and inequality: they are statements regarding how the strongest act towards the vulnerable and the marginalized, and the degree of mercy a collective body exhibits. Such civilizational values are profoundly undermined by the ways in which we ignore or marginalize hundreds of millions of vulnerable human beings, when we do not have to. This book also stands, then, as a comment on the hubris of liberal claims to civilization.

1 | HUMANIZING SECURITY?

Depending on one's perspective, human security is either a project whose time has come or one whose time has come and gone. This chapter is a response to the 'death through discourse' that has accompanied human security's efforts to negotiate for itself a place in security practices around the world, leaving us fiddling while Rome burns. It is a challenge to the reproachful lack of urgency vested in the millions of lives that end unnecessarily and prematurely around the world. The chapter discusses the isolation and marginalization of human security, along with the incoherence of mainstream security's priorities, before foregrounding a means of recovering the human security idea.

THE STATE AND SECURITY

State-centric security has rarely been concerned with the lives of human beings. Security concepts have traditionally been understood with regard to military hardware and, more lately, economic resources, technology and so on. The state in state-centrism is most ordinarily an anonymized entity at conflict with other anonymized states in a 'state of nature'. Mainstream IR has advanced into considering the role of international institutions in IR, but these are similarly anonymized and seemingly divorced from human creation and subjective determinism, as well as from the consequences of international institutional diktat. The discipline remains divorced from the social reality it claims to describe and in denial of the wider, global intellectual trend towards subjective normativity, as if, in the words of Slavoj Zizek, it is 'prepared, step by step, to accept as familiar a bizarre and morbid situation' (2002: 32). This is not to suggest that state-centrism has no place in security studies; but it is to highlight how security is studied almost without reference to the human population at large, prompting Professor Roy Preiswerk to ask, more than twenty-five years ago, 'could we study International Relations as if people mattered?' (1982). Nearly a quarter of a century later, Heidi Hudson was still asking the same question (2005). In the intervening period, IR broadly has moved a long way from its early, narrow confines; but it still rarely considers humans, either as actors in causation or as victims of security 'dilemmas', unless they are stipulated enemies of the progressive liberal order in which IR is situated (Sylvester 1994).

Realist argument has long been defined by assumptions of an immutable human nature and the fatalistic inevitability of violent interstate exchanges in an anarchic international environment regulated imperfectly by international institutions (Brown 2009; Crawford 2009; Booth and Wheeler 2008: 24–6). Furthermore, security is not 'real' unless it is possessed of certain characteristics. The 'real' matters of traditional security involve terrorism, nuclear weapons and rogue states, civil war, warlords and direct violence constituting 'hard' security. 'Soft' security is so labelled since it involves the abuse of human life on a very large scale, mainly by indirect causation, normally devoid of military weapons at the instant of their deployment, often absent obvious state involvement. For these reasons, the conditions of billions of people living in relative or absolute poverty, which threatens and/or extinguishes their lives routinely, is not considered a matter of security by the traditional security community. To securitize such issues is subjective, since it would allow for any 'existential threat' to accrue 'absolute priority' as a result of its dramatization, rather than its assessment according to 'objective' criteria (Patomaki 2008: 17). Such concerns are considered a matter of development at best, or human rights at worst, neither of which are considered priorities for or by public security policy. The focus of concern for those who inhabit this security domain lies with the state (the 'referent object'); international institutions (which are constituted of state membership); and global governance (which can be understood as the hegemonic process in international relations). The ability to maintain this security illogic is in part subsumed in its identity as 'traditional', since political tradition 'encodes power and hierarchy, allocates competencies (who may speak), constructs forms (how one may speak, what forms of discourse are proper), determines boundaries (what may not be named or conversed about), and structures exclusion (denial of voice)' (Baxi 1998: 129). In short, the dominance of such political traditions decides what we can think about in what context and disallows the potent notion that change is both possible and desirable.

This traditional understanding of security, to the exclusion of other imaginings, has been the case since the emergence of the state system itself in the seventeenth century, once memorably represented by Susan Strange as the 'Westfailure' system, on account of the effect on international peace and stability of the violence its rules make inevitable (1999). Despite a miserable record in its self-appointed role of managing the affairs of the world, its authority has become so deeply institutionalized over the intervening centuries that its legitimacy is profoundly resilient to challenge. The events of September 2001 in the USA reinforced state-centrism and reiterated the vulnerability of the state to non-state actors, as did subsequent attacks in Madrid and London. The proximity of armed violence to the state in these instances reinforced its primacy in international relations and security debates, and the boundaries of the state are again emphasized as barriers against social, civil, political and military threats from without and, increasingly, from within (Kirchner and Sperling 2007; Jackson and Sorenson 2007). So substantive are realism and neo-realism in international relations that until recently to question their most central arguments and beliefs was to invite incredulity and resentment (McSweeney 1999; Freedman 1998). Feminists who did so were marginalized, as were environmentalists and economists. The discipline remains sealed from within, by those who stipulate what may constitute security and who it affects (Booth 2005; Ackerly et al. 2006). The expansion of security by way of 'securitization' by the Copenhagen School is but a limited expansion, since although it accepts that security agendas change, it remains focused on mainly traditional purveyors and providers of security and insecurity in the form of 'the role of political leaders in the articulation and designation of threat' (McDonald 2008: 569).

Mainstream security and IR thinking in response to such threat perceptions and priorities revolves first around *prevention*. In realist and neo-realist terms, this involves self-help, statism and survival (Dunne and Schmidt 2008). It revolves secondly around *promotion*, based on the liberal assumption that a combination of democratic politics and neoliberal economics will eventually lead to the marginalization of troughs of poverty, the elevation of and concordance with individual human rights, and wider international prosperity, which will eradicate key sources of tension in the international system and undermine the propensity towards interstate war. These are its key concerns: to defend the established-but-flawed state system as it stands until interdependency and the democratic peace are successfully habituated and institutionalized and the borderlands are brought under control. Although such thinking tolerates a marginal and narrow discussion of human security at its fringes, it marginalizes the life and death of millions of people in the developing world as extra-disciplinary, and refuses to engage seriously, if at all, with the indisputable fact that millions of human beings' existential security is routinely terminated – people are killed by – the violence of extreme poverty. The narrow version of human security that mainstream security tolerates prioritizes 'death by politics over death by economics' and ensures that the threats addressed by this school 'are not the most prescient ones globally' (Bellamy and McDonald 2002: 374). Virgil Hawkins makes a similar argument in relation to Africa, regarding the propensity of international policy-makers to focus on smaller problems in Africa while paying less attention, or ignoring, the epic disaster in the Congo, measured not only in terms of war but in terms of its detritus and of wider maldevelopment (2008). Such distinctions reflect a refusal or reluctance to engage seriously with the security dilemmas that kill most people. We may reasonably conclude that mainstream security quite deliberately ignores – since it consciously selects the other matters it defines, labels and prioritizes as security – the lethal challenges that confront billions on a daily basis and which, in some cases quite preventably, kill millions annually. In so doing, mainstream security thinking eschews the imaginative and groundbreaking, but inconclusive, schools of human security that deal with global, systemic, structural violence against civilians; and with the concept of power as culpable in worldwide, mass avoidable mortality. The ontological and epistemological comfort zone in which it resides and which it sanctions marginalizes or precludes the consequences of socially constructed power transmitted through the organs of global governance as determinative of massive but preventable human fatalities. They are indifferent to, rather than maliciously complicit in, such suffering. These schools intellectually distance themselves from such arguments and deify an epistemology and ontology that claim ownership of and lionize social scientific impartiality and systemic neutrality and objectivity (Booth 2005; Ackerly et al. 2006). Concisely put, the discipline of IR is, according to its critics, dominated by 'a self-fulfilling militaristic paradigm obsessed with power and violence, interest and status' (Richmond 2008: 99).

The narrowness of mainstream security studies both invites criticism and begs explanation. Some critics have proposed that part of the explanation for the narrowness of mainstream security's ambit lies in the learned masculine character of the discipline, which associates matters of life security, either biologically or socially, with care and 'the feminine' (Sylvester 1994; Blanchard 2003; Walker 1984). Some critics suggest that such deeply habituated, institutionalized and socialized masculine behaviour not only disconnects from the feminine Other, but is also 'hard wired' to 'hard' security notions through association (Peterson 1992; Connell 2000). Certainly, this would seem to be borne out by the persistent prioritization of direct violence that kills very few, compared with a focus on indirect violence, which kills millions of (mainly female) human beings, from maternal mortality through to infanticide (explanations for and concern with which is primarily located in economics and resource distribution). Yet other critics have intimated that realist security is persistently blind to wider global lethality because considering such matters as security reveals extensive networks of partisan power across the entire field of international relations, since human insecurity is a function of asymmetrical power relations (Newman 2001; Roberts 2008a; Chandler 2008a, b). And, from the critical security studies perspective, if realism were to consider the implications of power and causation in human security, their ontological and epistemological foundations would inevitably be substantially challenged (Booth 2005; Booth and Wheeler 2008). Similar explanations for realist boundaries are to be found in social constructivist, postmodern and post-structural critiques (Wendt 2003; Ackerly et al. 2006; Berenskoetter and Williams 2007).

Global security is routinely defined, in the post-cold-war setting, with reference to the priorities and needs of the global North, or those in 'secure' states, as Mark Duffield refers to them. In this sense, security is far from global, since a wide range of subjective insecurities that plague billions of people in the maldeveloped world remain unaddressed. Furthermore, it is defined first in relation to vulnerability to direct violence, primarily from without, whereas security for the poorest 2 billion in the global South derives mainly indirectly, proximally from within but causally (mainly) from without. This latter point is important, since it underscores a central notion of this work: that power, expressed through the ideas and organs of global governance, produces indirect violence that results, quite avoidably, in millions of deaths. This relationship connects the 'production of suffering and responsibility for it' (Veitch 2007: 2). Those secure in the North hold great power; the insecure in the South, by definition, do not. Those who rank security in the former imperial metropolises are mainly white; those who die from lack of security in the ex-colonial peripheries are mainly people of colour. In gender terms, in the global North, those who prioritize security in terms of direct violence are mainly males, with a minority female element (normally white). In the global South, female fatalities from indirect violence outweigh male fatalities dramatically. The management of life through global governance, to which I shall turn shortly, differs for people of colour. It is impossible to sidestep the conclusion that those who have secured themselves from indirect violence prioritize security threats according to their remaining insecurities, reflecting Matt McDonald's question of 'why particular representations of threat resonate with particular communities, and how particular actors are either empowered

TABLE 1.1 Comparative global deaths from war and diseases, direct and indirect violence, 2002–05

	Deaths of soldiers and civilians in combat violence (direct violence)	Deaths from measles (indirect violence)	Deaths from malaria	Deaths from diarrhoea	Deaths from infectious and parasitic diseases and respiratory infections
2002	21,405[1]	611,000[2]	1,272,000[3]	1,798,000[4]	14,866,870[5]
2003	47,351[6]	530,000[7]	1,000,000[8]	1,788,500[9]	n/a
2004	41,586[10]	454,000[11]	1,000,000[12]	1,820,007[13]	n/a
2005	31,013[14]	345,000[15]	1,000,000[16]	n/a	14,018,871[17]

Notes: 1. Centre for the Study of Civil War, new.prio.no/CSCW-Datasets/Data-on-Armed-Conflict/Battle-Deaths-Data/, accessed 9 April 2008, upper limits. 2. WHO, World Health Report 2004.p. 120. 3. Ibid. 4. Ibid. 5. WHO, Revised Global Burden of Disease (GBD) 2002 Estimates, at www.who.int/healthinfo/bodgbd2002revised/en/index.html, accessed 22 April 2008. 6. Centre for the Study of Civil War, new.prio.no/CSCW-Datasets/Data-on-Armed-Conflict/Battle-Deaths-Data2/Battle-Deaths-Data/, accessed 9 April 2008, upper limits. 7. www.unicef.org/media/media_25308.html, accessed 8 February 2009. 8. www.who.int/malaria/malariandhivaids. html, accessed 9 February 2009. 9. WaterAid, 'Global cause and effect: how the aid system is undermining the Millennium Development Goals', 2007, www.wateraid.org/documents/global_cause_and_effect_mdg_midway_paper.pdf. 10. Centre for the Study of Civil War, new. prio.no/CSCW-Datasets/Data-on-Armed-Conflict/Battle-Deaths-Data2/Battle-Deaths-Data/, accessed 9 April 2008, upper limits. 11. www.who.int/malaria/malariandhivaids.html, accessed 9 February 2009. 12. Ibid. 13. Global and national estimates of deaths under age five attributable to rotavirus infection in 2004, as of 31 March 2006, www.who.int/immunization_monitoring/burden/Global_national_ estimates_2004_deaths_under_age_five_attributable_to_rotavirus_infection_2004.pdf, accessed 9 April 2008. 14. Centre for the Study of Civil War, new.prio.no/CSCW-Datasets/Data-on-Armed-Conflict/Battle-Deaths-Data2/Battle-Deaths-Data/, accessed 9 April 2008. 15. D. Elliman and H. Bedford (2007), 'Achieving the goal for global measles mortality', *Lancet*, 369(9557): 191–200. 16. www.who.int/ malaria/malariandhivaids.html, accessed 9 February 2009. 17. World Health Organization, World Health Statistics, Projections of mortality and burden of disease to 2030, www.who.int/healthinfo/statistics/bodprojections2030/en/index.html, accessed 22 April 2008.

or marginalized in "speaking" security' (2008: 564). These dissonances reflect the subjectivity of power and the asymmetries of opportunity and potential therein embedded. They reflect the subjectivity of the idea of security. Despite the unavoidability of this conclusion, the dominant security schools and policy-makers do not ask, in any substantial fashion, what security means to different people; who decides who and what is to be secured; from what risks and threats are they to be secured; and from what these risks and threats arise.

These questions are conspicuously absent from mainstream security debates. This neglect is considered by John Gerring, who identifies eight criteria for concept formation: familiarity, resonance, parsimony, coherence, differentiation, depth, theoretical utility and field utility (1999). As we will see in the following sections, human security is excluded and denied as a security concept by mainstream security debates not just because those who determine what counts as security cannot identify with those who are most vulnerable to avoidable death in the largest numbers (such as children in parts of Africa and Asia), but because human security and its mortal constituents are not familiar and do not resonate as security matters, since most security policy-makers have never been short of water or lived near landmines. Parsimony of security policy is a consequence of the limited economic pot and limited familiarity, while broad human security has been derided for incoherence because its lack of clear conceptualization has sometimes left it bereft of workable policy. Much of Gerring's account holds true, mainly with reference to familiarity and resonance. The matter of coherence, however, demands that we turn to substantial and valid criticism of human security, since such grounds are presented as justification for the concept's exclusion.

THE HUMAN AND SECURITY

Human security is about placing ordinary living human beings everywhere front and centre of the security question. It puts us, our vulnerabilities and our related needs, varied as they are, at the fore of all the calculations policy-makers make about security. It is about asking questions about our own personal security, rather than the security of an anonymous, bureaucratic entity we call 'the state' or 'the system'. If we consider that the kinds of avoidable mass violence illustrated in Table 1.1 deserve more than indifference, and if the route to that debate is to be considered as a security matter (since it is, for the people killed by such threats), then human security is presented as a means of bridging the gulf between those who determine narrowly what security is, and those who die for lack of a broader, but feasible, imagining. Human security marks a departure from how we normally think about global security, in terms of the state, of sovereign territory, of civil and ethnic conflict, of anti-state terrorism, of nuclear weapons and other such obvious challenges to state security, and in terms of the institutions of state used to address such threats. Perhaps surprisingly for some, relatively few people die in such traumas, as Table 1.1 suggests. Even amid the most extreme terrorist violence, more women were murdered in the USA in 2001 by intimate partners than died in 9/11, which is not to demean the brutal slaying of thousands of innocent civilians at the hands of al-Qaeda. It is, instead, to offer some perspective on the range of violences that human security addresses as beyond the conventional consideration.

Mainstream security has hijacked and narrowed the human security concept and agenda by defining and limiting its potency to civil wars and civilian casualties as the consequences of political violence. Mainstream, traditional security thinking has done exactly what Uppendra Baxi (1998) said traditions do: determine what is and is what is not legitimate and relevant; what should or should not be encompassed in their remit; what can and cannot be done. A broader imagining of human security, however, addresses mass threats that, every year and quite preventably, kill or maim millions without deliberately setting out to do so. Examples include under-five mortality (10 million every year), communicable diseases (17 million mortalities a year), maternal mortality (about half a million annually), and so on. At a yet wider level, human security is concerned with freedom from fear and freedom from want, and with human dignity for all. It is a more humane approach to thinking about security, and it is concerned with the billions whose lives are rendered insecure by a range of conditions which mainstream security ignores, but which are matters of security to the everyday existences of those people's lives. It is an attempt to place the human at the centre of the way we think about security. Human security therefore addresses a far wider human condition than conventional security, and the human security debate is designed to elevate these matters to a higher priority in the international system – something it has failed to do in any substantial fashion.

This speaks to the debate about who determines what security is by virtue of their ownership of the means of its production and imagination through what Matt McDonald refers to as the 'speech act'. McDonald writes that speech acts in policy-making situations can be thought of as 'securitizing moves that become securitizations through audience consent', meaning that once enunciated publicly and accepted by those listening to the speaker, the subject matter of the speech act forms a security subject or concept (2008: 566; Gerring 1999). Various 'securities' are 'securitized' over time, and these issues change; matters such as migration, or climate change, are posited by acts of expression that themselves are acted upon by those who respond to security threats. Human security is no different from this; but it departs substantially from mainstream security because it makes the human being the 'referent object', instead of the state. For some, it represents a profound shift, challenging centuries of assumptions regarding ontology, epistemology and the objective nature of 'reality', as opposed to its subjective social construction. David Chandler, for example, comments that this 'new paradigm' of security is seen by some as a 'struggle for the heart and soul of global policymaking' (2008b: 427), since it is suggested that whoever gains the high ground in this debate will determine the foreign and security policy of states. Some suggest human security already has: Gerd Oberleitner, for example, argues that 'the concept of human security has begun visibly to influence, change and challenge global politics, institutions and governance' (2005: 185). Others are less convinced of this primacy: Chandler suggests that human security has been delimited by realist domination of the security agenda and submerged into hegemonic institutions and methodologies, adding that although human security is debate rich, it is policy poor (2008b). Furthermore, he rightly notes that such change as claimed by some human security advocates is impossible while contemporary power structures remain intellectually unchallenged and denied (ibid.). The point is further made that certain elements of human security are tolerated by mainstream security because they are familiar, resonate with mainstream security policy and do not pass beyond the bounds of the expressible defined by mainstream security (Roberts 2008a). And, expressing scepticism commonly found in sympathetic liberal-realist writing, Roland Paris suggests that human security may be more 'hot air' than 'paradigm shift' (2001).

Like all social analysis, human security must inevitably be divided for the same reasons that all security debate is divided, epistemologically speaking, since it attempts to generalize security approaches when all 'individuals ... have different and differing security concerns' (Chandler 2008b: 429). This work takes the view that the search for a means of conceptualizing human security as a single absolute construct is wasteful of time and resources and is ontologically implausible, since there cannot and should not be a universal human security model or philosophy, since the variations in humans' security needs are so vast as to polarize security scholarship and stymie debate. These differences in understanding what human security can mean are found in the splitting of the concept into (at least) two schools, often referred to as narrow and broad, or minimalist and maximalist. And in turn, the subjective meaning of security as an inevitably contested concept (like all concepts examining human behaviour) splits even the mainstream IR discipline. That is, while human security studies are divided over narrow and broad interpretations, the wider arena into which that debate seeks to insinuate itself is similarly divided over what constitutes legitimate mainstream security matters. There can be no single meaning of human security for human security thinkers, just as there can be no single meaning of security for realist and neo-realist thinkers.

How has the human security concept become divided in terms of what the concept can mean? The narrow, or minimalist, imagining of human security is enunciated most obviously in the *Human Security Report 2005*, which abbreviated human security to the discourses of political violence, with some inclusion of casualties entailed as a result of the detritus of civil war (Mack 2005). In many respects it is not particularly far removed from mainstream IR, and it is the most popular representation of human security, perhaps because it diverges least from the boundaries of realism. Since it involves mainly political, direct violence and state actors, it leaves unchallenged the global structures responsible for threats to broader human security which kill hundreds of millions more than its narrow variant. Reflecting this dichotomy, Kyle Grayson notes that 'the human security discourse has been an example *par excellence* of how to manage [an] incitement to discourse in such a way that debates become subsumed within an allegiance that ultimately does little to challenge the power-relations constitutive of contemporary biopolitical regulation' (2008: 386). It is for this reason that Chandler is right to argue that narrow human security's integration into mainstream security 'has reinforced, rather than challenged, existing policy frameworks' (2008b: 428), and therefore brings into question the extent to which there has been a security 'paradigm shift' (Paris 2001).

Narrow human security has been absorbed into the mainstream in other ways, most obviously perhaps in its co-option into the security–development nexus. Mark Duffield argues that policy relating to human security is determined and deployed in order to secure Western states from threats that come from 'underdeveloped' regions. Duffield suggests this has become much clearer since the reach of the 'war on terror' has extended to include a broader range of threats to different

Western interests. For this reason, Duffield refers to narrow Western human security policy as an instrument or 'technology of governance' to manage potential threats from 'ineffective states' in a process that legitimizes intervention by 'effective' states (2005b: 1, 4). This represents a hijacking of the concept, proposed as a (developing world) human security priority but manipulated into a (developed world) state security priority. Duffield considers that in this process, human security becomes state-centric neo-imperialism; a tool to be used to achieve Northern goals over Southern populations. He argues that:

> This incarnation of security threatens to absorb development with, among other things, pressures to prioritise development criteria in relation to supporting intervention, reconstructing crisis states and, in order to stem terrorist recruitment, protecting livelihoods and promoting opportunity within strategically important areas of instability. (ibid.: 3)

David Chandler similarly considers human security as resulting in 'the problematization of the non-western state' sanctioning intervention and change (2008b: 435). From this perspective, the co-option of human security into the mainstream agenda provides the means by which to divide the world. The West has both a security 'interest' and a 'values-based' desire to 'secure', to 'develop', to 'protect' the Other, whose insecurity threatens the security of Western consumer society as the instabilities associated with conflict, poverty and alienation threaten to spill over into and destabilize the West. Chandler is concerned that intervention to protect human lives (in the narrow conception of human security) is being undertaken not for the sake of those lives, but to protect the West from the calamities that confound Western state-building and peace-building efforts in the global South (ibid.). This view finds sympathy among those suspicious of Western intent, especially when efforts to institutionalize sovereign violation are formalized in a concept such as the Responsibility to Protect (R2P), a proposal that both legitimizes narrow human security and undermines the fundamental proposition of sovereign inviolability – for some (Duffield 2008).

At the other end of the spectrum, the broad or 'maximalist' variant of human security has almost as many critics. The UNDP's early definition of human security, understood as the broadest imagining, identified 'freedom from want and freedom from fear' (UNDP 1994: 23). Inevitably, the concept has defied definition and made policy agreement impossible. A key problem is epistemological, since broad human security as the UN defines it seeks a universal, generalized vision, the realization of which is rendered impossible by virtue of the range of insecurities confronting individuals globally. But a larger problem involves Pandora's box. That is, very few broad interpretations of human security make sense because they are viewed in the abstract, remote from causation, and are therefore policy non-specific. They identify high ethical purpose and ambition, but rarely invoke discussion and inquiry into causation, as if the mere idea of the 'human' as a security referent would allow 'ethics to tame power' since 'human security is expected to have radical effects because the idea of the "human" is expected to be progressive and radical itself' (Chandler 2008a: 466). For example, the Commission on Human Security defines human security in terms of 'protecting the vital core' of human lives; but it does not supply an answer to the question of 'from what?' As a result, though undoubtedly morally laudable, Oberleitner suggests the concept is practically irredeemable (2005: 187). A similar fate confounds the idea of 'vital freedoms' that require protecting: no causation is explored, even if there are occasional intimations and hints as to structural determinism. They examine human security in a power vacuum, in the same way that systemic power, structure and causation are absent from some mainstream and popular explanations presented for illiberal behaviour in the global borderlands and periphery (Kaldor 1999; Sorensen 2001; Duffield 2001). Grayson argues that

> Human security's incitement to discourse is infused with a set of power-relations predisposed towards the ontological, epistemological and analytic status quo. In turn, these are conducive to the continued operation of contemporary biopolitical rationalities. (2008: 394)

It would be as if realism had proposed that states require protection, without suggesting what the threats to them might be. Opening debate on broad human security opens Pandora's Box: it reveals the causation of mass human insecurity in the hegemonic formations of power presented as rational ideas and instruments that we sanction as dominant and accepted global norms.

One of the consequences of the limits set by this discursive pattern of ontological and epistemological chauvinism is that the elephant in the room, of destructive and lethal asymmetrical power related to mass human violence of all colours, and which is caused by government, global governance and international biopolitics, is sidelined from security consideration by the identity and priorities of the security debate itself. Mike Pugh, among others, is concerned that 'silence surrounds the role of interventionary core capitalism in perpetuating poverty through neoliberal policies and the structuring of the global economy' (2005: 9). And, as Grayson puts it, in determining the terms of reference for human security and excluding a debate of substance on the role of neoliberalism, poverty and structured violence, 'cosmological realism functions as a gatekeeper, preventing the intrusion of anything that might unsettle [some] shared norms about what can count as knowledge' and what can count as security (2008: 394).

Unless multiple imaginings of human security engage with neoliberal power and are accepted and operationalized as far as their coherence allows, the concept risks becoming an empty signifier and a great waste of a remarkable opportunity to civilize ourselves by accelerating progress on global human security. In this sense, human security is a means of negotiating a space at the top table where global security policy is decided, for billions of human beings existing, rather than living, perilously close to the edge of life.

Even if it does not progress in this way, with real-world consequences, the concept has other utility. If it is destined momentarily to remain outside the mainstream, and if it cannot be adequately conceptualized, defined and turned into policy, it still remains a powerful critique of global governance. This book deploys it in part to evolve debate over global governance and human security, since the search for human security must inevitably prompt the question: what creates human insecurity? The concept itself is independently critical, meaning that, for Bellamy and McDonald, 'human security [could] operate less as a policy agenda within existing political structures and discourses than as a radical critique of these practices' (2002: 376). Another way in which its utility may be developed is by understanding it less as a means and more as an end. It eludes ready definition perhaps because it is an aspiration seeking a means of fulfilment. Rather than human security being 'a necessary but not sufficient precondition for human development' (Owen 2004: 381), the broad variant can be seen as the outcome of a nexus between successful socio-economic development and the curtailing of traditional sources of insecurity. It can also be understood as occurring when the legitimized rules, norms and procedures of the international system that cause millions of avoidable civilian deaths are identified as such and changed.

If realism is considered as defining the basics of security, and we are concerned that this is inadequate, then we may place human security farther along a growing security spectrum, first elongated in the aftermath of the cold war by matters such as environmentalism. Farther along this spectrum are broad forms of human security, and at the end there is a higher state of civilization to be achieved through the resolution of structural underdevelopment and concomitant insecurity, in conjunction with the eradication of international and internal violence as an institutionally sanctioned means of social transformation. None of these developments is impossible, but nor are they immediately probable. The practical utility of human security, then, may be that it represents both an objective to be reached, and a vehicle for illuminating the barriers to its achievement. But in addition, there also exists a way to navigate these conceptualizations of human security which avoids the pitfall of submersion in and co-option by the mainstream security debate; which offers a workable imagining from which active and effective policy can be energized without being stymied in discourse; and which provokes debate and analysis of causation without implying the necessity of total systemic or material change, or invoking arbitrary sovereign violation.

POPULATIONS AND SECURITY

If mainstream permission for human security grants it only a limited ambit, and if broad human security is beyond the means of universal achievement, a compromise position between the two can be enunciated. This approach discusses and describes the 'capillary power' of global governance, which reaches into the national policies of very poor states; notes the power structures behind the condition, which I have elaborated upon elsewhere in considerable detail (2008a); and generates a framework for identifying and prioritizing transnational human security issues. It therefore presents a means of enhancing human security; and also acts as a critique of the agency that causes the problem in the first place. And, rather than being an approach to human security 'disciplined by the desire to integrate [itself] into the power relations that constitute the dominant structures of biopolitical order in global politics' and 'a complement to existing power structures' with the purpose of 'mitigating some of their most abhorrent effects' (Grayson 2008: 395), this work identifies the 'biopolitical order' of global governance as causative in both creating and denying human security globally. This approach, of understanding human security and power in global governance as related matters, responds to Chandler's concern that those who are more interested in theorizing the concept of human security 'portray the human security discourse as somehow marginal to the articulation of power and the frameworks of international regulation and intervention' that characterize the contemporary international system (2008a: 465).

Narrow state-centrism largely ignores human beings but is rich in policy, effective or otherwise; broad human security overextends the security focus without being able to propose policy. A 'third way' may extend Michel Foucault's concern with state government to the domain of the global. Foucault wrote that as well as disciplining its population, a political regime, or ideationally driven set of rules, effectively 'exerts a positive influence on life, endeavours to administer, optimize and multiply it, subjecting it to precise controls and comprehensive regulations'. It is a situation where power is applied to 'the function of administering life' (1979: 137–8). Foucault argued that a 'biopolitics of the population … focused on the species body, the body imbued with the mechanics of life and serving as the basis of the biological processes: propagation, births and mortality, the level of health, life expectancy and longevity, with all the conditions that can cause these to vary' (ibid.: 139). Biopolitics, then, is the 'calculated management of life' (ibid.: 140). Foucault's work on power is receiving ever greater consideration in the study of international relations. Building on his interpretation of state power determining life outcomes, Giorgio Agamben refers to biopolitics as 'the growing inclusion of [hu]man's natural life in the mechanisms and calculations of power' (1998: 119); while Michael Dillon and Luis Lobo-Guerrero express the concept as 'power over life' (2008: 265). Elaborating further, Nikolas Rose explicates the role of government in the biopolitical sense as 'the deliberations, strategies, tactics and devices employed by authorities for making up and acting upon a population and its constituents to ensure good and avert ill' (2007: 195).

The concept of biopolitical security is distinct from state and human security in that it 'revolves around life and its properties rather than sovereign territoriality' or the individual (Dillon 2008: 311). That is, in conjunction with the preceding concept of the territorial state as the organizing body within which humans gather and exchange loyalty for protection from unknown contingencies, biopolitics expresses the relationship of state to population and the means by which life is nurtured and maintained (Foucault 2003). It is not concerned with universal human security, but with the security of a given body of humans organized in relation to the authority they cede to the state to discipline and protect them. Dillon and Reid abridge a range of Foucault's work and present biopower lucidly as:

> A positive and productive form of power that conceives the task of government in terms of the management of populations by systematically assaying their needs, composition, properties and dynamics in order to promote their welfare. Central to biopolitics is the intent to

govern by investing life through and through, by defining, analysing, knowing and promoting it. What is at stake is ... the continuous production and reproduction of life itself. (2001: 49)

The expression of such relations of power results in 'security practices [that] take species life as their referent object' (Dillon and Lobo-Guerrero 2008: 265). Duffield illustrates how this works when he talks about 'centrally directed hygienic campaigns and educational programmes, [and the] emergence of public health from curative medicine [as] regulatory biopower' (2005b: 4). This is familiar in the global North where state utilities have provided water, electricity and healthcare for their own populations, based on the needs of that population and the legitimacy of the state, as well as the objectives that both share and benefit from, such as health and productivity. Species-life, in the form of the organized and territorially bounded human collective, acts as the referent object of security. For Foucault, such national populations demonstrated observable characteristics of behaviour in relation to one another (Hardt and Negri 2004: 427; Dillon and Lobo-Guerrero 2008: 267), and state policy cohered around the shared needs that reflected the similarity of characteristics. We shall return to the power of this concept later, when formulating human security policy.

Biopolitical security has been directed towards population protection and punishment through regulatory control processes which vary depending on the ideological perspectives of the state's authority. Its evolution reflects the departure from agrarian group self-sustenance, to post-industrial atomization and industrial cash compensation (Foucault 2003: 251). Traditionally, states have managed population life according to ideological beliefs, such as liberalism or communism, and biopolitical processes have varied accordingly. Wherever the state, whatever its ideology, fails or ignores social need, people have relied on community self-provision. In the developing world, such practices are normal, legitimate and sanctioned; and are well documented (Eisenstadt and Roniger 1982; Roberts 2008c; Schmidt et al. 1977; Tambiah 1977). These practices mirror and echo those found in Europe centuries ago, before kingdoms and states assumed responsibility for their populations. The essence of the timeline comparison is the way in which people manage their own needs in the absence or presence of an effective state. A similar comparison may be made in the present, however, but across regions, which illustrates different values applied to the same question, and which implies strongly an asymmetry of power and an indifference to suffering on the part of global governance.

Duffield walks us into this unpleasant territory. He distinguishes life in the developed and undeveloped worlds as 'insured' and 'uninsured', respectively: protected by government or exposed by it. He argues that:

> The life-forms associated with mass consumer societies, such as Europe, are distinguished from an underdeveloped population by the degree to which life is supported by a comprehensive mixture of remedial and supportive measures, including public and private insurance-based safety nets, that cover birth, education, employment, health and pensions. (2005b: 4)

In the developed world, population-life is routinely managed by the state through the provision of social welfare systems that protect the vulnerable, whether they are rendered insecure by the social order or by biology. The social safety nets routinely found in 'overdeveloped' states (Gilroy 2002: 589) are biopolitical regulatory instruments managed by the state and, increasingly, the market. In the undeveloped world, the insurance Duffield refers to is absent or provided by state policy, and the supranational global governance norms that dictate national policy in developing countries through coercive conditionality can therefore be understood as biopolitical. Biopolitics, in its differing forms, then, can be understood as effective and empathetic or ineffective and indifferent life government, and global governance can be understood in a similar biopolitical sense because it has the power to determine the absence or presence of resources essential to modulate the biological requirements of life for national populations in the developing world. It is from a biopolitical perspective that we may advance a conceptualization and definition of human security that treads the path between the co-opted narrow and the unrealizable broad imaginings, as a basis for policy that may be derived from scientific foundations.

A DEFINITION

I propose a definition of human security as bio-life deliberatively secured: physiological necessities for human life to persist. Air is one that has yet to be rationed. But others that are rationed, by social mechanisms like the market, are water, nutrition and sanitation, for example. We know they are rationed because they exist in the global North in adequate, accessible form but not in the global South. All human life depends on these elements, yet tens of millions die annually from their inaccessibility. Human security as bio-life is governed by biopolitics: the means by which life is *managed* by ideas, beliefs and the institutions that project them. Presently, neoliberal global governance is the most substantial and wide-reaching regulatory manager of bio-life, since it reaches beyond sovereignty into the lives of millions of people in developing countries from its Northern liberal origins. The antithesis and nemesis of bio-life is biopoverty, whereby the elemental physiological needs for the persistence of human life are *mis*managed by those same global rhythms of socially constructed biopower. Bio-life is as biopolitically determined as biopoverty: it is a function of biopolitical management and mismanagement undertaken by neoliberal global governance. Bio-life (institutionally secured physiological security) is imperfectly predominant in the North; biopoverty (institutionally mismanaged physiological security) is a constant in the global South. Conditions in both hemispheres are determined by hegemonic neoliberal governance; neoliberal biopolitics begets bio-life and biopoverty. The danger of this hegemonic process is obvious: it quickly establishes who lives, who dies and how both are decided. This has always been the threat and challenge presented by the human security project; it connects cause, effect and culpability in the international system. It is not an emancipatory project just for humans, but also for intellectual and social truths.

CONCLUSION

Biopolitical analysis, then, may provide an intellectual bridge between the absence of power in both the realist and the human security debates. We may surmise that human security might be thought of as an end-state: that biopolitics can be understood as a way of describing the management process liberal government applies to a bounded population. However, neoliberal biopolitical policies are capable of the converse outcome: of mismanaging life so that the outcome is avoidable mortality. We may also surmise that the 'effective' and 'ineffective' *state* is only one source of biopolitical authority, in a much wider environment of international, global governance structures and institutions, since at both national and international levels neoliberal government and governance prescribe market costs to resources vital to life preservation and proscribe free provision of the same, placing them out of the reach of very vulnerable people. We may also understand human security in relation to power as bio-life. It is to an elaboration of this last area – of the power of global governance over human life – that the following chapter turns.

2 | GLOBAL GOVERNANCE OR GLOBAL HEGEMONY?

INTRODUCTION

This chapter discusses perspectives on global governance, power and its consequences for human security. The first part examines the literature that treats global governance and its transmitting institutions as objective, value-free and neutral processes that will eventually guide the world towards greater prosperity, equality and human security. This reflects a realist worldview. The second, from a constructivist perspective, examines the argument that power distortions in global governance and its instruments are responsible for global asymmetries and inequalities; and that these both sustain and undermine the ambition of human security. The third part discusses the elevation of biopolitics from the national to the supranational level, as a means to enhance human security and 'create on a global scale [aspects of] a mode of governance that corresponds in normative stature ... to the most humane public order systems that [operate] at the level of the sovereign state' (Falk 2000: 317).

GLOBAL GOVERNANCE AS BENIGN

Paralleling Dag Hammarskjöld's famous reflection on the United Nations (Tharoor 2005), Michael Barnett and Raymond Duvall critiqued the IR literature for imagining that global governance would 'bring out the best in the international community and rescue it from its worst instincts' (2005: 1). Global governance in this perspective is a response to globalization, a process described as 'the deterritorialization of traditional concepts, which are rhizomatically disaggregated from their indigenous contexts and resynthesized in unanticipated ways that make them globally efficacious among types of people and groups with certain shared interests' (Eade 1997: 5). Mainstream views consider global governance as functional and necessary to manage the unevenness of tumultuous globalization, since its range and scope far exceed the capacity of the state to manage such complexity. James Rosenau and Ernst-Otto Czempiel suggested that this 'governance without government' involved 'functions that have to be performed in any viable human system irrespective of whether the system has evolved organizations and institutions explicitly charged with performing them' (1992: 3). Gerry Stoker also referred to government, since global governance is concerned with 'creating the conditions for ordered rule and collective action' (1998: 21). Yakub Halabi described global governance as marking 'the acceptance of regulations at the global level out of a conviction that such regulations will enable actors to seek wealth in an orderly fashion and in accordance with the norms of the international system' (2004: 21). And Cornelia Beyer describes global governance as 'a system of rules that – given the absence of a central power – is carried out by a diversity of actors on different levels' (2008: 23). Global governance has thus been defined as 'the management of global political and economic space in the absence of a global state' (Solomon 2006: 327).

Such statements inevitably beg the question of who or what is managing that global space, if anything. But in this literature, the question goes both unasked and unanswered, instead reflecting the notion that global governance is necessary or exists unsatisfactorily to manage the uneven processes and outcomes of economic globalization. Where power enters the debate, it is normally in terms familiar to realist thinking. This literature is broad and dense but conceptually constricted, reflecting a preoccupation with a narrow interpretation of power in a very traditional format. In this context, power is primarily understood in a rather direct nature as the means by which 'one state uses its material resources to compel another state to do something it does not want to' (Barnett and Duvall 2006: 40). It constitutes sporadic impacts from manic behaviour, rather than routine consequences of chronic persistence, and power is not perceived as anything other than neutrally projected for a universal non-partisan good. Global governance is absent power, with the purpose of neutrally refining and regulating present global processes. Dingwerth and Pattberg emphasize this interpretation of global governance as impotent when they describe it as 'a specific mode of social interaction whose logic differs from that of both markets and government' (2006: 188). Similarly, Leon Gordenker and Thomas Weiss also neglect authority, defining global governance as 'efforts to bring more orderly and reliable responses to social and political issues that go beyond capacities of states to address individually' (1996: 17).

We may deduce from this element of the literature that, in this neutral form, global governance may be conceived of as a conglomeration of regimes and instructions mobilized primarily by states through international institutions to achieve a desired outcome of peace and prosperity amid the destabilizing forces of economic globalization. Rorden Wilkinson comments that this literature tends to emphasize how 'the steady development of international institutions and regimes have, when taken in the aggregate, led to the emergence of a web of international norms, treaties, and conventions that encourage sustained co-operation among states and, in so doing, generate a measure of international governance' (2004: 4). In a similar vein, James Rosenau defines global governance as something 'conceived to include systems of rule at all levels of human activity – from the family to the international organization – in which the pursuit of goals through the exercise of control has transnational repercussions' (1995: 13). And, within that broad rubric of global governance, which depends on multilayered multilateral institutionalism, Robert Keohane and Joseph Nye represent the main vehicles of global governance as politically passive systems (2000: 37).

Absent from such analyses is the role of ideational determinism, since 'neorealism and liberal institutionalism generally treat ideas as exogenous to states' interest formation and state interaction' (Bieler and Morton 2008: 103). In these senses, global governance and associated institutions may be thought of as a set of political management protocols based in liberal values and beliefs which must administer, as well as the uneven fallout from intensified and deregulated international capitalism, the paradox of the democratic right to resist authority that stems from those same protocols, and which is evident in many social, economic and political sites of resistance to globalization around the world, from Geneva to Seattle. This helps distinguish it from other social, political and economic civil phenomena, but it does not take us much closer to any notion of ideational authority and, without this, we are still left pondering what global governance may be, and whether and how it generates legitimacy.

Recent scholarship goes farther. The incoming editors of the prominent journal *Global Governance* declared in 2006 that there were many elements to global governance; but while they briefly alluded to the notion of a planetary rules regime being rooted in something called 'structure', the emphasis in the journal is very clearly on what they describe as 'multilayered regulation' (Carin et al. 2006: 3). Like much of the literature on this subject, the respected *Global Governance* journal largely conceives of its subject matter in power-neutral terms; identifies its core elements as institutional in nature; and has little to say about global governance in ideological and ideational terms (Diehl 1997). Cornelia Beyer's observation, that 'the concept remains empirical, is not normative or prescriptive and provides a description of real processes of change in the international system', affirms this perspective (2008: 23). Similarly, the Commission on Global Governance remarks that global governance is 'not founded on domination but upon accommodation' (1995: 2–3), while James Rosenau is equally clear about the neutrality of global governance when he writes that 'the organizing perspective is that of governance in the world rather than governance of the world. The latter implies a central authority that is doing the governing, an implication that clearly has no basis in fact' (Wilkinson 2004). Global governance, then, relates to a system of multilevel arrangements that exists to manage, and equally to mismanage, the fluctuations, distortions, accidents, trends, moods, transformations, traditional security dilemmas and other disasters and developments that routinely punctuate and characterize contemporary global life. In a sense, this literature tends to treat international institutions and regimes *as* governance.

GLOBAL GOVERNANCE AS ASYMMETRICAL POWER

More recently, and inevitably from alternative epistemologies and ontologies, another perspective recognizes most of the technocratic determinism outlined in the liberal-institutionalist literature, but then departs radically from the claim that partisan power is absent from global governance. According to Barnett and Duvall, persisting in considering power in terms of a liberal-institutionalist/state-centric 'central authority' is not just intellectually moribund but also carries with it very real risks in the 'real world' of everyday human lives. They argue that 'failure to develop alternative conceptualizations of power limits the ability of international relations scholars to understand how global outcomes are produced and how actors are differentially enabled and constrained to determine their fates' (2006: 41). In short, they argue that 'concern with power ... brings attention to global structures, processes, and institutions that shape the fates and life chances of actors around the world' (2005: 7–8). There are inevitable implications for broad human security in observing the relationships between governance, power and outcomes.

Barnett and Duvall are not alone in this view. Others have considered power in global governance and identified a variety of forms. Kapstein, for example, suggests that international institutions, at the heart of global governance, may change or maintain conditions or processes in ways that benefit some more than others (2005). When power is added to the equation at the international level, it is clear that global governance creates and/or perpetuates hierarchies of advantage and disadvantage by dictating and maintaining uneven preferences and practices in a range of economic regimes that aggravate post-colonial asymmetries of relative prosperity and poverty. Affirming such a proposition is the wealth of qualitative critical international political economy scholarship that identifies distorted practices and uneven playing fields that challenge neoliberal claims of free markets and fair practices (Payne 2005; Williams 1994; Greig et al. 2007).

Of great importance also, Ian Johnstone identifies a second type of power present in global governance as 'productive' (2005). This refers to the ability to represent a subjective, incomplete and partisan claim as an objective, absolute and neutral truth. Economics, for example, is presented in the neoliberal mainstream as a neutral science when the plethora of contending perspectives and priorities suggest it cannot be so; human nature is presented as universal and a scientific fact when no such scientific evidence has ever existed; common sense is claimed as an absolute when it is a subjective and shifting collection of prejudices and preferences. All claim a universality and reliability that none can prove, but they enjoy productive power since they are accepted and taken for granted by many, in part because they normally enjoy hegemony; they are dominant norms.

A third form of power in governance, discussed by Barnett and Duvall (2006), involves structures, or transnational social rules systems, which, when combined with the hegemony of productive discourses, are responsible for creating and perpetuating material and capability inequality. And, since these concepts of power permeate the institutions and practices of global governance and are projected by them, governance itself is a form of power. Even from such an enlightened perspective, however, structure as power is still considered in relatively conventional terms, such as class and related social and economic divides.

Felix Berenskoetter takes this conceptual evolution farther, however. He argues that power at the global level maintains the institutions, beliefs and practices that underpin it. Perhaps yet more importantly, Berenskoetter maintains that power can also be applied to challenge and change a given scenario, implying clearly that power is 'responsible for both change and continuity' in the international system (2007: 13). That is, intentional or unintentional activity is required both to maintain a status quo and to transform it. Berenskoetter further contends that if the exercise of power makes a difference, then 'identifying power is analytically indistinguishable with identifying cause' (ibid.: 13). He adds that 'this is significant because it also means identifying who/what is responsible for the ways things are, or are likely to be'. According to this perspective, 'power can be made analytically responsible for phenomena of both change and continuity' (ibid.: 13). For this argument constructively to be pursued requires that traditional conventions relating to power and global governance be left behind, in search of a more nuanced framework in which to pursue human security. It is also important to consider how power as Berenskoetter, Barnett and Duvall and others express it (above) is maintained; I turn to this matter first.

GLOBAL GOVERNANCE AND HEGEMONY

Hegemony in the realist sense normally involves a dominant state capable of disciplining the errant international system through reward and punishment of various actors in accordance with neoliberal global governance values or in accordance with quite different values such as those of realism that routinely justify the support of murderous klepto-crats, tyrants and dictators around the world. Jeffrey Kentor summarized this understanding well when he wrote that 'the concept of hegemony ... refers to the distribution of power among the developed, or core, countries of the world economy'. He referred to power as being economic and coercive (military), and to hegemony as referring to fluid hierarchies in anarchic systems where states compete for top positions (2004: 74). Hegemony in the traditional literature is often understood as relating to the domination of a given nation-state at a particular time through its command of economic and military power. The concept of hegemony is limited in this sense by the distance mainstream thinking will take it.

For other inquiry, however, hegemony is more concerned with 'how the logic of the capitalist system came to be so dominant, the conditions under which certain choices came to be understood as rational, and how power has been understood in different contexts and the consequences of this understanding for how power has been pursued' (Rae 2008: 131). Hegemony from this perspective is domination by consensus: we agree to be led and to accept 'natural' outcomes because we and most other people appear to benefit, or can expect to, if we stick to the rules. As Robert Cox put it, 'world hegemony ... is expressed in universal norms, institutions and mechanisms which lay down general rules of behaviour for states and for those forces of civil society that act across national boundaries' (1983: 172). It is these rules which underpin neoliberal organization and production. The near-universality of the process lends hegemony its legitimacy and ostracizes opposition on the grounds that the majority consensus must be right. For Jonathan Joseph, hegemony is 'a reality that is ordered in a certain way and is relatively enduring' (2008: 112). In relation to the world we see around us, hegemony constructs, and projects as normal, the potential for wealth and security.

But it also constructs and projects 'a scenario in which poverty, massive social injustices and sheer relentless violence in many of the richest countries in the world, let alone the poorest, appear all too familiar' (Zalewski 2006: 26). Such conditions we often agree to be normal and unchangeable, and we arrive at these conclusions without being forced in any easily perceptible way. Where we challenge hegemonic norms, we may expect censure at best and violence at worst. Those who challenge hegemonic conventions are normally a very small minority, so their credibility can be eviscerated on the grounds that they must be wrong (since there are relatively only a few of them). In Cox's words, 'coercion is always latent but is only applied in marginal, deviant cases' because 'hegemony is enough to ensure conformity of behaviour in most people most of the time' (1983: 164).

This interpretation increasingly challenges realist perceptions and is epistemologically and ontologically distinct from that deployed in realism. While for the latter the state is the hegemon, the former view ideas coupled with material resources as the key hegemonic forces. For many social constructivists, structure, or the rules that generate, bind and exclude international behaviour of all forms, derives from ideas, and structure maintains the hegemonic idea. Summarizing, Armstrong et al. suggest that, from such a perspective, 'ideas provide the social context for, and hence make possible, meaningful action, and the influence of such social facts on behaviour may, and indeed must be, subject to scientific study' (2007: 96). Such an approach suggests that hegemonic power and authority may be less obvious but nevertheless may exert leadership and agency through the manipulation of knowledge and the production of legitimacy, subjective normality and 'common sense'.

Robert Cox moves the meaning of hegemony from anonymous states to social elements within states, and from this it is only a small step to being able to conceive of hegemony as ideational, material and transversal, rather than located in a few states capable of monopolizing extreme military force and wealth. Cox writes that 'hegemony derives from the dominant social strata of the dominant states in so far as these ways of doing and thinking have acquired the acquiescence of the dominant social strata of other states'. That is, hegemony is transverse, in that it is construed from individuals and groups of individuals in public and private institutions (for example) that are linked by dominant common beliefs. Furthermore, these values, beliefs and the actions that accompany them are accepted by enough of a majority for the ideas not to be overturned, even though they may be challenged. Cox argues that 'in a hegemonic order these values and understandings are relatively stable and unquestioned [and] appear to most actors as the natural order' (1993: 42). These values, shared among enough influential powers and institutions to generate legitimacy, are then shored up by particular claims about their veracity that may or may not be reasonable. Furthermore, non-acquiescence may be punishable by hegemons in order to generate conformity where it is absent.

Cox argues that in the international system, 'the dominant state creates an order based ideologically on a broad measure of consent, functioning according to general principles that in fact ensure the continuing supremacy of the leading state or states and leading social classes but at the same time offer some measure or prospect of satisfaction to the less powerful' (1987: 7). Hegemony projects key priorities relating to economic development and prosperity from understandings shared among leading states and social elites in the metropolitan and peripheral areas of the international system. This creates a dominant and authoritative consensus capable of instigating and projecting a particular worldview. For a majority of people in 'satisfied' Western states, the 'measure of satisfaction' comes from the capacity to consume goods relatively freely, within the confines of their disposable income, increasingly coupled with their debt-carrying capacity. For the world's poorest people (about one-third of the total global population, since nearly one-third 'lives' on less than $2 per day), and for those who want to believe that this can change, a 'prospect of satisfaction' might be the 'trickle-down effect'.

If, on the other hand, the USSR had shaped the post-war economic order, a quite different hegemony would have become dominant. This is because, according to Stephen Gill and David Law, 'the significance of hegemonic leadership for the power of capital depends crucially on the nature of the political economy of the dominant states, and their domestic coalitions which control international economic policy' (1993: 115). These different versions confirm the social construction and potential for variation and transformation that characterize hegemony: the world can indeed be quite different. Cox's earlier writings conveyed these tiered relationships of hegemony, acquiescence and consent, patronage and clientelism and elite status quo preservation, when he wrote that hegemony 'necessarily involved concessions to subordinate classes in return for acquiescence in bourgeois leadership, concessions which could lead ultimately to forms of social democracy which preserve capitalism while making it more acceptable to workers and the petty bourgeoisie' (1983: 163).

Beyer similarly ascribes to hegemony the notion of acceptance when she describes it as 'a relation, not of domination by means of force, but of consent by means of political and ideological leadership' that results in 'the organization of consent' on a worldwide scale in which 'the hegemon would always attempt to make his leadership to appear consensual, even if it was based on force' (Beyer 2008: 17). In this manner, it is argued, Gramscian hegemony produces 'a subtle but totally pervasive system of influence' (Kingsbury 2007: 33). While Gramsci's model of hegemony applied initially at the level of the nation-state, Robert Cox famously proclaimed a constellation of social forces that produced domination through consensus, which maintained its legitimacy and authority through the production and control of knowledge (1993). Describing global governance, Cox referred to a supportive 'nebuleuse', or a constellation of social (and therefore human) forces that underscore neoliberalism. These forces consist of 'the unofficial and official transnational and international networks of state and corporate representatives and intellectuals who work towards the formulation of a policy consensus for global capitalism' (Cox and Schechter 2002: 33). It is constituted of 'a loose elite network of influentials and agencies, sharing a common set of ideas that collectively perform the [global] governance function' (Cox 1997: 60). Cox proposes that this nebuleuse 'has no fixed and authoritative institutional structure' but instead emerges from the discussions of powerful and influential hegemons of global neoliberal governance.

At this level, such a hegemon achieves mass consensus through the indirect coercion, or manipulation, of 'reality'. It is both dominant and directing, 'implying leadership with ... consent' (Cox 1983: 163). Where dissent exists, it is represented by the dominant social forces as wrongful divergence from normalcy and therefore becomes delegitimized in public consciousness. Challenge is perceived as deviant since it rejects normality and then loses legitimacy. The ways in which Cox reframed Gramscian thought on hegemony at the international level open the door to a range of interpretations of what might constitute hegemony itself. Specifically, Cox referred to ideology as actually or potentially hegemonic, but more broadly he introduced the notion that hegemony can be considered in ideational terms – that is, as an international structure derived from pre-eminent ideas and beliefs.

Craig Murphy demonstrates the combination of ideation and hegemony in global governance. Murphy addresses the hegemony of neoliberalism globally, in economic and, to a lesser extent, political forms. He argues that liberalism projects norms that 'exert power not due to their inherent validity or rightness, but because they are regularly enacted

... because some international actors have become convinced of their rightness and validity' (2000: 797). Within liberal regimes, power is applied to preserve continuity or structure change using, for example, the World Trade Organization (WTO). This body's objective is to set the rules of international economic intercourse, which are dominated by the preferences of its most powerful members. It is one of the key instruments of global governance, regulating relations between states and economies. It is ideologically aspirational, not neutral, in that it favours, sustains and projects a variant of neoliberalism that can be bitingly un-kind to those states, societies and systems that are already marginalized by historical relations between centre and periphery. It presides over a series of rules that it requires developing countries to adhere to, but does not insist on similar compliance in the developed world, whose elite social strata determine its policy, thereby orchestrating an uneven relationship. This process, whereby institutions are empowered as organs of governance charged with transmitting and regulating a particular agenda, reflects the considerations of Barnett and Duvall (2005), as well as Williams (1994) and numerous others. Murphy proposes that such institutions 'usually remain the creatures of the most powerful of their state members' (2000: 793). The WTO, a 'creature' of the West, thus uses its influence, power and authority to *preserve* and *refine* the current status quo, which distinctly favours developed countries. The same argument can be made of the International Monetary Fund (IMF) and the World Bank (WB). These institutional vessels (the means by which neoliberalism is projected and maintained) require developing countries to surrender social policy (for example) to the market and to privatize public services like healthcare. Similarly, trade regulations preclude state subsidies of domestic private businesses because this may provide national actors with an unfair advantage over their international competitors. This is an inversion of policies enjoyed by a variety of states and corporations, which have been openly afforded advantages to ensure that specific economies or goods prosper in the start-up phase; this approach is partly responsible for the rise of the Asian 'Tiger' economies, and it is practised presently to protect vulnerable states and their economies in Europe and the Americas (Bello 1989; Chang 2002). In this sense, the 'free market' is a myth and a nonsense, perpetuated by lies, propaganda and misinformation achieved on the back of, and consequentially reinforcing, neoliberal hegemony.

Ideation and hegemony are also evident politically speaking. Economic neoliberalism's political counterpart, democracy, is a parallel projection of global governance. Democracy is advanced, rightly or wrongly, as the means by which we may secure a less violent interstate system; as the institutional architecture in which to embed liberal economic practices; and as a panacea for producing peace in conflict and post-conflict environments (Paris 2004; Chesterman 2004; Sorensen 2006). Western states and international institutions coerce democratic development through lending conditionality, human rights bodies observe concordance with democratic practices concerning prison conditions, media freedom and judicial impartiality, and democratic standards like accountability and transparency are applied in Weberian fashion to audit, evaluate, reward and punish conformity and non-conformity with liberal values and practices. Even where the evidence shows that political liberalization fails to change elite behaviour, or fails to enhance everyday lives in any meaningful way, the idea of liberal democracy and the Liberal Peace enjoys institutional, productive and ideational hegemony and authority (Roberts 2008a; Richmond 2008). Global governance is biopolitical in this sense: it disciplines the international system into conforming to liberal political values, reaching into supposedly sovereign territory and, where conformity is absent, punishing a state and its people. Transiting states are audited for such conformity; there is no shortage of organizations in the West, public and private, that scrutinize the Other for conformity with global governance demands. Transparency International, Amnesty International, Human Rights Watch, the World Bank – all act to check that particular liberal political and economic processes are being adhered to, with requisite punishments for nonconformity. The power of global governance is profoundly capillary in this sense; but it is focused primarily on top-down institutional transformation that anticipates trickle-down democracy. In practice, liberal peace is often a limited peace for a limited minority, since institutional democracy is not meaningful in any immediate sense for the majority of a 'democratizing' society because its top-down institutional metropolitan emphasis has very limited impact on urgent everyday needs in very poor societies, since immediate-to-medium-term needs are normally governed by and a product of access to socio-economic resources, rather than abstract political rights (Roberts 2008c; Mac Ginty 2008). Thus, both political and economic liberalism are advanced as means to ends as well as ends in themselves. Gill calls this the 'new constitutionalism', which is 'the political project of attempting to make transnational Liberalism, and if possible liberal democratic capitalism, the sole model for future development' (1995: 412), in a discourse that parallels Tom Young's consideration of the 'Liberal Project' as a means of assimilating the non-liberal Other into 'Westernity' (1994). The means by which they are propelled are the institutions and productive values of global governance with the explicit intention of disciplining and assimilating the non-liberal Other. Global governance, then, can be understood as the ideationally hegemonic biopolitical process by which neoliberalism disciplines and punishes polities, economies and societies globally through asymmetrically orientated public and private international institutions.

GLOBAL GOVERNMENTALITY, TRANSNATIONAL POPULATIONS AND BIOPOLITICS

The following section elevates Foucault's analysis of state power over national life (governmentality) to the international level (global governmentality). Governmentality refers to the rationale that guides states to manage the lives of their populations (Foucault 2003). Governmentality is variable, but in the liberal sense, it refers to the values that drive state responses to population contingencies and which regulate the means by which a population is kept in conformity with the ideas and values of the state, or sovereign. Foucault expressed government as the means by which population-life was modulated: disciplined and punished, with the sovereign owning, ultimately, the right to end life in certain circumstances. He suggested that government power was not solely centralized but was 'capillary', in the sense that the power of the state circulated through a national territory by way of decentralized organs and instruments of state tasked with socio-biological management. Although his work famously considered institutions such as schools and prisons as means by which life was managed, contemporary liberal practices that fulfil the same functions include on-line self-employed tax declarations, airport facial recognition and recording systems, digital traffic management and revenue-raising cameras, digitally encoded driving licences and bio-data identity cards, all of which further the biopolitical rationale defining governmentality, allowing for the comprehensive monitoring and regulation of life by the state. It is biopolitical in the sense that it represents the 'calculated management of life' (Foucault 1979: 140). It is, however, human, in that it will, inevitably, make mistakes and mismanage life. The mismanagement of population contingencies by governments is as routine in mature democracies as it is in dictatorships. This is perhaps most obvious in the calamitous failures of state to regulate neoliberal excess in the downturn to the late noughties; but it is also equally evident in the loss, by government departments, of confidential data containing private records of 'their' citizens, for example. Mismanagement of population matters is as normal as successful management.

If biopolitical management and mismanagement apply at the national level, they also apply at the international level, according to a growing body of scholarship. Michael Merlingen argues that extending Foucauldian imaginings of government to the global level 'with a view to assembling a larger picture of the biopolitical character of the international' would facilitate 'a powerful critical sociology … for the exploration of world order' (2008: 272–3). Ronnie Lipschutz comments on this potential, suggesting that 'although Foucault wrote only about governmentality within states … the extension of his idea to the international arena is rather straightforward'. Lipschutz writes that:

> Global governmentality is more than the sum of national governmen-
> talities; it is more than the state system and its associated organs; it
> is more than the standard definitions of global governance. It is an
> arrangement of actors and institutions, of rules and rule, through
> which the architecture of the global articulation of states and capital-
> ism is maintained … The management of human populations and
> their environments – the exercise of compulsory and institutional
> power – is the task of both the agencies of government and the
> populations themselves. (2005: 235–6; see also Albert and Lencon
> 2008: 265)

Although a descriptive tool, a neo-Foucauldian approach to global governance helps us understand what global governance does and how it does it, and it helps us account for differential outcomes in developed and developing worlds. Biopolitical approaches to global governance offer an alternative way of seeing and describing the world that circumvents the epistemological and ontological arrogance of neoliberal institution-alism and the concomitant nonsense of an international system devoid of asymmetrical and partisan power. A neo-Foucauldian approach allows us to describe in detail global flows of ideological power, through thousands of international and national institutions, which socially construct the security and insecurity of billions of people worldwide. It constitutes a more balanced – and therefore more intellectually reasonable – approach to interrogating and understanding the uneven and routinely lethal outcomes of global governance, globalization and international relations. In management must also be mismanagement.

Fleshing out this approach, Michael Dillon and Julian Reid argue that 'global liberal governance' involves 'a varied and complex regime of power, whose founding principle lies in the administration and produc-tion of life'. They continue that global governance 'is substantially com-prised of techniques that examine the detailed properties and dynamics of populations so that they can be better managed with respect to their many needs and life chances' (2001: 41, 46). Biopolitical liberal global governance, or global governance, is concerned 'with the detailed knowledgeable strategies and tactics that affect the constitution of life and the regulation of the affairs of populations, no matter how these are specified' (Sorensen 2001: 12–13). Jo Rowlands notes that governance of this kind 'affects us all', adding that this process 'refers to social, cultural and political phenomena that deeply shape and govern daily life and what happens within it' (2008: 801). It affects almost everyone on the planet in different ways, determined in part by the specific values of govern-ance invoked at particular times, reflecting the numerous and varied manifestations and multifarious consequences of different imaginings of this means of extending power, control and direction over human life. Global governance at the international level, then, is as biopolitical as government at the national level. Governmentality and biopolitics can be understood to operate at the global level through:

> a pervasive, complex and heterogeneous network of practices. Structuring the desires, proprieties and possibilities that shape the operation of life, working on and through subjective freedoms, gov-ernmental rationalities typically develop around specific problematics, such as those of health, wealth, security, poverty, esteem, culture or migration. (Dillon and Reid 2001: 48)

We may develop other aspects of Foucault's approach to the manage-ment of life. Just as Lipschutz applies Foucault's discussion of national government to the international, he also proposes that Foucault's con-sideration of populations with shared biopolitical characteristics and contingencies can also be conceived of in a transnational sense. Lipschutz writes that:

> Populations are not composed of sovereign and autonomous individuals, as normally conceived under liberalism. Rather, they are regarded and treated as homogeneous collections of people who are molded institutionally into particular categories and forms, who regard themselves as belonging to those categories and forms, and who act accordingly. Individuals comport themselves according to the standards of normality of their specific population ... For example, those with HIV or AIDS are managed as a population with a specific set of characteristics for which treatment is available. (2005: 237)

Put simply, where national governments exert biopolitical influence over national populations and create policy in accordance with specific issues like 'health, wealth, security, poverty, esteem, culture or migration' (above), global governance similarly exerts biopolitical influence in such matters in transnational populations globally. We can see this if we recall that external global governance prescription determines domestic social policy in parts of Africa and elsewhere by making World Bank lending conditional on states accepting this policy, a substantial matter I will address in greater detail in Chapter 4. Particular 'problematics' are confronted according to the neoliberal ethos of global governance, and downloaded through and around developing states on the assumption that neoliberalism will resolve contingencies like health, poverty or education.

Even though Foucauldian approaches have opened up novel ways of interpreting governance and analysing power more substantially, however, it has been a largely one-sided account of the role of biopower in the management of human life. A key rationale for this book and its critique of human security scholarship as lacking in engagement with a broad imagining of the concept is to demonstrate the role of power not just in production but also in reduction: in the destruction of human life en masse, quite predictably and preventably. Whereas Foucauldian analyses have normally been applied with a view to conceiving power in more sophisticated and nuanced terms than any other ontology in IR so far, this work applies a Foucauldian lens to destructive power in global governance: the power to reduce life. Just as global governance can be understood as the calculated management of life, then it must inevitably also be considered in terms of the calculated mismanagement of life, since its methodologies and ontologies, assumptions and values, practices and priorities must and can only ever be subjective and ultimately therefore prone to failure as well as success. It is no different from any other form of management in this sense; global business leaders, captains of finance and industry and policy-makers generally are all prone to miscalculation, an inevitability writ large in the latest global economic meltdown. The architects of global governance are all human and are responsible for socially constructing its ordinance, and they must be as subject to failure and miscalculation as any other group of humans tasked with managing resources and crises. Global governance cannot, empirically and reasonably, be any different and we must therefore consider its role in miscalculating the management of life. This approach bypasses what Merlingen calls the 'sanitised accounts of governance in which elements of domination, exploitation and violence (figuratively and literal) become largely invisible' (2006: 191; Fraser 1989). It is a step beyond the analysis of power as asymmetrical and productive in global governance, as Berenskoetter, Barnett and a number of others (above and below) have demonstrated, into the domain where socially constructed asymmetrical power reduces and destroys human life. Biopower begets bio-life and biopoverty in numerous developing countries, whether those policies descend directly from national government or in more capillary fashion from global governance. But some clouds have a silver lining.

Such transnational human groups with shared characteristics and contingencies like biopoverty may provide the basis and focus for a more coherent reorientation of human security directed not at the universal-individual but towards the 'calculated management of life' (Foucault 1979: 140) of human groupings not specific to territories. Groups of humans with shared contingencies and shared solutions can be targeted by the institutions of global governance exercising biopolitical force. The identification of influencing 'conditions' on such groups of people other than from 'effective' or 'ineffective' states (state-centric analysis) allows for an expansion of causal analysis to include the structure and power of biopolitical governance itself where its impact is negative, allowing for critique but also for policy reform. This overcomes a key challenge in mainstream security writing to broad human security's 'coherence'. Inevitably, this must further inquiry into the impact of neoliberalism, since 'the grid of intelligibility for biopolitics is economic' (Dillon 2008: 309).

In short, applying Foucault's interpretation and description of government power at the national level to the idea of governance at the global level helps us both describe and rethink the consequences of global governance and its impact on transnational human life. As Lipschutz and Rowe argue,

> what is most provocative and thought-provoking about the application of governmentality to contemporary social orders is that it does not stand as a 'theoretical' alternative to realism, liberalism, radicalism, or constructivism, or fall prey to the false dichotomies drawn between and among those theories. Global governmentality is an empirical phenomenon whose specific features are determined by contingency and context, and which may fit one or more of the conventional theoretical framings of international relations that themselves are products of power as deployed in particular places at particular times. (2005: 15)

If global governance is seen as the means by which planetary life is modulated, we can conceive of it in ways similar to national governmentality, since it is founded in and bounded by similar liberal assumptions of power and responsibility. Just as liberal national government extends centralized values through decentralized and disparate extensions of metropolitan authority such that it impacts directly and indirectly on the organization of population life, the same can be said of global governance. Global governance is determined by long-ascendant hegemonic neoliberal values regarding the use of power and the self-assumed responsibility to subsume all others to liberal prescription in a process the consequences of which fall not far short of assimilation and neo-imperialism. Global governance regulates, disciplines and punishes through multiple formal regulatory frameworks in the form of elite-designed covenants (like those that stem from the WTO) founded on and able to project with consensus the central values of the system, such that people in 'far distant lands of whom we know little' are forced to work to consume and pay taxes to maintain a state with which they experience an often coercive and disruptive relationship. Their political elites and organizational methods aspire, voluntarily and involuntarily, to the liberal model of the state through which global governance may dissipate metropolitan values, and the political, social and economic institutions of the state and the international system form the Foucauldian capillaries of power that extend the influence of global governance to the peripheries of the planet. As Merlingen writes, 'Governmentality theory offers researchers a toolbox – containing ... the concept of political rationalities and a complex notion of power – which enables them to excavate, map ... and interrogate quotidian and inconspicuous relations of power ... In short, governmentality designates a space of governance in which the negative and positive dimensions of power come together' (2006: 192; Larner and Walters 2004). It is especially with regard to the negative dimension that this work is concerned, such that policy solutions can be imagined and advanced.

Underscoring the wider, broader and deeper global governance and neoliberal process, normalizing it, lending it legitimacy and creating the consensus required to maintain hegemony is the drive to force consumption. The capacity demonstrated by Malthus's Irishman (it could have been anyone) to reject the legitimacy of consumption is increasingly eroded in the West by an ever more intrusive insemination of false consciousness in which neoliberalism uber-commodifies, for example, human emotions (an ever-expanding range of conventional and digital cards exploiting a range of emotional experiences like Valentine's Day, for example) and normalizes the commodification of human relationships (exploiting millions of people's emotional bonds and reinforcing archaic

gender roles, lately including music CD compilations arranged to ener-
gize and invigorate 'Mum' while she does 'housework', for Mothering
Sunday, as a 'reward' for being a mother). The momentum of the Neoliberal Project, conducted through the architecture of global governance,
is exceptionally difficult to critique because of its seeming normalcy for
so many people and because of the hegemony that normalcy underscores
and reinforces. The system that manages resources and numbs critical
curiosity with purchasing 'choice' and 'power' in the global North is
the same system that mismanages, by virtue of the choices it stipulates
for very poor people, bio-life necessities for hundreds of millions of
people – for many millions of those with lethal consequences – in the
global South. Human security, bio-life and biopoverty are regulated
differently for some than others by the supranational architecture of
global governance.

BIOPOLITICS FOR HUMAN SECURITY?

If global governance is biopolitical, and if biopolitics constitutes the
means by which some are secured while others are insecured through
the social construction of biopoverty, how might it be a useful tool for
making human security workable? After all, it still falls foul of the same
problem that confronts the human security approach, namely which
humans should be prioritized for securing from what, since not everyone
who is rendered insecure can have their lives secured simultaneously.
Yuen Foong Khong identified this dilemma when he asked which groups
of humans 'deserve priority attention and on what grounds?' With this
conundrum in mind, he declared that 'at a minimum, proponents of
human security need to specify criteria for distinguishing between [differ-
ent] security [issues]' (2001: 233). Khong's work does not identify such
criteria, but Alexander Bellamy and Matt McDonald invert the concept
to identify causation of human insecurity, using the seven sources of
insecurity identified by the UN (including economic, environmental,
political and so on), from which they recommend analysing the role
of the 'effective' and 'ineffective' state in causing or preventing such
insecurities (although they do not use such terms) (2002). Although this
approach boldly invoked structure and power, it was state-centric, and
it fell at the hurdle of universality of treatment, as must all approaches
focused on the level of the individual in the current economic system,
and the concept went no farther in policy terms.

Taylor Owen's threshold-oriented approach, however, puts some
meat on the bones. He suggests that human security could be focused
around severity of threat rather than the cause of insecurity. He argues

that this allows 'all possible harms to be considered, but selectively limits those that at any time are prioritized with the "security" label' (2004: 381). Owen proposes that, 'as there is an unlimited number of possible threats [to human security], only the most serious, those that take lives or seriously threaten lives', should form the basis of a conceptualization and definition of human security (ibid.: 383). This is a useful compromise that develops the idea of prioritization by severity of threat. When this approach is coupled with Roberts's delimitation of human security around preventable death and discernible causation (2008a), and focused on human groupings facing shared contingencies that require similar exigencies, the outline of a biopolitics of human security emerges. Lipschutz sketches the trans-boundary ranging of biopolitics (above); it could be organized and prioritized around the severity hypothesis articulated by Owen and the avoidable lethality notion identified by Roberts. We arrive at a situation where human security is defined in relation to biopoverty, and where large transnational groups of human beings experiencing shared, avoidable lethal biopoverty can be identified, prioritized and treated biopolitically.

Developing these strands of thinking in both biopolitics and human security, we may propose the following criteria for identifying, prioritizing and treating human security bio-life threats. First, there must be a trans-boundary, national or subnational population characterized by similar and discernible immediate threats to mortality en masse. Second, this threat must be caused through the social institutions and biopolitical processes of government and/or global governance. Third, such threats must be preventable, so that policy may cohere around evident causation. The third criterion is contingent on the second, since if a lethal threat derives from government or governance, it is necessarily human, institutional in causation and socially constructed. There are numerous groups that fit such a schema. Lethal female genital mutilation is one. Infanticide is another. The example I develop here is under-five mortality, since there is very broad agreement that vulnerable children are worthy of adult care; it is a clear outcome of biopolitical management and mismanagement; because the differentiation of rates between states and regions is compelling evidence of distortions in approaches and priorities that could be policy responsive and homogenized (to some degree); and, finally, because the present levels, although falling slowly, are shaming and intolerable. Under-five mortality fits the criteria identified because it is sub-state and trans-boundary; it is caused, according to medical epidemiology (Chapter 3), by a combination of immediate and proximal social processes that have their origins in biopolitical management and mismanagement; and according to the same sources, roughly two-thirds of the mortality rate is easily preventable. There are further benefits to this approach, since considering causation reveals much about the structures and institutions that account for different child mortality rates in different parts of the world. The nature of causation affirms the biopolitical content of global governmentality and the essence of power that underscores this global system, and acts as a critique of biopower, in much the same way that the human security concept can. Finally, this approach engages directly with David Chandler's concern that human security cannot be considered without reference to power in the international system (2008a).

CONCLUSION

If we challenge the reliability, utility and efficacy of traditional IR epistemology, and consider that subjectively directed and asymmetrically projected power is omnipresent in the international system, we may draw a number of conclusions regarding what global governance might mean and, as importantly, what it might do and cause to be done differently. First, global governance, or the authorization of political and economic neoliberal values maintained through ideational hegemony, creates and presides over political and economic conditions globally, except where it cannot, in which case it attempts to discipline and punish into conformity. The international system is policed by the values of global governance, which determine what are and what are not to be considered matters of security; these values and preferences are a key cause of the very problems their authors claim they can solve. Second, the ideas that underpin global neoliberal governance have achieved and maintain hegemonic status, despite substantial intellectual challenges to their veracity, utility and applicability, affirming neo-Gramscian interpretations of hegemony. This pyrrhic achievement reflects what Oliver Richmond describes as the 'hubris' widely associated with liberal peace (2008: 96). Third, the institutions that radiate from this ideational structure exert power over life: both to evolve it, and to expose it to lethal contingencies. That is, while there is a very broad expectation that global governance will manage life, it will also mismanage life en masse. Global governance can in this sense be considered biopolitical. The effects of global governance are both constructive and destructive of human security. This perspective places global governance at the scene of the crime, not as police but as perpetrator: as well as curing some of the ills of the world, global governance also causes the very illnesses it is supposed to cure. The following chapter introduces an epistemic community representing a counter-hegemonic 'nebuleuse', borrowing from Robert Cox, which further elaborates an understanding of human security and human insecurity as functions of constructive and destructive global governance.

3 | A NEW 'NEBULEUSE'?

INTRODUCTION

Although neoliberal global governance is hegemonic, this does not mean to say that there is no challenge to its authority. Indeed, just as Robert Cox proposed multiple powerful social forces (a nebuleuse) as creating and maintaining hegemonic governance, he also noted the inevitability of a counter-hegemonic process. This parallel 'nebuleuse' is also composed of social forces, but these are value-inverted in relation to the hegemonic social order and are responding, in Polanyian tradition, to the expansion of the market, the contraction of the state and the subsequent mass inability of people to create a buffer between themselves and the international economy (Polanyi 2002). They are materially weaker, lack political authority and are less legitimate in the eyes of those who support the dominant hegemony and its associated normality. They are 'abnormal' and they will be less influential and less able to access the offices of those who cement the consensus of hegemony. In the post-cold-war world, Cox maintains, such counter-hegemonic social forces that 'arise within domestic societies ... increasingly coordinate their resistance to globalization and ... elaborate alternative visions of what the future might look like' (Cox and Schechter 2002: 33). This chapter sketches the contours of a counter-hegemonic nebuleuse that provides a rich vein of literature able to consider global governance and human security more broadly and with a different range of tools, beliefs and approaches that expand the authority, legitimacy and coherence of the present debate. This is perhaps what Upendra Baxi had in mind when he referred to a 'discursive insurrection' (1998: 129).

Cox is not alone in identifying counter-hegemonic development, in terms of those who challenge the ideas and outcomes (the structure and agency) of neoliberal governance. Peter Evans, for example, identifies 'three different but interrelated kinds of ... counter-hegemonic globalization' able to connect 'disprivileged Third World groups and communities to political actors and arenas that can affect decisions in hegemonic global networks' (2000: 231). These networks, he argues, reflect 'efforts to constrain the power of global elites, both by pushing for different rules and by building different understandings'. Evans adds that 'they are not likely to overturn the whole apparatus, but they constitute challenges to "business as usual" both globally and locally, and are in this sense "counter-hegemonic"' (ibid.: 231; Richmond 2008: 127). Martin Hopenhayn also considers counter-hegemony at work, but describes it in more detailed form as

> global thinking that encompasses the United Nations system, a pro-fuse range of non-governmental organisations and academics around the world, connected through crossborder networks [concerned with] greater social justice, greater regulation and a global order based on rights. In addition, counter-hegemony is rooted in a set of local actors who may or may not be part of transnational networks and who construct practices and discourses from the margins and interstices of economics, politics and global culture. (2004)

For Bob Deacon, such counter-hegemony reflects the need for a 'shared international political project to secure a socially just world through some combination of restored and equitable national social policies, strengthened and effective regional social policies and a measure of global social redistribution, regulation and rights articulation and realization' (2005b: 433–44).

The counter-hegemonic forces that Cox discussed and which Polanyi predicted as a response to deregulated, unrestrained 'consensual' neo-liberalism cover challenges at both ideational and material levels. Most contemporary literature and argument concerns the latter and represents critiques of sporadic, manic, specific global governance outcomes. They tend less to be concerned with counter-hegemony that challenges the legitimacy of the underlying ideation (structure) that has crystallized through socialization, institutionalization and habituation to substanti-ate the present normality and its hegemony of discourse and public worldview. Of those who have, Cox has been criticized as being both too utopian and too pessimistic. But his work was also criticized because it did not clearly enough elaborate upon what a counter-hegemonic nebuleuse might look like, how it might coalesce, or how it might impact on the dominant hegemony and thus alter the consequences of global governance and its regimes. W. Andy Knight summarized these critiques, writing that 'the chief problem with Cox's work is that he does not provide a programmatic set of policies that could unite the multifarious protest movement into a potent enough force to combat … globalization' (2003: 404). Knight also queried how and where the necessary coalescing of multifaceted resistance would occur, since Cox had not covered this problem (although it seems a little harsh to expect one person to provide all the answers). Later, however, Cox presented an argument that identified a multilevel challenge involving 'a Gramscian war of position of probably long duration', although he did not elaborate on detail (2005: 152–3).

Departing from, but also loosely attached to, Cox's tradition, and following the ontological and epistemological assumptions that consider the likelihood of cosmopolitan universality and mono-global policies presently unlikely and in some ways undesirable, I will attempt to paint a more detailed picture of what a counter-hegemony may look like. To begin with, I connect a set of otherwise disparate and multidisciplinary contributions that mainly lie beyond the narrow ambit of international relations. To this end, I suggest that there is an emerging counter-hegemonic constellation of actors and forces that are confronting both the ideation of the present hegemony as well as the violent agency and outcomes that derive from global governance values and preferences.

I propose that a compromise achieved through counter-hegemony would be helpful to all concerned. Rather than a long-lasting attempt to build new 'historic blocs' or to change the entire structure of world order and its social relations, I suggest that ongoing critiques within an evolving counter-hegemony are adopting middle-ground responses to the challenges to human security caused by global governance. That is, the 'nebuleuse' upon which I will expand (below) is able to propose relatively moderate policy change without attempting, or even desiring, to subordinate or overthrow completely the underlying beliefs of global governance. In essence, it is an attempt to manage the biopolitical consequences of neoliberal governance that persist in emphasizing economic growth while underemphasizing the importance of social care for anything other than sporadic financial shocks, as opposed to long-term structural inequality (Craig and Porter 2006; Spence 2008). Despite its failings, neoliberalism is here to stay for the time being; and despite, or perhaps because of, its gross inadequacies, its form is mutable, and a revised and less damaging version is readily imaginable and envisioned with relatively minor transformations at institutional levels.

In this tradition, of moderation and tampering, rather than mutiny and termination, David Held argues that regulated neoliberalism might in some form 'provide a powerful impetus' towards growth, human security and development. But in its unregulated form, he adds, it 'falls short of managed economic change geared to the prosperity of all', since 'the current rules of global trade are heavily structured to protect the interest of the well-off and are heavily structured against the interests of the poorest countries as well as the middle-income ones' (2008: 104). Growth, then, is a necessary, but not sufficient, requirement for meaningful poverty reduction, because not everyone can engage with the carefully designed and articulated self-serving rules of hegemonic neoliberalism. Millions will remain excluded from participation in equitable economic growth because neoliberalism's rules ensure unequal participation through protectionism and many other covenants central to key hegemonic institutions and the processes that maintain them in their present modes. Present hegemonic consensus in key neoliberal national and international institutions continues to authorize, condone and legitimize an ever more unregulated economy claimed to end poverty through growth, despite having failed over the last sixty years to eradicate poverty in Africa, or to create wealth in eastern Europe without establishing debt where it did not pre-exist (ibid.). The 'creative destruction' of neoliberalism identified by the Commission on Growth and Development in 2008 is claimed to be 'economically natural' (Spence 2008; Harvey 2007). But such quixotic oxymorons dignify with a sense of reluctant inevitability an often brutal system rent with internal contradictions, inconsistencies, fallacies and myths. There is, in fact, nothing natural at all about a socially constructed neoliberal system that perpetuates structural inequality and entropy, and aggravates international political disequilibria while precipitating conditions for hard security crises.

Indeed, neoliberalism is considered by some (Sorensen 2001; Duffield 2001) to be the cause of illiberal behaviours in the global peripheries (as responses to an exclusionary and stratified globalization) that prompted Mary Kaldor (1999) to urge cosmopolitan police-keeping in an effort to subdue the uncooperative borderlands whose behaviour she disconnects from its structural causation. It is this disconnection of structure and outcome, governance and mismanagement, power and consequence, which permits mainstream security to hold broad human security at arm's length and to sanction the pacification of the unruly Other; but it is no reason to propose the dismantling of the entire neoliberal system, nor is it necessary to do so. The counter-hegemonic nebuleuse is mostly in favour of a 'third way' response at the international level to manage the socially constructed and mutable inadequacies of hegemonic, unregulated neoliberalism. The achievement of such a 'middle way' was described by Peter Evans as a 'partial hijacking by progressives acting globally'. He added that this 'is not a bad compromise, [since dominating hegemons] are much better off if [a nebuleuse] combines the task of providing stability and predictability with efforts at well-being-oriented regulation' (2000). Evans proposes a compromise and a 'bargain': one which is 'not all that dissimilar from the one that produced the welfare state and embedded liberalism, except that it must be constructed at the global level'. Evans went as far as to suggest that this approach 'may well be an integral part of the only political project that can provide the institutional underpinnings that the current global political economy needs to survive' (ibid.: 239–40; Held 2004). The strength of this proposal is its familiarity and closeness to the existing regime; the weakness is that neoliberalism is not yet ready for social subsidies in developing countries, even if it routinely ignores them in the developed world.

A NEW NEBULEUSE?

I turn now to a prospective nebuleuse: an evolving body of thought concerned with challenging the consequences of unregulated neoliberal governance which constitutes a counter-hegemonic movement aimed not at global revolution but at aspects of particular institutional reform. I undertake this analysis through the lens of the under-five mortality rate, which I stress here and in an earlier work is largely avoidable (Roberts 2008a; Chen and Narasimhan 2003; Thomas and Weber 2004; Pogge 2002). This should be uncontroversial, since there are few grounds on which to eschew care of children, even if some states, such as Somalia and the USA, have rejected the Convention on the Rights of the Child (CRC). Using the U5MR as a source of broad consensus parallels the use by Paul Diehl, Charlotte Ku and Daniel Zamora of genocide to illustrate a debate on norms, because of the uniformity of its rejection by the international community (2003: 62). One may assume that the U5MR is similarly abhorred and uniformly condemned. Not to challenge the barbarism of the dominant international norms that neglect tens of millions of avoidable child deaths implies that the status quo is acceptable (Box 1983; Reiman 1979). It is not. Virginia Held claims that:

> The ethics of care recognizes that human beings are dependent for many years of their lives, that the moral claim of those dependent on us for the care they need is pressing, and that there are highly important moral aspects in developing the relations of caring that enable human beings to live and progress. All persons need care for at least their early years. Prospects for human progress and flourishing hinge fundamentally on the care that those needing it receive, and the ethics of care stresses the moral force of the responsibility to the needs of the dependent. (2006: 10)

Children need care wherever they are. If this argument is insufficient to challenge neoliberal determinism of the biopoverty that kills millions, then we may argue, uncomfortably, that there are profound economic advantages in a neoliberal system in ensuring children are well cared for in terms of health and education. Those children will be less of a drain on weak health infrastructures and more able educationally to enter the production and consumption arenas essential to the propagation of neoliberalism. In addition, there will be a 'trickle-up' effect in terms of adult human security, if the basics of child health security like clean water and sanitation are provided, enhancing growth and prosperity – within the ultimate ideational and material limitations implicit in competitive, individualist neoliberalism. I do not suggest that this is the most that should be done, or that economic benefit should be the key rationale for reducing child mortality and enhancing human security. It appears, however, that this may be the only argument acceptable to the Post-Washington Consensus (PWC), and may therefore function to shift the trajectory of an otherwise brutal and malfeasant dystopia.

The counter-hegemonic nebuleuse I suggest is evolving is comprised of four elements. Each is distinct in itself, but the concerns of some overlap with the interests of others. The first element draws from the interests and concerns of global public health professionals. There is growing evidence in the scholarly literature that medical doctors, psychologists, psychiatrists, surgeons and other practitioners of medicine, as well as public health advocates, scholars, policy analysts and researchers, are considering their work within the broader fields of human security and global governance. They are engaging in scholarly debate and in advocacy. These engagements range from the British Medical Association's (BMA) condemnation of boxing on grounds of ill health, to critical intellectual inquiry into the socio-economic causes of a range of preventable illnesses and the technologies that can reduce attendant mortality rates, by way of human rights legislation and international law.

A second element of such a counter-hegemonic community might involve social policy scholarship and policy design. Although there has for many years been debate about what might constitute effective and appropriate social policy in most of the mature democracies, social policy scholarship has effectively 'gone global'. This has been in response to the question of national social policy in developing countries increasingly being determined as a result of the demands of the Post-Washington Consensus. Such critical inquiry and challenge are primarily concerned with the notion that neoliberalism excludes the principle and practice of publicly provided social 'safety nets', a prevalent state function in most of the global North, but considered perhaps all the more necessary where conditions are more extreme and where elemental preventable diseases are rife and deadly. This element has in fact triggered its own peer-reviewed and widely respected *Global Social Policy* journal.

A third element has become increasingly vociferous in its intellectual critique of the foundational beliefs and routine practices of neoliberalism. Critical international political economy is increasingly concerned with the epistemological and ontological inadequacy of neoliberalism's underpinnings; with its discursive hegemony; and with the inequality attached to a deeply flawed and problematic economic system. This grouping of scholars provides evidence of the unequal and uneven outcomes of 'impartial' and 'neutral' neoliberalism and provides us with an effective counter to the intellectual claims of the neoliberal project, and is essential for demonstrating how poverty is caused and aggravated by neoliberal policies, rather than by the failure of people, states and societies to adhere closely enough to neoliberal practices.

The fourth element involves scholarship concerned with how the international system may be changed. There is little doubt that the expectation of change locates the study of norms dynamics, as it is sometimes known, firmly within the epistemological assumptions and ontological worldviews of social constructivism. Recent work has identified a range of conditions that 'tip' change, and further work is being conducted on the platforms necessary to carry 'norms entrepreneurs' within the international system. It is an important conceptual approach that carries with it significant potential, when applied at the practical level to the theoretical musings of the other elements of this nebuleuse. In short, if the consideration of medical science, social policy scholars and critical economists can make sense of alternative propositions on how to reframe the rules of global governance around humanizing security and securing the human, then norms scholars' intellectual inquiry considers how to convert those ideas into mainstream practices. I turn now to the first of these elements in greater detail.

MEDICAL SCIENCE AND HUMAN SECURITY

Medical science, like other branches of the natural sciences including atomic physics, has long played a role in international relations (Jenssen 2001; Evans 2002). Traditionally, this has been in terms of warfare: the medical scientific approach to battlefield trauma has long been deeply embedded in international institutions like the Red Cross and, more latterly, the International Committee of the Red Cross and Red Crescent – ICRC (Watts 2003). This reflects a desire to respond to immediate casualties of conventional security problems. At another level, medical science has entered the debate on more structural issues such as human rights (Evans 2002). Physicians for Human Rights, for example, are concerned with a wide range of assaults on human dignity around the world. These bodies might be classified as agency oriented.

More recently, medical science has taken a direct interest in the concept of human security and the causes of its denial in an approach that might be classified as both structure and outcome oriented, implying a cause-and-effect relationship. One might suggest it acts as a palliative to consequence but also as a critique of causation. Jack Piachaud, for example, argues that 'global health and human security are inextricably bound to [human] survival'. As editor of *Medicine, Conflict and Survival*, his concern is clearly enunciated when he states that 'the primary issue for [this] journal [is] ill-health as a measure of suffering [as] the yardstick by which we judge the nature of our global society and the progress of our ... policies' (2008: 1–3). Thus, health protection is held up as an element of broad human security. In line with these arguments, medical scientists have increasingly chosen to engage with matters of power and health. Within this debate, their scientific expertise has turned to human security as it is determined by neoliberal institutions and beliefs.

It is this broad conceptualization of human security which vexes many conservative security specialists, who are concerned that this kind of imagining of human security 'would destroy its intellectual coherence and make it more difficult to devise solutions to any of these important problems' (Buzan et al. 1998: 3–4; Stoett 1999; Krause 2004). Scholars and practitioners of medical science, however, present intellectually solid and reliable epistemologies and mechanisms for rendering coherent aspects of broad human security such that it covers mass avoidable civilian deaths caused by the preferences, priorities and values of global governance processes. In short, if structural impoverishment caused by international regimes causes millions of avoidable civilian deaths, medical science can identify causation and provide solutions using positivist, scientific methodologies.

Among such scholars, Nathan Taback and Robin Coupland discuss health as human security and vice versa. They conclude that there is a significant role for medical science in the wider multi-sectoral treatment of public health as human security. They further argue that 'the big issues in human security relate to the impact on health of any type of violence of one sort or another whether it is, for example, structural or physical' (2008: 23). For them, and many other health specialists, health and human security are inextricably interwoven. They argue that 'when different disciplines examine human security ... it is people's health that is the irreducible element; indeed health becomes a measure of insecurity' (2007: 3). Having recognized health as a human security issue, inquiry is turned towards causation and, inevitably, this is structural in character. From outside the domain of security studies, they propose a multidisciplinary approach to such problems, since such health insecurities derive from a combination of political, economic, security and developmental challenges. They advance a 'science of human security', which describes a 'newly emerging multidisciplinary field', and propose a scientific methodological basis involving the collation of a range of research data from primary fieldwork and secondary patient records using a number of verifiable and proven methodological approaches (ibid.: 5–7).

Alan Buchanan and Mathew Decamp parallel this intervention. They write that

> due to the revolution in information technologies and the emergence of transnational epistemic communities equipped with powerful empirical methodologies for measuring and explaining health and disease, we now know more about the health problems of people in other countries than ever before.

Having established the impact of medical science in examining and explaining health securities globally, they add that 'we also now have greater institutional resources, both within wealthier states and through international and transnational organizations, for applying this new knowledge to ameliorate global health problems' (2007: 506). Recognizing and responding to the concerns of the traditional security sector regarding research data reliability and policy coherence, Taback and Coupland maintain that avoidable deaths in the under-fives, the second-largest single group of victims of neoliberal and state policy choices and restrictions, 'could be measured via an epidemiological study and hence would clearly be an instance of a scientific method applied to human security' (2008: 24). Black confirms the vitality of this claim, writing that 'child health epidemiology is developing and increasingly can provide information ... on causes and determinants of death [which] would be available for planning at national or subnational levels' (2003: 2234). Scientific disciplines outside IR challenge and undermine essential realist critiques of human security and confirm the viability of coherent policy derived from positivist methodologies and epistemologies.

Taback and Coupland elaborate: if 'avoidable deaths in the under fives [are] an instance of the wider conceptualization of human security', then they fall 'within the science of human security' (2008: 24).

Furthermore, one of the world's leading and most respected medical journals, *The Lancet*, declared that if low-level interventions were made available globally, 63 per cent of child deaths would be preventable. This is clearly a fixable problem and the necessary interventions are available (but not necessarily accessible) to reduce the child mortality rate by almost two-thirds. This means that active processes are prioritizing other issues that relegate the U5MR to the point where more than six million infants die needlessly every year. Of these, roughly four million die in the first twenty-eight days of life (UNICEF 2007: 24–5). The prediction model used by *The Lancet*, and the data from the World Health Organization, 'identify pneumonia, diarrhea and malaria as causing the greatest numbers of deaths in children younger than 5 years' (Black 2003: 2231). According to globally recognized health expertise, these are mainly identifiable, treatable and preventable (WHO 2008; UNICEF 2007; Thomas and Weber 2004).

Furthermore, although it is correct that some of the countries in which the U5MR is highest are least able to provide reliable national data through vital event registrations, Black identifies 'alternatives to the reporting of vital events [including] use of data from nationally-representative surveys and special study populations' with which 'ascertainment of death is usually very complete ...' (2003: 2231). While there are problems in identifying exactly which children have such conditions, the problem is almost always exacerbated where levels of clean water are inadequate and where sanitation is absent or compromised.

The suggestion, then, that human security is indefinable and incoherent is wrong. Perhaps the largest segment of broad human security, in the form of 10 million deaths per year in the U5M grouping, makes this demonstrably clear. We may therefore argue that any claim to reject broad human security on the grounds that it, or aspects of it, is indefinable neglects available conceptualizations (Roberts 2008b; Owen 2004; Newman 2001; Grayson 2008) to which medical science can relate epidemiological data (Taback and Coupland 2007; Jones 2003; Piachaud 2008). Since there are 10 million deaths annually, there will be more than enough epidemiologically and methodologically reliable data to establish immediate causation from which preventive policy may be determined (WHO 2008; Chen and Narasimhan 2003; Taback and Coupland 2007; Jones 2003).

Medical science also considers proximal or indirect causation, based on the science of medical diagnosis. *The Lancet* remarks upon the social construction of poverty and multiple sequential and/or concurrent causes of death in the under-fives, noting that this invariably complicates verification of cause of death. It argues, however, that in most cases 'the likelihood of contracting initiating or subsequent diseases and illnesses is diminished with access to appropriate nutrition and relevant healthcare and basic needs interventions' (Black 2003; Bloom and Canning 2007). *The Lancet* confirms proximal causes of U5M as deriving from 'socioeconomic factors, such as income, social status, and education ...' (Black 2003: 2173; Gordon 2007; McMichael 1999). The consequences of national and supranational policy are lethal. The WHO annual report for 1995 codes poverty in its International Classification of Disease (ICD) as Z59.5, and it is worth quoting at length to allow the mind to absorb the staggering breadth, range and depth of human consequences:

> Poverty is the main reason why babies are not vaccinated, clean water and sanitation are not provided, and curative drugs and other treatments are unavailable and why mothers die in childbirth. Poverty is the main cause of reduced life expectancy, of handicap and disability, of starvation. Poverty is a major contributor to mental illness, stress, suicide, family disintegration and substance abuse. Poverty wields its destructive influence at every stage of human life from the moment of conception to the grave. It conspires with the most deadly and painful diseases to bring a wretched existence to all who suffer from it ... For many millions of people for whom survival is a daily battle, the prospect of a longer life may seem more like a punishment than a prize. (WHO 1995; Gordon 2007: 252)

Although global governance and its financial institutions objectify poverty and propose the neutral market as solution, the denial of its social construction, its subjectivity and its gross inefficacy in relation to poverty alleviation is evident to medical science in ways that it is not to mainstream security scholarship. Medical practitioners writing in *The Lancet* painted the picture of relationships between socially constructed poverty, inequality, ill health and broad human security in stark terms:

> Socioeconomic inequities in child survival ... exist at every step along the path from exposure and resistance to infectious disease, through careseeking, to the probability that [a] child will receive prompt treatment with effective therapeutic agents. The odds are stacked against the poorest children at every one of these steps ... Poor people ... are least able to afford water connecting and usage charges, non-polluting heating and cooking fuels, and houses of appropriate size. Low

income enhances the chances of hunger and malnutrition, thereby reducing resistance to disease. Absence of income also constrains use of appropriate medical care both directly – because user fees cannot be paid – and indirectly because the other costs associated with using health services, such as transport costs, are not affordable. (Victora et al. 2003: 235; Hemson et al. 2008)

Similarly, Benjamin Meier, public health law project manager at Columbia's Centre for Health Policy, argues that the broad effects of economic globalization are responsible for a social pathology of ill health. Globalization, for Meier, 'has harmed the public's health through myriad, overlapping causal pathways' (2007: 545). These might include an absent or denied education, wherein mothers remain ignorant of the need for immunization in children or basic health actions like boiling river water before consumption; and it is women who experience exclusion from education more frequently than men. Often, this is because girls (rather than boys) are taken out of schooling to take up the slack in household finances caused by ill health and other contributors to impoverishment. Girls also have their education rescinded and drop out of school in their millions because of inadequate sanitation, 'consigning them to a future of illiteracy and restricted choice' (UNHDR 2006: 22; Sen and Ostlin 2007). The causative chain can therefore be very reliably located within neoliberal policy, which increases the costs of healthcare provision through privatization and decreases accessibility of free public healthcare through the prohibition of subsidies and through associated lending conditionality.

Allyn Taylor confirms and expands upon the move towards interrogating international neoliberal policies and national neoliberal prescription in national health matters. He notes the 'proliferation of cross-border determinants of health status ... undermining the capacity of nation states to protect health through domestic action alone' (2007: 525; Gable 2007). Peters et al. also refer to supranational determinants of public health provision when they argue that 'when health care is needed yet delayed or not obtained, people's health worsens, which in turn leads to lost income and higher health care costs, both of which contribute to poverty' (2007: 1). Pemberton (2004) and Gordon (2007) demonstrate this simple relationship and the former elaborates the means by which it is denied. Perhaps Meier expresses it best when he declares that it is the 'neoliberal economic paradigm [which] undermines the supply of public goods, crippling public health systems and diminishing their ability to prevent disease and promote health' (2007: 547). Innumerable others demonstrate how neoliberal strategy and policy also discourage reliable and efficacious nutritional supplies to the poorest by demanding debt repayment strategies that demand the cash-cropping of national food supplies for export when they are needed indigenously (George 1989; Roberts 2008a; Pogge 2002 among others). Neoliberalism urges state retraction from health subsidies and promotes the market as the only efficient means by which medicine and healthcare provision may be efficiently distributed. The poorest people can never afford fully marketized nutrition and care. The poorest people number more than two billion, since it is this number who struggle to survive on less than two dollars per day. Nor should it be forgotten that two dollars per day is not the minimum people live on. According to the World Bank, the per capita income in Liberia, for example, is 79 cents per day (World Bank 2007a: 3); while in Sierra Leone it is between 65 cents and $1.70 (UNDP 2008: 31). Furthermore, although this method of measuring the number of people in such extremes of difficulty helps us make sense of the problem in terms of proportionality, it reinforces the idea that people are earning in a market system that may improve, when in fact the opportunities for improvements measured in such terms may be non-existent. In such conditions, and when sudden economic shocks aggravate existing insecurities, women and girls experience the consequences more, since males are normally prioritized for care because of their slightly better relationships to economic production (Sen and Ostlin 2007). This distortion and inequity reflect unequal distributions of power within political elites at all levels (Harrington 1992; Peterson 1992); and this is a consequence of the reality that men

> in many parts of the world exercise power over women, making decisions on their behalf, regulating and constraining their behaviour and constraining their access to resources and personal agency, and sanctioning and policing their behaviour through socially condoned violence or the threat of violence. (Sen and Ostlin 2007: xiv)

To put this in relative political perspective, the U5MR affects boys and girls differently, and is higher in the peripheral conditions shared by billions of human beings who are prevented from influencing neoliberal global governance policy-making that affects them lethally.

However, the conditions generating such avoidable mayhem also provide the context for transformation. In 2003, Paula Gutlove and Gordon Thompson presented the relationship between health, power and human security as 'a context within which to build partnerships across disciplines, sectors and agencies' (2003: 17). This cross-disciplinary approach recurs frequently, as we shall see, where medical science confronts human security. Gutlove and Thompson argue that human security as a concept 'offers particular promise as a framework for debating and acting upon humanity's shared interests and vulnerabilities', and propose considering human security as falling within the domain of public health (ibid.: 18). They conclude that 'proven principles of public health can, with some expansion of their traditional scope of application, make major contributions' to human security threat reduction (ibid.: 18). They suggest that:

> Health is a crucial domain of human security and a human security approach rooted in international consensus can bring added value to existing policies and programmes. The world would benefit from a comprehensive strategy for enhancing public health within a human security framework. (ibid.: 31)

Clearly, some medical professionals identify strongly with the relationship between human security, public health and global policy. They describe the operation of a system designed to confront public health problems that are national and transnational in impacts in terms of 'existing institutions' that will 'promote collaboration by national governments, international agencies, private foundations, academic institutions, professional groups, citizen organizations and businesses, [and] pharmaceutical companies' (ibid.: 31). This approach recognizes the distribution of public health as a national matter, but also sees existing international structures as sources of transformation, if differently used.

Medical science provides us with epidemiological and methodological reliability in ascertaining causation of avoidable mortality en masse and links it to neoliberal policies, as we have seen; but it also, crucially, generates data with which to design and implement effective policy responses that will reduce the U5MR. Medical science, then, gives us tools to apply to the problem of broad human security; it gives us coherent groupings and the means of identifying avoidable mass mortality; and it gives us the means with which to address this problem at a relatively low cost. It also confirms which policies *not* to apply in order to reduce the U5MR as an element of global human security. Medical science helps render human security both coherent and policy-potent, with potential for immediate and telling positive impacts. At least two options present themselves. First, the neoliberal hegemony of global governance continues to undermine public health provision for the most vulnerable people in the world and, increasingly, this approach expands in the global North as public sectors shrink. Second, health infrastructure and policies might be influenced by epidemiology analysis and funded by international financial institutions.

POOR HEALTH, WEAK GROWTH?

Contemporary neoliberal arguments and policy are presented as necessary for growth; and growth will propel people from excruciating poverty. There is little question that the first part of this statement holds some degree of truth. Europe and North America have experienced phenomenal growth since the end of the Second World War, despite a series of derailing downturns. But the second element of the argument – that growth lifts all boats and will spur people out of severe poverty – is deeply problematic. Growth, it would appear, is a necessary, but not sufficient, condition for the foreclosure of poverty. This is because numerous other factors must be present, such as a level playing field on which to compete for profits (to name one); and because people must be able to engage with the gears of neoliberal practices. The first of these two is widely understood now, but the second is less clear. In different places, different conditions undermine people's engagement with growth opportunities at the most basic levels. To benefit from the mechanisms of capitalism, certain conditions must be present. These conditions are normal in many developed countries, and in some metropolises in developing countries. But they are absent for hundreds of millions of people in the developing world and, increasingly, people in deprived areas of the global North are also denied the basic means by which prosperity is legally and formally acquired.

Those whose lives are suspended in conditions of poverty and who are unable to read or write, for example, are inevitably disadvantaged compared to those who are literate, when it comes to participating in the neoliberal project. Those able to read a computer manual (and access a PC) have acquired certain skills, as have those able to write a business plan or a contract. People denied literacy have more problems opening bank accounts than those able to identify their postal or zip codes, filling in an application form online or in an office, and acquiring the necessary documentation needed to support endeavours like these that are important to legal business. And as neoliberal institutional values spread, the bureaucratization of the social world increasingly creates barriers to illiterate or innumerate people in the kind of practices taken for granted by orthodox neoliberal economists. To take a job with an employer as a driver, the rules of global governance increasingly dictate that a candidate may have to have a driver's licence, and in most developing countries such matters have not been enforced traditionally. Surmounting the bu-

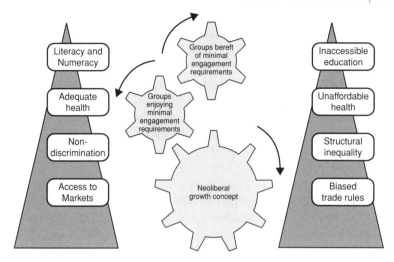

Figure 3.1 Facilitators and inhibitors for engagement with neoliberalism

reaucratic procedure requires particular skills which have to be acquired over time, without which the licence is unobtainable and the labour opportunity is lost. Such experiences are commonplace in many parts of the world. And people denied numeracy are even more disengaged from neoliberalism, since it is primarily evaluated quantitatively. The ability to count well is central to growth development and cash acquisition and accumulation. It is taken for granted in the global North, but it cannot at all be relied on to a reasonable degree for many people in many parts of the global South. And in an obvious but inadequately contemplated causal chain, disease inhibits education, which in turn undermines the ability to engage in growth activities. The UN Human Development Report (HDR) notes that 'water-related diseases ... cost 443 million school days each year ... and diminish learning potential' (UNHDR 2006: 22). In the global knowledge economy, this is a serious inhibitor to participation in neoliberal growth agendas.

There are other inhibitors to participation in neoliberalism. Ill health is one of them. Poverty, lack of adequate nutrition and vulnerability to avoidable illnesses weaken the body and undermine cognitive development and the ability to engage with the intellectually demanding challenges associated with neoliberal growth projects, such as business or law, or applications for microcredit or larger loans for start-up purposes (Bloom and Canning 2007). Exposure to life-threatening illnesses cripples the ability to grow and develop. It also imposes a burden on an already severely strained family structure, because for the billions in absolute poverty, financing recovery from critical illness either privately or publicly requires that other essential needs are marginalized. Malaria, for example, simply reducible with cheap interventions like nets and sprays, is described as 'a major constraint to economic development' which can constitute a 'growth penalty' of '1.3 percent in some African countries' (RBM 2008). This 'growth penalty' is made up of the medical costs in human and material resources required to treat it, once caught; the cost of trying to prevent it, either at local levels or in terms of vector management (the redirection of malaria-carrying mosquitoes en masse); and growth lost owing to illness incapacity. The UN Roll Back Malaria (RBM) campaign also notes that 'in some countries with a heavy malaria burden, the disease may account for as much as 40 percent of public health expenditure, 30–35 percent of inpatient admissions, and up to 50 percent of outpatient visits' (ibid.).

Furthermore, areas known for endemic infection deter investment and production, perpetuating poverty. In Cambodia in 1992, mass area denial for settlement, growth and production in the north-west of the country was ascribed to the presence of two killers: landmines, and malaria (Roberts 2001). The Roll Back Malaria campaign also describes growth losses from 'lost workdays' and 'the value of unpaid work done in the home', as well as 'the discounted future lifetime earnings of those who die'. It notes further inhibitors on growth from lost tourism to infected areas, and lost market opportunities due to the unwillingness of business people/traders to travel to malaria-infected areas (ibid.). Nor can malaria be analysed remote from its economic context: conditions of poverty, such as poor housing, increase exposure risks. The better the housing, with mesh-protected doors, electricity, air conditioning and sealed water pipes, for example, the lower the likelihood of malarial mosquitoes thriving and infecting. The poorer the housing, with no doors, weak electricity for fans, no air conditioning, no sealed walls and water stored in buckets and pots outside, the greater the likelihood of exposure to mosquito bites.

The consequences of crippling diseases like malaria, polio and measles lock out the millions infected from neoliberal growth opportunities. The young boy and girls in Phnom Penh who crawl across the main street in the baking midday sun, chasing cash from tourists on Achar Mean Boulevard, their legs bent out of shape by diseases that could have been prevented, will likely beg until they die prematurely. Some of them will be ruthlessly exploited by street gangs and criminals who facilitate such a child's contact with a beneficent tourist trade, and then

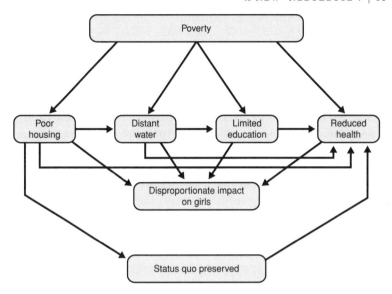

Figure 3.2 How poverty and ill health prevent engagement with neoliberalism and maintain the status quo

rob them of the money given to them by well-meaning foreigners who see only part of the problem. They remain imprisoned in this cycle to a significant extent because they do not have the ability to engage with neoliberalism as most educated, healthy people in other parts of the world do. Such factors seem absent from the calculations of neoliberal economics. In short, as Peters et al. put it, 'The relationship between poverty and access to health care can be seen as part of a larger vicious cycle, where poverty leads to ill health, and ill health maintains poverty' (2007: 10).

The above are some of the conditions that are necessary for engagement with neoliberal growth and escape from poverty and ill health. But those conditions are aggravated yet further by the unfair rules of hegemonic neoliberalism. Institutional inequities sanctioned by international conventions and international law (for example, the WTO) tilt further an already uneven playing field to the detriment of those who are denied adequate education and health by the very conditions of poverty from which they seek to escape. We may therefore make a strong case that if health is undermined, growth and poverty reduction will remain elusive for the millions whose health needs it the most (Millen et al. 2000). Neoliberal growth strategies are incomplete, inadequate and ignorant of the essential requirements for engagement with their primary processes.

GOOD HEALTH, STRONG GROWTH

We may make the opposite case also. If health necessities are financed accessibly rather than at market rates that very poor people cannot afford, growth will more likely follow (Agenor and Moreno-Dodson 2006). The Commission on Growth and Development, which favours neoliberal approaches, also identifies the importance of accessible nutrition and health provision in the acquisition and maintenance of cognitive and non-cognitive skills essential for personal growth and employability (Spence 2008; Kilburn and Karoly 2008). Two public health experts based at Harvard, David Bloom and David Canning, confirm that 'health follows income' and that 'income is a consequence of health'. They also argue, however, that 'health may be not only a consequence but also a cause of a high level of income' (2007: 1; Bloom et al. 2002). Furthermore, they argue that 'relatively inexpensive public health interventions and policies can have remarkable impacts on population health even in very poor countries', adding that 'in practice, the major force behind health improvements has been improvements in health technologies and public health measures that prevent the spread of infectious disease, and not higher incomes'. They conclude that 'health interventions can improve population health, without the need for prior improvements in income' (2007: 3; Cahill 1993; Crow and Thorpe 1992). Specifically, reducing the number of deaths from avoidable illnesses is likely to have a positive impact on economic growth, since it means more potential workers. Bloom and Canning also publish research relating to Africa, where the U5MR is particularly severe. They conclude that 'investing in health, with the aid of the international community, could make a big difference in Africa's economic prospects. Moreover, some feasible, low-cost interventions would likely have high returns' (2004: 57). Elsewhere, Bloom, Canning and Sevilla identify more causation between health and economic growth and argue that 'good health has a positive, sizable, and statistically significant effect on aggregate output' (2001, 2004; Suhrcke 2006).

We may reasonably conclude, then, that increasing health provision will reduce the infant mortality rate with a concomitant increase in prosperity to be anticipated. We may reasonably assume that a larger number of surviving children represent greater human capital with which to engage neoliberal economic governance precepts and create growth and prosperity. The human and health security of infants are directly related, and good health (survival, in the case of the U5MR) is positively related to economic growth. It is a necessary, but not sufficient, element of growth from poverty to prosperity. The paradox lies here: health provision is essential for the millions of penurious infants who die avoidably; but global governance rules demand that people with almost no money are charged for essential-to-life biopolitical needs like water and sanitation. Neoliberal governance provides excellent healthcare opportunities, but only for those who can afford it. Privatization, deregulation and the removal of state subsidies by fiat maintain deep inequity, high mortality rates and lower growth outputs. The problem is aggravated because the solution is pyrrhic. Perpetuation of neoliberal governance stands in direct opposition to the achievement of the Millennium Development Goals (MDGs) in the poorest environments, since insistence on claiming water as an economic good that should be distributed by the market is a large part of the problem the MDGs face in ensuring social access to water for the poorest people. It comes as a surprise to many people that there is more than enough water in, for example, Africa for the entire population; that it is inaccessible to large numbers of people is a function of the organization of its distribution both within and without the continent. Hemson et al. describe the problem lucidly and simply when they declare that 'water scarcity is the result of the interplay between resource availability, consumption patterns and the (mis-)management of the resources', adding that 'water scarcity is thus linked to water governance rather than to shortage in the absolute physical sense of the term' (2008: 5). This argument mirrors the more sophisticated comprehension of famine that evolved from it being misunderstood as an unfortunate tragedy to being seen as a matter of resource availability and then as one of accessibility to available resources.

THE EUROPEAN EXPERIENCE

The contemporary neoliberal diktat regarding the retraction of the state from public provision in the developing world stands in stark contrast to policies instigated in Europe when it experienced similar developmental challenges to those presently facing many states in Africa and Asia. In the 1800s, people in the UK, for example, faced similar conditions of extreme poverty and extensive exposure to waterborne diseases, with a state that had very little role in public health. These conditions were aggravated by growing population movements from the countryside to towns and cities attendant upon the Industrial Revolution. The increasing concentration of large numbers of people, coupled with enlarged international trade, brought a greater number of people into contact with a greater concentration of disease (Hobsbawn 1997a; Rosen 1993).

According to the UN, the infant mortality rate in the UK during the period of early industrialization was roughly equivalent to Nigeria's in 2007. A combination of massive state investment in the provision of clean water and improved sanitation led to a substantial decline in infant mortality from 160 deaths per 1,000 live births to 100. The UN notes this represents 'one of the steepest declines in history'. Although other factors were at work, these giant public investments, which 'displaced private water operators as the main providers of water in towns and cities' in England, were essential ingredients in the reduction of infant mortality from waterborne diseases (UNHDR 2006: 29). The WHO points out that, for Europe, a combination of vaccine development and public sanitation procedures 'helped industrialized countries, which had reliable access to them, to eliminate or markedly decrease the infectious disease threats', adding that 'improvements in hygiene and standards of living in these more prosperous parts of the world altered the conditions that had allowed the diseases to flourish' (2007: 6; Mehrotra and Delamonica 2005: 142). Public health investment by European governments, as well as scientific advances (which are now available for dissemination globally), was an essential element in the improvement of health for very poor people and facilitated their self-maximizing engagement with industrialization, capitalism and early elements of contemporary neoliberal approaches to growth and prosperity (Mehrotra and Delamonica 2005). In these conditions, the British government recognized the relationship of public illness to national growth when it amended poverty legislation to reduce the economic costs of infectious disease. Although social investment and public health infrastructure took decades to develop, 'in the end they had a major effect on mortality, reducing health costs and increasing economic output potential' (Mackenbach 2007: 2; Bhaskar 2008). The approach was successful because of state commitment to and investment in national public health (Hamlin and Sheard 1998: 587; Hobsbawm 1997a). Private arbitrary provision was replaced by expansive public protection in a process that is widely accepted as having contributed substantially to UK and European economic growth. It is all the more surprising, then, that this approach, which reduced mortality rates and increased growth, is rejected and denied by neoliberal prescription for people in the global South (Reinert 2007; Chang 2002).

It is not an unreasonable intellectual leap to suggest that the reduction in infant (and broader adult) mortality and concomitant growth in

Europe a century ago could be replicated substantially in other parts of the world, since the issue is primarily scientific, rather than 'cultural'. The underlying biopolitical *force majeure* was the subjugation of the market to state intervention in conditions of widespread poverty for the purposes of public health, since the market will not supply where those demanding have insufficient money to pay market rates. The same conditions in essence apply in many developing countries: large-scale health infrastructural interventions are required in a context of abject penury that market provision will not respond to. The huge cost borne by European governments is considered by most to have been a wise and munificent investment, as it is still essential to the maintenance of good health, the prevention of lethal diseases and the productivity of a healthy workforce in what was clearly a biopolitical engagement between state and society. The principle is transferable and relevant, but is subject to the biopolitical choices and directives of neoliberal global governance.

MEDICAL SCIENCE AND HUMAN SECURITY: A WAY FORWARD?

In contrast with the claims of mainstream security, medical science's engagement with human security suggests that a meaningful, practicable and broad conceptualization of human security can be evolved. From this perspective, human security expands as biopolitical regimes that create biopoverty contract. A key barrier to the achievement of expanded human security, then, is the persistence of neoliberal beliefs in deregulation and privatization. Medical science's epidemiological apparatus confirms that the U5MR is related directly to impoverishment and inadequate hygiene and sanitation infrastructures. Medical science also confirms that the greatest extent of avoidable child mortality happens in identifiable areas, for identifiable immediate and proximal reasons. Institutional-structural cause of death is readily traceable from immediate and proximal conditions. This scientific approach confirms beyond reasonable doubt that, although there are variations across regions and within states, the essence of causation lies in inadequate health infrastructure, from hospitals to electricity to hygiene provision. Any effective approach to reducing the U5MR must necessarily entail a holistic approach to deal with all levels of challenge. Illustrating this holism, the esteemed *British Medical Journal* (BMJ) concluded a review of sanitation and hygiene with three central observations regarding health, human security and growth. It argued that:

Firstly, effective intervention does not always need accurate knowledge of disease causation (the development of sanitary measures largely preceded the germ theory). Secondly, environmental measures may be more effective than changing individual behaviour ('passive' protection through piped drinking water and sewerage systems worked better than educating the public to improve 'active' hygienic practices). And thirdly, universal measures may be better than targeted measures in reducing health inequalities (better water supply and sanitation reached people at all social levels). These lessons [are] part of the 'collective consciousness' of public health. (Mackenbach 2007: 3)

The essential contribution of medical science to this aspect of the broad human security debate is the scientifically concluded argument that the provision of clean water and sanitation will quickly reduce U5M through either targeted or universal approaches. Targeted approaches can be applied where there are extant data, reflecting the literature's concern with different conditions in different places. There is also agreement that the challenges to generating comprehensive medical data can be surmounted or at least confronted by methodologies that scale up specific planning and distribution of interventions to national level to reduce avoidable child mortality. But the essence of the U5MR lies in its biopolitical nature, whether specificity or universality apply. It is a combination of biological essence and political organization, where the former is a consequence of the latter. The biological element allows for universality, since it is clear beyond doubt that the provision of clean water and sanitation where it is absent will reduce under-five mortality rates anywhere, regardless of specific conditions. All children need clean water and sanitation to prevent the intestinal diseases from which they die in their millions. Significant improvements far in excess of those sought by the Millennium Development Goals could be achieved readily and cheaply because, regardless of specific conditions, the provision of targeted or universally applied clean water and sanitation will produce sudden improvements. Indeed, specific approaches to geographical areas, social groups or diseases are proposed complementarily with wider, more universal methods that saturate accessible populations. Victora et al. argue forcefully that 'we know enough now to move ahead to reduce health inequities in children', adding that 'complacency is not an option' (2003: 236). In short, 'policy makers designing child health initiatives should give serious consideration to both targeted and universal coverage as potentially effective approaches for improving equity in child health care' (ibid.: 239; Gillespie 2003: 326). Indeed, Victora et al. later elaborate on the potential and drawbacks of a universal approach and find in favour of it (2004), while Peters et al. also affirm the potency of such approaches (2007). The scientifically understood, tested and proven solutions are available; the choices of policy which render them accessible are political, since we may choose whether to facilitate water and sanitation or to withhold it. The supranational structures that determine policy are inevitably biopolitical.

Already-fragile child healthcare in water-poor environments would be dramatically damaged by (supra)national policy that attempts to charge very poor people at rates they cannot afford for water. Reliable data from the WHO, UNICEF and independent scholarly medical research confirm the highest prevalence of avoidable child mortality in some of the very poorest places on earth, where income is routinely below $2 per day. Buchanan and Decamp suggest that humanity has the knowledge and capacity to change this. They argue that:

> Having reliable information about the nature and causes of global health problems, the capacity to ameliorate them, and a cosmopolitan ethical perspective that regards the need to ameliorate them as urgent is not sufficient, however. It is also necessary to move from the judgment that these problems must be addressed to concrete discussion about who should do what to solve them. (2007: 506; Box 1983)

Since strategic, structural causation is demonstrably rooted in the biopolitics of global governance, part of the solution lies in the adjustment of its practices and institutions. The application of neoliberal rules as they stand – of deregulation and privatization with the expectation that the invisible hand and impartial market mechanisms will rapidly reduce child mortality – is absurd in the context of extreme poverty. States in the most seriously affected parts of Africa and Asia cannot afford and are discouraged from supplying sufficient healthcare provision, or they choose to prioritize other policies, such as security sector reform, arms races or space exploration. Even if they could afford to subsidize healthcare for the under-fives, they are actively discouraged from doing so by neoliberal rules and the international financial institutions that enforce them. Poor people experiencing very high rates of infant mortality can rarely afford the costs of adequate nutrition, schooling and multiple disease prevention and avoidance interventions. Urging a market pricing mechanism of any kind is clearly incongruous with reducing child mortality, since the most vulnerable and exposed are least able to pay. Thomas and Weber note how orthodox economic approaches inevitably exclude 'those who cannot pay through the imposition of user fees and other cost-recovery mechanisms', and add that this 'market-based logic ... is set apart operationally from concerns and problems that cannot be expressed in terms of the logic of an economic system' (2004: 193). Richer people can afford private water provision better than poorer people. It seems necessary to restate the obvious, since the converse seems to elude neoliberal thinking. *The Lancet* urged that international agencies involved in the process of determining child mortality 'must ensure that equity considerations are an essential part of the design of all new projects, must address equity issues in dialogue with countries, and must ensure that impact evaluations provide data on equity' (Victora et al. 2003: 239). Applying markets to achieve this is quixotically oxymoronic. Very poor people cannot afford expensive water, and water does not have to be very expensive to be unaffordable if people struggle on less than two dollars a day.

Medical science illustrates the biopolitical nature of child mortality; it helps render policy-relevant definitions of human security possible and, from this, it can design interventions that will reduce child mortality. Central to this process, both from the perspective of epidemiological analysis and the European experience, is the need to manage the supply of water and the provision of sanitation. Both require substantial financial commitments and both require national and subnational implementation, but marketization must not be undertaken to the extent that accessibility is compromised for people with no money. This is not to exclude market forces, since no other form of distribution is presently deemed tolerable; but it is to argue that market provision alone will not reduce the U5MR among the poorest people in the world. Victora et al. argue that 'we must change trends and present conditions, rather than simply perpetuate them'. They add that 'approaches are available to reduce inequities; the challenge is to ensure they are implemented' (ibid.: 239). There are numerous alternatives available that have worked in the developed world to reduce the U5MR in developing countries which are eminently transferable; and there are variations on neoliberalism that can be applied to accelerate this process while bypassing some of the shortfalls of public provision. The trend, however, still shows no signs of departing in any substantial way from the present, and lethal, model of neoliberal governance that kills through the perpetuation of biopoverty.

4 | NEOLIBERALISM, WATER AND SANITATION

This chapter surveys key beliefs and assumptions associated with neo-liberal practices before critiquing them from the second, critical inter-national political economy, element of the counter-hegemonic nebuleuse inferred by Robert Cox (Chapter 3). It then examines the outcomes of water and sanitation privatization (WASP), finding that water privat-ization in developing countries is increasingly expensive for consumers and short on gain for providers in urban centres; is absent from most rural areas; and largely ignores sanitation needs. It then turns to other elements of the counter-hegemonic epistemic community for alterna-tives, finding them intellectually sound but widely contested, presently impractical and lengthy in implementation.

NEOLIBERALISM AND PRIVATIZATION

For Wendy Larner, and millions of others, neoliberalism can be understood in part as a 'policy framework' for marketization and de-regulation (2006: 200). Since the 1980s, privatization of significant tranches of traditionally state-owned public provision has become the international norm and has extended and reinforced the hegemony of neoliberalism. The evolving legitimacy of this model became enshrined in and projected by the so-called Washington Consensus (Held 2008; Craig and Porter 2006). The Washington Consensus is a term that reflects agreement between key economic powers, especially the USA, which has led in this advocacy, that a rather extreme version of neoliberalism is the way to growth and prosperity for all, in which a rising tide will float all boats. The key to this outcome is strict adherence to market discipline, key aspects of which are privatization of the state and deregulation of markets. This approach was superseded by a refined version which ac-commodated a number of criticisms of the Washington Consensus, and became known as the Post-Washington Consensus. Numerous economic devices claimed to compensate for the inadequacies of Washington Consensus neoliberal economics, such as Poverty Reduction Strategy Papers (PRSPs), were patched on to the old model, allowing the World

Bank to claim to its stakeholders and critics alike that it is a responsive institution able to accommodate criticism. I shall turn to this shortly.

At the heart of this orthodoxy lies privatization. Privatization is ideological and, like any ideological debate, it is deeply contested. Privatization, as a core aspect of neoliberal economic policy, is promoted as having universal applicability and benefits (Payne 2005). Politically, privatization frees the state of onerous responsibilities it is ill suited to deliver effectively; economically, intensified levels of competition lower prices and make production more efficient; and socially, traditional groupings of people confined to a particular station in life have become socially upwardly mobile. In the UK, for example, the system was jump-started in the 1980s with the sale of public housing at low costs, empowering a wide range of people who would usually have rented from the state instead to enjoy the advantages of household ownership and the personal and financial security associated with such liberation, such as increased access to personal credit, among other things. While neoliberalism is ideational, the World Bank represents the material and institutional power of global governance to create change. The Bank, as we have seen, attempts universally to apply strategies that convert the poor to effective producers in the service of capital, while simultaneously financially coercing as many states as remain susceptible to such persuasion to adopt and enforce market-friendly practices like deregulation and privatization. The Bank is, in this sense, a key element of global governance and the neoliberal agenda; it is an institutional instrument of ideational delivery.

Privatization is deeply embedded in the dominant values and institutions of global governance. Global governance values focus on achieving certain outcomes related to particular ideals. One involves the democratization of the state globally, in part so that alleged endemic corruption can be brought under control (Freyberg-Inan 2006: 421). Commenting on this matter, Antony Anghie suggests that 'for the proper beneficial effects of globalization to be felt' requires political democratization in the developing world, and states need 'to be reformed in accordance with the principles of accountability, transparency, and good governance', reinforcing and prioritizing political human rights above their economic and social co-dependents (2000: 260). It also remains widely held that democratization globally will increase levels of international peace and enhance human rights, so adding to the arguments supporting the liberalization of polities globally. The economic variant, capitalism, further removes the opportunity for state larceny where it remains, especially important since it is increasingly understood that the institutionalization of democratic values does not happen overnight. It also brings prosperity by releasing the potential of humans to maximize their own gains, rather than having them determined or dictated by the state. The net result of this dual strategy of political and economic neoliberalization is expected to reduce the scale and role of the state and, concomitantly, the diversion of public funds into private coffers, especially since the state is claimed to be a poor provider of public services. The state is presumed to become more efficient, less costly to taxpayers, and less corrupt. Simultaneously, the cost of previously public-funded social operations declines through the opening of pluralist competitive markets, financial deregulation and greater efficiency and economies of scale. These global governance values and expectations are believed to produce greater accessibility for the domestic population, greater trust of the state, and faster growth and increased poverty reduction, resulting in what neoliberal advocates describe as development.

These beliefs, values and expectations represent central elements of the neoliberal Post-Washington Consensus regarding growth and development in the developing world in relation to the public sector, sometimes severely swollen through patronage and clientelism (Held 2008; Serrand and Stiglitz 2008). The bureaucratic state, with extensive civil service employment, rent-seeking behaviours and extensive reach into and control over society, is seen as an enemy of the objectives of economic and political liberalization, and its role in all sectors is to be minimized (World Bank 2004: 16; Williams and Young 1994). Mehrotra and Delamonica note that 'even immunization and public health campaigns are said to be left out of the state's purview' (2005: 143). The overall beneficiaries of this project are 'the poor', sometimes in neoliberal literature a seemingly homogeneous grouping to whom universal neoliberalism is presented as the solution to 'their' predicament. In fact, this dehumanizing categorization of billions of human beings sanctions 'their' education and preparation for submersion in underpaid and brutally competitive labour markets. IFIs are the mechanisms by which such practices are transmitted, and form a substantial element of global governance. Accordingly, they can be expected to be responsible for the biopolitical outcomes of such hegemonic beliefs.

CRITICAL INTERNATIONAL POLITICAL ECONOMY

In the face of this hegemony, there is growing criticism of the intellectual validity of neoliberal ideation and practice. Such criticism, although dominated perhaps by critical development scholarship, is increasingly complemented by critical international political economy (critical IPE). This school of thought is a second element of the post-realist nebuleuse: a counter-hegemonic challenge to the critique of hegemonic neoliberal orthodoxy (Watson 2007). If once on the fringe of development, globalization and global governance debates, critical IPE now stands as a compelling challenge to the fundamental epistemologies and ontologies of its mainstream counterpart and its claims to scientific objectivity and consistency, and acts as a powerful commentary on the complex interrelationships of international economics and political relationships. One scholar went so far as to suggest that 'the old orthodoxy in development thinking should be quickly put behind us', adding that 'many of the conventional prescriptions for development are at risk of being put to the torch' (Taylor 2008: 543). Like all studies of the social, however, its broad church is divided, in this case between those who are more ardently opposed to the destructiveness of neoliberalism, and those who seek amendments and amelioration rather than ideological annihilation.

Either outcome may still be premature; but critical IPE considers far more thoughtfully the great questions of resource distribution in relation to subjectivity, qualitative research and argument, and social construction, among other things; and it does this with a concern for everyday lives as well as high theory. It is concerned with the nature of domination: of the conversion of the Other to Westernity without reference to the desires of the Other, or to the efficacy of the mechanisms of conversion and their suitability to other people. Richard Kozul-Wright and Paul Rayment make these points well when they identify a dissonance of objectives between neoliberalism and the developed world, on the one hand, and development and the developing world, on the other. They write that:

> For developing countries ... the problem for policy is not only balancing economic and social objectives in a more globalised world, but whether the pursuit of economic efficiency by private actors in the developed market economies is compatible with the pursuit of catch-up growth and structural transformation at lower levels of development. (2007: 15)

Critical IPE is concerned with a mismatch between the hegemonic domination of a belief system (neoliberalism) and the experience of the failure of development for billions of people (everyday lives). It charges that the approach of the Post-Washington Consensus will ensure that structural inequality is perpetuated. Craig and Porter, for example, while supportive of certain aspects of the neoliberal agenda, suggest that it is destined to maintain poverty in certain circumstances (2006). This is because of the narrow range of permissions in neoliberal economic thought. Erik Reinert argues that orthodox economists' adherence to quantitative methodologies and associated epistemologies constricts development praxis in the same way that 'someone writing a thesis on various types of snow would [be] if she or he chose to write in Swahili' (2007: 46). In short, it will fail to capture the human in development, since epistemologically, the human is as absent from orthodox economic calculations as snow is from the experiences of Swahili speakers in lowland Africa. Helleiner similarly moves that neoliberal economics is 'ideologically encrusted' (2001: 245) and Kozul-Wright and Rayment that it is abstracted from its social and political context (2007). Yet others charge that its reductionist, one-size-fits-all approach is destined to fail by virtue of the range of different circumstances it will encounter in different parts of the world (Payne 2005; Grugel and Piper 2007).

Ultimately, it is impossible to escape the conclusion that neoliberal claims rest on substantial myths, such as those of free markets (protectionism is standard globally); the absence of alternatives (there are many socially responsible variations adopted in various countries and by various corporations); the level playing field for all (the present system grew out of imperial domination and its institutions maintain this asymmetry); the objectivity and rationality of markets (they are designed by subjective humans prioritizing subjective preferences, the outcomes of which may be profoundly irrational, such as City bonuses for failure); and that they operate free of subjective interventions (the oil cartels selectively and openly manipulated supply in the 2008 oil price fiasco, and farther back in the OPEC price hikes of the 1970s, rather than objectively responding to demand fluctuations). Helleiner argues that 'empirical reality ... presents us with an imperfection-ridden market system – imperfectly competitive and imperfectly formed, with many markets entirely missing [and] characterized by grotesquely inequitable "initial condition"' (2001: 246; Baumol et al. 2007). In an echo of the realization of the contribution to capitalist growth of unpaid and unrecognized female home-maker labour, he rejects the 'simpleminded' market assumptions that quite deliberately deny and ignore the contribution to economic development globally of the mass of human activity that preoccupies humankind everywhere. There is, he writes:

> A vast, unrecorded sphere of extremely valuable daily activity that should be described as 'economic', involving the care of one's fellow human beings, notably children, the disabled and the aged. In the

economy of care, to which feminists have correctly directed attention, there are typically minimal, if any, material rewards. Market
behaviour, involving the rational pursuit of self-interest, has very little
to do with its functioning, except in the minds of some benighted
economists forever warped by their own crude assumptions that no
other kind of behaviour exists. (2001: 246)

Ultimately, dependence on quantitative methods guarantees that
orthodox economics will miss the obvious qualitative problems such
as structural inequalities among different labour forces and differential
engagement and exclusion within and between societies at different
levels of development. At its heart, and of necessity for the system to
function, neoliberalism is intrinsically and inevitably deeply divisive,
since it is based on individual self-maximization and the suggestion of
biologically inherent competition, the outcome of which requires winners
and losers in a system that requires, creates and promotes hierarchical
organization and rivalry in behaviour, with inevitable inequality as
a result. The claim that this is part of human nature is unverifiable,
since no gene or other natural scientific experiment has ever mapped
its presence in human beings, and since not everyone is competitive.
These assumptions and expectations are uncritically embedded in the
directives of global governance and the IFIs, along with parallel security processes also based on hierarchies and rivalry, and they define
and prescribe the limits to our social behaviour, placing humans on
multiple collision courses of competitive behaviour that are inevitably
destructive to their own needs. The environment is but one example of
this paradox, while evidence is gathering which suggests that economic
inequality – a hierarchy that sustains profit-making endeavours – causes
widespread social ills (Wilkinson and Pickett 2009). The neo-Gramscian,
hegemonically sanctioned, mainstream and mass behaviours contrast
with human and planetary needs in the early third millennium, which
appear instead to require subnational and pan-national mutuality in a
revised international system based on reduced rivalry and enhanced
cooperation in the face of multiple shared contingencies.

That such global threats to human and planetary needs and security,
such as mass poverty for 2 billion people, devastating environmental
collapse and transglobal child and maternal mortality, to name but a
few, do not drive substantial and structural change in international
policy demonstrates the power of neoliberal hegemony to procrastinate,
obfuscate and prevaricate. On the one hand, there is overwhelming
evidence of a need for change. On the other, there is stasis. How are these

dissonances and distances to be explained? It is worth thinking a little more deeply about the means by which myths can be considered and upheld not just as truths, but as truths whose validity is demonstrated and affirmed by the legitimacy attached to the scientific Enlightenment methods that have been co-opted by orthodox economists and political 'scientists' whose ethos is enshrined in and protected by the hegemony of neoliberalism. The co-option of Enlightenment scientific approaches to social study is commonplace, as Horkheimer pointed out (1974). But the denial of demonstrably falsifiable assertions within a broader hegemonic discourse is worthy of further interrogation. Tony Evans writes that 'the Liberal consensus has elevated [economic practices] to the status of "common sense" [creating] legitimate habits that are part of a natural and rational approach to the current world order to which everyone should subscribe' (Evans 2002: 205; Muzaffar 1995). Consensus is generated and maintained from ideological power bases in dominant states; by their counterpart elites in metropolitan countries; by the overwhelming success of wealth generation represented in the media and transmitted globally; and by those who benefit from the system and enjoy genuine fruits of liberal economics or are rendered critically mute through false consciousness. Such is the expansive spread of propaganda that even people who are prevented from engagement with neoliberal practices have been led to believe that the system works for the majority.

This consensus is maintained through denial. Stanley Cohen elaborates a framework that helps outline and typologize what denial is in formal terms. This helps bypass the often emotive abstractions attached to such a powerful word and process and renders the concept constructive rather than merely critical. In this framework, Cohen identifies three forms of denial useful to us here. The first is what he calls 'literal' denial; the second is 'interpretive' denial; and the third is 'implicatory' denial. The first involves denial of facts. The second involves manipulation, so that responsibility for fault is transferred to others: thus, 'by changing words, by euphemism, by technical jargon, the observer disputes the cognitive meaning given to an event and re-allocates it to another class of event'. The third involves recognition of a problem without a responsibility to act. Interpreting neoliberal claims against this framework reveals the routine practice of denial (2008: 7–9). First, the ontological claim that there is no alternative to neoliberal practices is fallacious, and clearly denies the range of variations proposed by critical scholarship. For instance, numerous 'world' leaders routinely argue that neoliberalism is inevitable in the absence of alternatives.

Former US president Bill Clinton and former British prime minister Tony Blair described neoliberal forces as 'not a political choice but a fact' and as 'irreversible and irresistible'; many others have made similar claims (Evans 2002: 205–6). Such claims fall into the same worldview that treats poverty 'as a fact of nature impossible to control by direct intervention', leading some to conclude that 'inequality is ... a natural, irrefutably given fact of industrial society' (Procacci 1991: 155). Evans writes that 'it is the "naturalisation" of liberalism that provides ... international financial institutions and international organisations with the rationale for denying responsibility for structural violations of human rights' (2002: 205). This type of claim stands in clear contrast to the presentation of alternatives from innumerable general sources and from dozens of globally recognized scholars aimed at reducing massive inequality through reforming the structural asymmetry on which the neoliberal system builds. The neoliberal claim regarding systemic and consequential inevitability is demonstrably falsifiable and falls into Cohen's category of 'literal denial'.

Second, the epistemological claim that the market is a purely rational and objective concept is falsifiable, as are the claims regarding the freeness of the market and the fairness of its environment. That the economy is set, designed and fixed by human beings with subjective preferences is demonstrated clearly with reference to the European Common Agricultural Policy (CAP), US farm subsidies, butter mountains and wine lakes, government subsidies to major industries such as aerospace, state subsidizing of arms exports to very poor countries, Super 301 anti-dumping penalties, dumping policies, fishing quotas, state bail-outs of bank shareholders in crisis, all forms of market protection, quota privileges for favoured allies, tied aid undermining competitive practice, supermarket and oil price fixing and hundreds of other demonstrable, recorded and formal policies at state and sub-state levels. And, since part of the function of the WTO is to manage disputes over differing economic approaches to issues like protectionism, it would be hard to deny the subjective human creation and shaping of neoliberal practices as routine, institutionalized and variable. Neoliberal epistemological claims to objectivity, impartiality and neutrality can all be falsified empirically, so the claims fit Cohen's classification of 'literal' and also 'interpretive' denial.

In this context, Cohen's 'literal' and 'interpretive' denial merges with Zygmunt Bauman's notion of 'adiaphorization' (1998: 78). Adiaphorization is the means by which we come to believe the world cannot be changed when it can. Adiaphorization, or adiaphoric denial, refers to the authorizing and tolerance of the obscene on the lie that it is inevitable.

It is important because this form of denial creates and sanctions a gap between what we are told we can achieve and what we are actually capable of, and it denies the extent of human imagination and agency. In its domination and censoring of security and governance discourses, adiaphorization is a tool by which realism defines the scope of what we may envision, limits the alternatives we may envisage by excusing the unconscionable as inevitable, and disconnects us from our capacity and potency to improve human security. Bauman identifies in this process the 'social production of distance' that separates cause from effect and reflects the imbalance between consequence and culpability. As he puts it, 'morality seems to conform to the law of optical perspective' (ibid.: 78). Or, as Simon Pemberton puts it, as the distance between those who invoke policy and those who suffer from it increases, responsibility decreases (2004: 78). Both distance and its corollary, denial, then maintain the capacity to reify and fetishize the market, for example (Aldridge 2005: 50).

A third claim of neoliberalism that sustains its hegemony reflects Cohen's 'interpretive' denial. Since all social systems are fallible, and since neoliberalism is a socially constructed social system, neoliberalism will inevitably fail to deliver what its supporters claim. When it does, responsibility for such failure is normally transferred to developing countries. It is normal to hear neoliberal supporters argue that developing countries' elites are corrupt and siphon off substantial funding; or, more frequently, that developing countries have failed to adhere to neoliberal practices (Abouharb and Cingranelli 2008; Phillips 2006; Payne 2005). This might be through general disinclination, or because of institutional under-endowment and a shortfall in capacity. Responsibility for failure is transferred and blame apportioned elsewhere, and the outcome of failed neoliberal policy is reinterpreted. Combined, the ability authoritatively to deny responsibility ontologically and epistemologically, and the capacity erroneously or disingenuously to transfer blame to others, creates the social distance that underscores Cohen's third, 'implicatory' variant of denial. 'Implicatory' denial 'is not a refusal to acknowledge reality [the U5MR, for example], but a denial of its significance or implications' (Cohen 2008: 8). In the case of water privatization, there are very clear implications for the life chances of very poor people and their children; but such implications are excluded by the denial processes associated with neoliberal propaganda and dogma. This elaborate architecture of denial and 'refusal of contrary evidence' (Aldridge 2005: 49) is crucial to any explanation of the means by which neoliberal hegemony is maintained, and any counter-hegemony must be fully cognizant of such processes. The Post-Washington Consensus, then, is not malicious but misfeasant and indifferent; it is well meaning but erroneously guided and protected from critical consciousness by adiaphoric denial.

CRITICAL IPE AND THE POST-WASHINGTON CONSENSUS

Aware of such intellectual and amoral morbidity, IPE has much to say about the Washington Consensus. In the first instance, critics claim that the Post-Washington Consensus is not structurally different from its predecessor (Cammack 2004; Novitz 2008). That is, the transformation in nomenclature is not matched by change in more substantial matters of underlying belief and policy, in a practice reminiscent of communist states' periodic public vilification of disgraced elites to restore flagging legitimacy or control. Anthony Payne describes the change as 'the piecemeal addition of a number of new ideas to the core of the original consensus in a series of attempts to rescue it from its own inadequacies' (2005: 85). As the PWC's inability to resolve a broad range of developmental problems has become ever more apparent in places like Kosovo, Bosnia and East Timor, a range of systemic adaptations has emerged that imply some degree of variation in neoliberalization, an effect typologized by Oliver Richmond (2005). This has involved the establishment of a range of different public bodies and processes in different places to ameliorate the inevitable dysfunctionalities consequent upon the internal contradictions and paradoxes of extreme liberalization applied to human security conditions in peace-building environments (Caplan 2004). While such responses have prompted some writers to declare the Washington and Post-Washington Consensuses dead (Maxwell 2005; Ritzen 2005), critical IPE and critical theory arguments maintain that the underlying assumptions of the PWC have not evolved substantially, nor with an interest in bottom-up emphases or shock absorption methodologies to neoliberal structural economic failures, meaning that 'development' and its relative corollary, human security, persistently fail. As Mike Pugh writes:

> The debate on development generally has evolved to the point that the Washington consensus has been declared 'dead' except as an inaccurate term of abuse. Certainly, the neoliberal agenda is now contested more seriously than in the 1990s, so that it has ceased to be an unquestioned 'common sense', ideology or doxa ... However ... the evolving debate marks out dynamics in the liberal peace project that protect and reproduce its core assumptions. The old-style unthinking Washington consensus about development may be merely

a virtual death, with a pro-poor liberal peace *redivivus* emerging from the ashes. (Pugh 2005: 5)

It would be quite wrong, however, to suggest that the approach of the Post-Washington Consensus is incoherent. In fact, the converse is true. The World Bank, as a strong-arm of neoliberalism, attempts to condition all countries similarly within a broad economic framework, whether they are Northern or Southern. In 2009, the IMF berated the UK's fiscal policies, for example, with knock-on effects in terms of Britain's international credit ratings. Growth is the first objective, with the expectation that poverty reduction will follow as a consequence for all countries. In Paul Cammack's words:

The Bank's commitment to poverty reduction is real, within limits, [but] it is conditional upon, and secondary to, a broader goal. Its principal objective is the systematic transformation of social relations and institutions in the developing world, in order to generalize and facilitate proletarianization and capitalist accumulation on a global scale, and build specifically capitalist hegemony through the promotion of legitimating schemes of community participation and country ownership. (2004: 190)

Both Washington and Post-Washington approaches are ideationally, ideologically, locked into the belief that a genuinely competitive and efficient world market system able to exploit the greatest range of the cheapest human labour will improve any state's growth, whether it is high or low in global ranking, and that poverty reduction will inevitably follow strict adherence to neoliberal practices. This strategy is coherent and continuous. The objective in applying these processes is a genuine belief in their virtue, rather than a malicious intent to impoverish, and it is presented, although not equally rigorously, to all societies, economies and polities. This should not be seen as incoherent; nor should it be seen as conspiratorial, for it is the expected outcome of a conviction in the nostrums of neoliberalism. This is why Cammack can reasonably claim that the World Bank

Has been systematically engaged in promoting the proletarianization of the world's poor (their equipping for, incorporation into and subjection to competitive labour markets) and the creation of an institutional framework within which global capitalist accumulation can be sustained, while simultaneously seeking to legitimate the project through policies of controlled participation and pro-poor propaganda. (ibid.: 190)

The process is recognizable in Europe and North America. The insemination of 'entrepreneurialism' into education agendas prepares for and facilitates participation in a production-based ethos via ever more competitive labour markets, with the purpose of 'empowering' people to consume increasingly irrelevant materials to enhance profit and accumulation and prevent capitalism collapsing under the weight of its multiple internal contradictions. The Bank's orthodoxy, set carefully within the wider authority of global governance, is limited primarily by the capacity of a recipient state to reject such diktat. Little has changed, then, in terms of the underlying ideas, beliefs and priorities associated with privatization of public services that are designed and delivered to benefit all, sometimes known as 'public goods'.

Having considered criticisms of neoliberalism broadly, I now turn to a more specific consideration of privatization. Again, critiques from critical IPE merge with development scholarship (as opposed to neoliberal growth thought). The two schools have much in common, since they counterbalance the assumptions and arguments of modernization theory, postulated first after decolonization, upgraded through neoliberal hegemony presently, and advanced innocuously enough through the vanguard of liberal peace-building and global governance. In this view, privatization is claimed to accelerate growth in part by eliminating that perennial bugbear of development and growth, corruption. In so doing, it underscores another neoliberal ethos concerned with restraining the size and role of government in order to minimize state regulation and free the market (Riley 1998). The presence of widespread corruption is used to justify privatization of state sectors in the developing world, even though endemic privatization in the developed world has conspicuously failed to eliminate it from the same neoliberal polities and economies (Doig 1984; Neild 2002). Corruption, in its many forms, is inescapable in all societies and all systems of governance, which does not necessarily make it right. It should be more carefully considered, however, because what is presented as corruption by Western thinking exists as an alternative form of socio-economic distribution that is in its demeanour as biopolitical as neoliberal governance. It bears careful consideration here because it is both endemic and socially sanctioned where effective and humane governance is absent and where poverty is unrelenting and opportunity unavailable. It applies at all levels of society and has different purposes depending on determinism. Its most common manifestation in Western consciousness is in the form of a range of notorious kleptocratic and authoritarian elites in rich urban metropolises in the developing world, but in a different form, it finds expression as a routine matter of organization and survival for a majority of very poor people. I refer to this system as common social patronage (CSP), to distinguish it from elite larceny, whether in corrupt dictatorships or democracies. It is this form of social organization which I will consider in greater detail below, since its operation is essential to understanding human, political and economic organization in very poor societies; and since its necessity, endurance and permanence indicate both that people need it, and that privatization cannot and will not prevent it in the short term.

Corruption as it is presented in the mainstream literature is largely a monolithic notion. In such sources, it is routinely poorly understood and oversimplified, and uncritically thought of as the use of public office for private gain. There can be no doubt that, in its commonly understood elite guise, it robs millions of people of billions of dollars in social and other entitlements, decelerates potential development and undermines growth, aggravates poverty and enriches state elites through greed. As Stephen Riley wrote, 'corruption often has a "Robin Hood in reverse" character: the losers are likely to be the exceptionally poor, female and marginalized, whilst the winners are already wealthy and part of an inefficient, swollen state' (1998: 131). But the informal and unequal redistribution of national resources is a far more complex concept; and it is not restricted to formal public institutions. In the first instance, although self-evidently harmful at state level, the practice represented in mainstream literature as corruption is also an essential part of human survival for millions of people around the world, and it is far from specific to developing countries. Recognizing the role of such social forces is not necessarily to argue that they can make a contribution to development, as some scholars have suggested (Abueva 1966; Leff 1964). It is, however, to consider the role of common social patronage in sustaining the everyday lives of very poor people for whom there is no alternative than to be beholden to a more powerful patron, even if that patron is still relatively poor.

Most significantly for this work, it is to argue that privatization will not end this practice, as long as people are disconnected by the market or the state from their basic needs, a serious question given the number of people struggling on less than $2 per day. Development scholars and anthropologists have long understood such social practices as necessary and indigenously legitimate for managing the absence of essential provision, practised formally and informally among hundreds of millions of people who rely on them for everyday survival and basic nutritional-physiological needs (Harrison 2007; Sissener 2001). As far as the preservation of life in extreme contingencies is concerned, it is biopolitical in nature (see below). In both situations, of elite greed and social need, it revolves around patronage and clientelism, an enduring characteristic of developing countries, as it was in Europe in the last century and as it persists in some European states presently (Roberts 2008c). Such practices tend to be relatively small scale and involve informal exchanges and transfers of publicly controlled goods for private consumption. Eisenstadt and Roniger offer a useful and insightful characterization of such ubiquitous relationships, which they refer to as 'generalized exchange' (1982: 49–55). They argue that the 'gift giving' in such networks and relationships is 'distinct from the usual "specific" market exchange in that it is seemingly nonutilitarian and disinterested. But at the same time it is highly structured, being based on elaborate rules of reciprocity, which nevertheless differ from those of utilitarian, specific market exchange' (ibid.: 52).

In the societies in which such forms of social behaviour are legitimate and routine, Randall and Theobald note that people 'often live at the margin of subsistence'. They go on to comment that 'not infrequently, [they] are driven below this margin by the vicissitudes of their existence: flood, drought, diseases, sickness, death, violence and intimidation by outsiders ...' (1985: 52). Family and kin may provide vital sustenance in a process sometimes referred to as 'informal' welfare, and these exchanges and gifts will often be reciprocal and equivalent. Where the family or local community (kin and extended kin) cannot or will not intervene to ameliorate such conditions, however, and when the state and the market do not provide, vulnerable people often turn to a more powerful individual such as their landlord, or a village chief, or a wealthy business person. These relationships may compensate for the absence of important or essential human security provision, but they do not do so in a regulated, transparent democratic sense at the grassroots level, where priorities are often decided by a non-elected 'official' linked to a particular identity or other such grouping. Wood and Gough write that where 'both states and markets are sufficiently problematic to the pursuit of livelihoods ... people have to rely to a greater extent' on informal practices which, outside the family, 'are more likely to be hierarchical and thus clientelist' (2006: 1696). Indeed, such social practices are not recognized as corrupt by the people pursuing them. Noting this distinction, Anna Kubiak remarks that 'for people who are not interested in political matters, corruption quite often is a word not understood'. Kubiak confirms the distinction between common 'corruption' and elite larceny when she identifies the majority of those engaged in such practices as mainly 'farmers, old age and disability pensioners, the unemployed and unskilled workers, elderly persons, respondents with low educational attainment, low-income respondents [and] people who read the daily press rarely or not at all' (Kubiak 2001: 4). Reflecting the ignorance of most perspectives on the social legitimacy of what would otherwise be described as corruption, Randall and Theobald characterize widely applied patronage and clientelism as: 'A relationship which involves an exchange between a superior patron or patron group and an inferior client or client group [in which] the low-status client will receive material assistance in one form or another whilst his patron will receive less tangible resources such as deference, esteem, loyalty [or] personal services' (1985: 52)

Dogan and Pelassy broadly concur. In their view, 'clientelism forges a relationship between two persons of unequal status, prestige, and influence, thus constituting an original factor of vertical stratification. The clientele relationship is engendered by an asymmetry in the situations of patron and client' (1990: 87). An earlier definition describes patronage and clientelism as 'not a distinct type of social organization, but different modes of structuring the flow of resources and of interpersonal interaction and exchange in society: different modes of generalized exchange' (Eisenstadt and Roniger 1982: 164). More recently, Daniel Ogbaharya has referred to these practices as 'the social norms, customs, and networks that allocate and manage the economic and environmental resources of communities' at sub-state levels (2008: 396).

These definitions leave sufficient room to understand how the practices of hundreds of millions of people in the developing world, which would otherwise and commonly be called corruption by foreigners, are actually essential mechanisms for survival in very harsh environments. This is antithetical to neoliberalism in the sense that neoliberalism is claimed to generate horizontal equality for all through informal impersonal relations governed by the impartial rule of law. In contrast to this, patronage and clientelism are based on and perpetuate vertical lineages of power for specific people and specific gains through formal personal relationships that function in many ways outside or parallel to the rule of law, which is in any case routinely subverted to the personal requirements of both patrons and clients. Indeed, this may be said of neoliberalism, since, as I have noted above, that system of economic distribution is also characterized by profound inequality, vertical hierarchies of power, opportunity and advantage, and basic rent-seeking and corruption. Privatization will not eradicate patronage and clientelism unless very poor people benefit from neoliberalism. The record in this matter is grim, since despite decades of Washington and Post-Washington Consensus, nearly a third of the world struggles on less than $2 a day. Neoliberalism demands disruptive behaviours with which people are unfamiliar and which the liberal-democratic rule of law disciplines them to adopt, but which do not provide the sustenance generated by the systems that have been outlawed. Nor can millions of indigenous people even engage with institutional international neoliberalism equitably. Neoliberalism therefore disrupts indigenously legitimate biopolitical social organization and prohibits the old ways without offering any means by which often precarious life might be maintained. This is not to say people do not resist, however. Indeed, as Adrian Smith, Alison Stenning and Katie Willis write, 'people and organizations challenge and contest the ways in which neoliberal practices threaten livelihoods, social cohesion and environmental conditions'. They further argue that while this can be seen as political resistance, it 'may also be seen as economic and social strategies for "getting by"' (2008: 3–4). It is in this sense an indigenous biopolitical response to exogenous biopolitical intervention.

It is not solely neoliberalism which is at fault, of course. The poverty of the state itself and its attitude towards the people within its boundaries are major contributing factors to these relationships and the conditions that sustain them. As a consequence, in some parts of the world it is the family's moral obligation and responsibility to sustain their poor and vulnerable, not the state's. And at the nexus of these two systems, the relatively low-level public servant working for the state in close proximity to his or her hungry and poorly kin cannot reasonably be expected to direct loyalty to the state before family and extended family needs.

This attitude is further underpinned by the state's customary neglect of various elements of society. The colonial state traditionally was not established for the benefit of the population at large but to discipline the aberrant, recruit soldiery and extract taxes, with a few exceptions, and this tradition was replicated by post-colonial elites that also viewed the state as a means of self-enrichment (McCloud 1995: 40; Kelsall 2008). This perspective speaks to other liberal assumptions regarding the social contract, because dominant social practices and relations reflect pre-state functionality and remind us that the Weberian state is a quite recent, artificial and socially constructed intervention in asymmetrical biopolitical largesse. The 'corrupt' behaviour associated with developing countries in the literature is thus far more sophisticated, and considerably less acknowledged, than the simplified version presented as a justification for intervention. Many people depend on diversions of resources from low-level state employees whose families and kin depend on their ability to extract small rents from public coffers. These behaviours are recognized by global governance institutions, and used to reject arguments for formal social welfare provision (Kopits 1993; World Bank 1989). The IMF, for example, maintains that such vital informal social organization 'operates relatively well as an informal social security scheme obviating the need for the urgent introduction of large-scale public pensions' (Deacon et al. 1997: 64). As Duffield puts it, 'conveniently for neoliberalism, a large part of humanity apparently exempts itself from the need for expensive systems of social protection through its own communal resilience' (2008: 152), a resilience that is often over-imagined or poorly contextualized. This is problematic, since these forms of patronage and clientelism provide in many instances for only the most basic needs. They are also subject to social whims and may be removed by forced migration to new networks, the social ostracism of women who separate from abusive partners against local social rules, familial deaths, local disputes, unaffordable medical needs and reduced circumstances of patrons, their departure from a locale or their political deselection, as well as downturns in local and global economies. They are substantially different from formal social safety nets in this respect since they are unreliable, inconsistent and may be absent in times of crucial need (Schmidt, Lande and Guasti 1977; Eisenstadt and Roniger 1982; Hall and Midgley 2006: 209).

The importance of such awareness is twofold. First, what is normally represented as corruption is homogeneously and simplistically expressed in terms of greed and is normally related to high political office. This is not the case commonly. Petty transfers, or common social patronage (CSP), are necessities of life for millions of people (Roberts 2008e; Mehrotra and Delamonica 2005). In this sense, we may consider CSP as a form of economic self-government, with the purpose of maintaining life systems. It is biopolitical in the same sense that neoliberal governance is biopolitical, because its exercise through hierarchies of power determines, *in extremis*, who lives and who dies in harsh environments of poverty and resource inaccessibility. It is the calculated management of life, as Foucault suggested (above). Second, the consequences of privatization will inevitably mean that very poor people will continue to face shortfalls that mean they must continue to act in 'corrupt' ways (Cornia 2001; Mehrotra and Delamonica 2005). Those basic needs that are governed by CSP routinely create a union between civil society and public institutions, at the interface of which is the routine petty corruption of low-level public office for economic survival. In 1991 in Phnom Penh, for example, state doctors were rarely paid on time, if at all, and could wait several months for a $7 monthly salary. It was unsurprising if they were selling state medical assets to feed their own families. As is commonly the case, some were also working informally as taxi drivers, and their absence from state posts further damaged wider medical provision. Similarly, other state servants, such as policemen and women, were bribing the local and expatriate community, sometimes out of greed, but mainly to subsidize meagre or impossibly small wages in conditions that necessitate larger families as substitutes for pension provision where infant mortality rates are high. Success in such dealings socializes and habituates the process further. Such practices are commonplace in the developing world (Van Lerberghe et al. 2002; Hall and Midgley 2006). These forms of public–private corruption cannot be ameliorated in the short to medium term by privatization, especially since privatization is inevitably associated with a reduction in state jobs. In very low-income circumstances, the benefits of privatization where they exist will not be felt by the poorest, since they are routinely unable to engage effectively with institutionalized neoliberal practices. Claims that privatization will end corruption must be tempered by a more sophisticated comprehension of what 'corruption' entails; and a more nuanced recognition that the predominant form of 'corruption', or common social patronage, will not be eliminated by privatization of essential-to-life services where people have no money to avail themselves of such provision. Privatization in this context is biopolitically counterproductive and unlikely to undermine common social patronage used to source vital biopolitical needs.

Indeed, the reverse is true. Where costs of essential goods and services increase through marketization, which they routinely and ordinarily do, CSP will necessarily persist (Walton and Seddon 1994). The argument that privatization will undo 'corruption' needs comprehensive rethinking. But suggestions that privatization and corruption are antithetical are problematic for other reasons. Privatization in wealthier environments does not have a pure record of being corruption free; indeed, it functions at levels of personal greed that would make many a Third World dictator blush. It is both erroneous and disingenuous to claim that the private sector cancels large- or small-scale corruption, or that liberal states are corruption free. They are not. In the UK, the state and its international allies have intervened in criminal investigations of public figures and offices with the result that such investigations are derailed, undermining the essential doctrine of a separation of powers between state and legislature, and preventing the opportunity to publicly confirm or refute such widely held allegations (Porta and Meny 1997; Gilby 2008). Furthermore, the benefits of parliamentary expenses claimed by British MPs that were exposed in 2009 infuriated a public whose declining wages fund such old-world elite opulence in a practice that, while not legally corrupt, corrupts the trust of a society in its political leadership, which is similarly damaging (*Daily Telegraph*, 6 April 2009: 4). Nor are private corporations paragons of virtue. For example, corruption in very large, very visible private enterprises such as Enron is commonplace (Johnstone and Brown 2004; Tiihonen 2003; Hall 1999). Western transnational corporations (TNCs) commonly use corrupt methods to secure contracts offered during the privatization of European state operations (Hall 1999). And in the water sector specifically, from Europe to Asia, there is substantial evidence of extensive corruption in both the public and private spheres. Charles Kenny records that the European Commission (EC) learned in 2003 that '90 per cent of EU funds intended to help improve water service in fifty communities in Paraguay had been diverted' (2008: 45). Transparency International (TI), a respected monitor of democratic and undemocratic practices, recently published a thorough report in which it identified 'a range of problems, from petty bribery in water delivery to procurement-related looting of irrigation and hydropower funds; from covering up industrial pollution to manipulation of water management and allocation policies' (Labelle 2008). A World Bank economist painted a devastating picture of the consequences of corruption in the water sector and its relationship to avoidable child mortality, which is worth quoting at length. He argued that in South Asia, a survey taken between 2001 and 2002 showed that:

> Bribes on average ranged from 1 to 6 per cent of the contract values. Kickbacks ... escalated the costs to companies by up to another 11 per cent ... 'Sanctioned cartels' ... helped push prices 15–20 per cent higher than what the market would have demanded. What is worse, these payments actually facilitated companies' failure to meet contract obligations. Kickbacks tended to cover low-quality work and the non-delivery of goods. Materials worth between 3 and 5 per cent of the contract value were never supplied. The economic cost of each dollar of missing materials can be calculated at US$3 to $4 as a result of the water network's shorter life and limited capacity. These costs add up to another 20 per cent ... This double impact of corruption in the construction of water networks may raise the price of access by 25 to 45 per cent. (Kenny 2008: 16)

From such evidence, we may reasonably conclude that the neoliberal claim that privatizing public provision will eliminate corruption misses two crucial points. First, informal widespread common social patronage will persist where essential resources remain inaccessible for millions of very poor people. This practice has widespread social legitimacy and may be deemed necessary for life preservation. In this sense, it is indigenous biopolitical resilience in the face of exogenous biopolitical diktat. Second, it is the case that large-scale corruption in the state is matched in the private sector, and neither is immune to substantial larceny and abuse of public funds. Furthermore, corruption and grand theft also occur in liberal public institutions, including the World Bank and the United Nations (ibid.; Labelle 2008; Porta and Meny 1997). The argument that privatization will cure corruption, then, is fallacious, unrepresentative, disingenuous in the light of the evidence, and wrong. Indeed, we may invert the Kaldorian relationship of 'criminality' and aliberal behaviour in the borderlands. Kaldor maintains that criminality and non-liberal practices are a function of a refusal to endorse and apply neoliberal values and practices (1999). Ongoing non-liberal behaviour, however, is also a consequence of neoliberal political and economic determinism disrupting pre-existing, traditional forms of biopolitical organization without facilitating or permitting alternatives.

I turn now to another problematic neoliberal prescription, which assumes that the state will fail effectively to deliver public goods like health or water, in contrast to privatized performance in the same area (World Bank 2004). In addition to the arguments made regarding corruption (above), it is regularly claimed that the hundreds of millions of people without basic public goods provision are in this situation because the state is corrupt, inept, unwilling, in debt, or a combination of these and other factors. This is true in some cases, but it is not the rule, and the deployment of this falsifiable propaganda sustains a key element of neoliberal argument. In practice, the state does deliver public goods, often where no alternative exists, and no matter how corrupt it is claimed to be. Much existing public provision in water and sanitation, where it was made, has either been a result of investment during colonization which is now state owned and municipally delivered, no matter how well or poorly, or is provided from state funds and donor support. According-ing to a report presented at the Third World Water Forum in Kyoto, Japan, in 2003, 'the public sector contributes 85% of the finance and operates more than 90% of water systems' (Hall 2003: 4–5). WaterAid, a global NGO, corroborates this analysis, confirming the extent of attempted public provision of water and sanitation in comparison with private sector input (Annamradju et al. 2001). Hall adds that 'the same picture emerges if we consider the estimates of numbers served'

(2003: 5). Independent research claims that between 5 and 7 per cent of populations in developing countries are reached by private companies (Tagliabue 2002). In contrast, between 93 and 95 per cent 'are served by the public sector' (Hall 2003: 5). It is illusory to suggest that the state fails to deliver public services, for example water and sanitation, when the proportion of investment and connections confirm that the state has been far more widespread in this domain than the private sector. This does not mean, however, that all is well. Nor does it mean that there is no room for private provision to evolve and contribute, no matter how seriously flawed neoliberal ideation is in a wider sense. The state does not satisfy all its population in any society. In some of the poorest parts of the world, this is especially so. In many developing countries, state water provision is centred in metropolitan areas, while rural sectors are routinely neglected. Furthermore, supplies in both metropolis and periphery are often unreliable and subject to regular interruption, lack of maintenance and variable quality. The state is often committed to providing water and sanitation in its own political and social interests, since it is rarely a profit-making industry.

This is in contrast to TNC privatization of public services, which is never social and rarely political. A private sector water provider made this clear when he stated that 'no private company will lay a water connection until it can identify a clear stream of revenue to repay the investment' (ibid.: 6). Private enterprise exists first and foremost to make profits. In the case of water, decreasing investment and commitment to water and sanitation provision on the part of the major water TNCs have resulted in market failure. It is because of the low likelihood of cost recovery that major private water companies are withdrawing from tendering for contracts unless a range of risks they face is mitigated by public funding (Hall and Lobina 2006: 8; Hall 2003: 5). The risks about which they have shown concern include political instability, costs of competitive tendering, and failure to recoup investment. TNC water providers are concerned with 'developing guarantee mechanisms against political risks [and] protection against currency risks' (Hall 2004: 3). Political risks associated with currency instability and inconsistency in leadership (and therefore public policy and relations with multilateral lenders) also tax the private sector, which as a result has increasingly been reluctant to invest in water provision in very poor societies. Despite risk being an inherent aspect of privatization, endorsed by orthodox economic thinking, TNC water suppliers are increasingly seeking to have the associated costs of contingencies met from the public purse; a case of having their cake and eating it. Rather than accepting the risks attached to large investments as the downside of market entre-preneurialism, water TNCs submit budget proposals to the World Bank and other public funding agencies which include demands for money to compensate them financially if events turn foul, and for the costs of the bid to the target state, which will be substantial. Public money therefore subsidizes TNC risk-taking. The World Bank has supported this approach, despite it being in contravention of neoliberal competi-tion values and despite it applying only to large TNCs rather than small-business people. A local company in Laos presenting a budget for a bid to take over water provision in Vientiane, which included a section devoted to compensating for failure in that bid, would be sent packing; but the World Bank supports subsidies for TNCs considering investing in foreign water markets (Camdessus 2003). The European Union Water Initiative (EUWI) promotes similar approaches to sustain-ing private sector involvement (Hall 2003: 4). J. F. Talbot, CEO of one of the largest water providers, writes that investment requirements are too high for the private sector, contracts are too unreliable and hard to enforce, and profits too unreliable as a result (2002; Lobina and Hall 2003: 29). Similarly, Charles Kenny notes that 'the formal private sector may be reluctant to provide service to low-income areas' because poor people may 'fail to pay bills or will vandalize the infrastructure once it is built'. The international private sector is also conscious that 'the costs for directly connecting households to the water network are often prohibitive for poor people' (Kenny 2008: 43). Incentives and returns are very low, demanding, for TNCs, public monies for private risks, in antithesis to the common understanding that capitalist enterprise must take self-funding risks as a matter of course.

The combination of unwillingness to supply water without public risk management funding, low returns on metropolitan investments and the near-absence of TNC provision for very poor people who might 'vandalize' infrastructure and fail to pay bills that are routinely many times higher than Europeans and North Americans pay has led to waste and underdevelopment. Hall and Lobina observe that:

> Private contracts have failed to deliver investment in new infrastruc-ture as promised. After 15 years, only about 600,000 households have been connected as a result of investment by private water operators in sub-Saharan Africa, South Asia, and east Asia (outside China) – representing less than 1% of the people who need to be connected in those regions to meet the UN Millennium Development Goals. (2006: 8)

According to WaterAid, 'decades of developments in water infra-structure involving billions of dollars have not only largely excluded the poor from benefiting from these investments, but have exacerbated their lack of access to [water]' (Calaguas and O'Connell 2000: 2). Hall estimates that 'an extra 1.5 billion people will have to be connected to water supply, and 2 billion to sanitation and wastewater treatment' to meet the Millennium Development Goals (2003: 5). Talbot confirms the relative paucity of investment capacity in relation to needs, determining that this cannot be achieved by the private sector (2002). Even the World Bank recognizes the dearth of privatization success (Hall and Lobina 2008: 6). Furthermore, even if privatization could provide equitable access to essential water and sanitation provision, which is oxymoronic since the market cannot be equitable, differing interests, investments and timing of key processes mean that separate private operations would be highly unlikely to be complementary. The vagaries of market provision in giant state infrastructures would not be 'joined up'; and they would not constitute or support a broad national developmental strategy able to 'trigger … synergies among health, family planning, water and sanitation, nutrition and education inputs and outcomes without simultaneous investment in each' (Mehrotra and Delamonica 2005: 144; Grant 1993). An effective approach to maldevelopment requires a coordinated strategy to both stimulate, and benefit from, the cross-fertilization of each separate element, because 'each intervention has ramifications that lie outside its "sector"' (Mehrotra and Delamonica 2005: 144). For example, education impacts upon health and nutrition, nutrition affects health, health affects maternal mortality, and so on. An effective national development strategy requires coordination that is highly unlikely to match the interests and priorities of competing privatization interests. Mehrotra and Delamonica write that 'national development is a multidimensional synergetic system … If the investment is left to the private sector, there is much greater risk of coordination failure and lower efficiency than if the state was to provide the services, instead of merely financing them' (ibid.: 144). Ultimately, these problems perhaps account for why water provision is the least popular private sector investment prospect, relegating it behind quicker fixes like telecoms and electricity. This means that in water poverty conditions, the private sector will, inevitably, provide mobile phones for market opportunities before sanitation for life. The pro-market, World Bank-housed Public–Private Infrastructure Advisory Facility (PPIAF) estimates that water would be at least three years behind telecoms provision in the peacetime 'development' scenario (Schwartz et al. 2004). People do not die in their millions from the lack of a mobile (cell) phone, but they do from the lack of clean water and sanitation; but the market prioritizes the former, affirming the absence of the human from market outcomes.

All of these arguments matter, in the sense that they represent intellectual and practical challenges to the justification for privatizing per se. They constitute a challenge to the hegemonic consensus that directs neoliberal global governance policy, and they offer convincing evidence that, and arguments why, privatization is unable to deliver. World Bank and IMF programmes have slashed

> whatever modest governmental programs existed for the improvement of the life of the people in poorer countries and [have] taken the task out of the public policy arena ... [Consequently,] social improvement is to be left to development via the privatized market-driven economy in the hands of private profit-orientated concerns. (Fields 2003: 138)

Arguments from private corporations' executives bolster this perspective and confirm the 'bottom line' involved. Evidence from failed water privatization, such as in Tanzania or India, is ignored (Dwivedi and Dharmadhikary 2006; Dharmadhikary 2005; Hall and Lobina 2006). While this undoubtedly leaves very poor people exploited in cities and neglected in the provinces, however, it overlooks the most obvious problem. The bottom line is that poor people with no money cannot buy water, and will not be able to pay for sanitation. Nor will cash-strapped public institutions like local schools be able to provide adequate sanitation to ensure that children who do have the opportunity to get an education will not be exposed unreasonably to human waste. Most of the people most vulnerable to fatal water-related diseases are children in the poorest families that will be unable to pay private fees for water and sanitation, whether in the home, the school or the workplace. They are also the least attractive to the transnational water companies, since those companies will be unable to recover their costs and will therefore not invest in such a fragile 'market'.

The 2 billion people struggling on less than $2 per day will be less able to pay for vital, life-giving, life-preserving water, and it will not be provided privately for free. As well as affecting children's development and survival potential, the failure to render water accessible disproportionately affects women, since it is normally they who must perform the arduous task of collecting and carrying water from distant turnpikes, rivers, lakes and boreholes back to their communities and families (while it is mostly males who determine water distribution policies at the national and international level). Nor does this onerous burden end here. Water collection can take many hours per day, trebling many women's workloads as they labour in the household with children and domestic provision and attempt to eke a meagre living from subsistence or exchange farming or other low-yield, labour-intensive activity. This undermines yet further their chances of entering and remaining in education and of breaking the chains of their labour imprisonment. Water is just one more burden; privatization is unlikely to increase access in rural areas since private corporations are reluctant to engage with low-income people. Furthermore, where privatization does happen, prices will still too often be beyond the poorest, meaning women will still have to travel to collect and carry water, and existing free supplies (minus the cost of female transport) may be diverted in the course of privatization, extending the distances travelled and the time spent away from home. The poorest women and children, then, will inevitably be hit hardest in water privatization. The 'bottom line' is that without cash, people cannot access privatized clean water to drink, and they will go without sanitation systems to deal with deadly fecal matter. Vulnerable infants will be on the front line of this latest assault on poor people concomitant on the privatized governance of water (Hemson et al. 2008). Neoliberal attitudes to privatization continue to brook little opposition and universalize a one-faith church of human development which sanctions 'high transition costs' outweighed by 'the prospects for delivering positive aspirations in the future' for the poorest people in the world (Evans 2002: 202; Lee 1996). The highest transition costs, reflected in the failure to improve even basic living conditions for 10 million infants per annum, will remain lethally high as long as global governance adheres to the myth of the 'trickle-down' effect. Positive aspirations for the present, for people without the most basic physiological necessities, incline towards water. Without water, there are no 'positive aspirations in the future'. As John Turay, Chief of Crab Town Slum Community, Freetown, Sierra Leone, commented recently, 'water is life' (2009).

The state offers unreliable delivery in the capitals and fails the provinces in the poorest parts of the world; and privatized enterprise is disproportionately expensive in the cities and is disinclined to invest in such high-risk, low-return ventures in the countryside. A possible solution, however, treads a middle path between the state and the market without surrendering sovereign policy to global governance while thoroughly exploiting the motivating capacity of profit. Dani Rodrik, for example, recognizes the critiques of neoliberalism presented above, but is more reluctant to dismiss the project out of sight, either ideologically or pragmatically, identifying the crux of the matter as the one-size-fits-all dimension to neoliberal advocacy and prescription. He argues that each setting into which neoliberal precepts are inseminated should be considered in its own context, 'not because economics works differently in different settings, but because ... environments differ in terms of the opportunities and constraints they present', a notion that considers the ability of humans to engage with the mechanisms and means of neoliberalism discussed in Chapter 3 (2007: 4). This said, Rodrik's emphasis on what is being missed by neoliberal growth ignores more fundamental prerequisites of and for growth, since his focus is on fiscal calculations, rather than the provision of life-saving resources.

It is perhaps this which prompts Mathew Taylor to suggest that 'some aspects of development may be as important as ends in their own right as they are means towards growth', adding that the approaches to thinking about development economics outlined by the likes of Baumol et al. and Rodrik might not 'prioritize some ends (such as education and health) as [development objectives] in their own right' (2008: 554). So, if we were to couple private indigenous water provision as a precursor to health and inevitably, therefore, growth with exogenous neoliberal lending and grant-making, we might be able to synthesize and reconcile the reformation in development thinking advocated by Baumol et al., Rodrik and others with the more obvious everyday needs of very poor people and their untapped social and economic entrepreneurialism and potency. I will come to such a synthesis in Chapter 5. In the absence of such approaches in the present everyday lives of insecure people in the global South, however, I turn to the third element of the counter-hegemonic nebuleuse, which is concerned with social policy responses to privatization with the intention of limiting the fallout from neoliberal prescription and proscription in developing the poorest parts of the world.

GLOBAL SOCIAL POLICY

The tension between hegemonic global governance processes and their biopolitical consequences is confronted in the third element of a counter-hegemonic nebuleuse that we might identify. This is the concept of global social policy, which arises in parallel with global governance efforts to retract state activity in markets and reduce social provision, and which considers the best ways to fill the gaps in essential human security provision caused by this economic ethos. Bob Deacon defines the idea of global social policy as an extension into the international arena of the principles of redistribution, regulation and rights found at the national level in parts of the developed world. He writes that global social policy refers to:

> The mechanisms, policies and procedures used by intergovernmental and international organizations, working with other actors to … influence and guide national social policy and … provide for a supranational or global social policy … Global social policy is about global social redistribution, global social regulation and global social rights. (Deacon 2004: 5)

Global social policy scholars are concerned broadly with 're-embed[ding] free floating global capital in a set of international institutions which might ensure that the global economy had a social or public purpose' (ibid.: 5). This is another angle on Ruggie's embedded liberalism, whereby social responsibility for the consequences of market practices is formalized and institutionalized. The purpose of this process is to create, in the words of K. P. Kannan, 'collective care arrangements to meet contingencies' (2007: 19). From such perspectives, at least two critical concerns frame the debate. One is that national state policy everywhere is increasingly controlled from beyond state borders (Deacon 2000; Grugel and Piper 2007; Yeates 2005; Suleiman and Waterbury 1990). A well-understood example affects Europe, whereby some European Union legislation removes sovereign control of national matters from national parliaments and places it under the authority of a regional body. For example, recently most European states switched from a national currency to the common euro, subjugating national economic policy-making to supranational control.

Scholars of global social policy, when considering such supranational influence, have pointed to the way in which national welfare policy is subjugated to neoliberal global governance expectations (Deacon 2005a; Yeates 2005). That is, the Post-Washington Consensus makes lending conditional upon state withdrawal from public provision of basic welfare. This has been the case since decolonization and the domestication of the state in the global South, when cold war terms and conditions engendered massive and ineffective lending from international institutions on condition of allegiance to one superpower or the other. Probably the best-known example involves the World Bank and a procession of kleptocratic African dictators. After 1989, large-scale loans became contingent on good governance, or political reform in line with liberal democratic benchmarks, rather than on Third World client–superpower-patron loyalty. This political tool of control was later upgraded to cover economic reform in accordance with preferred neoliberal economic policies. According to Stephen Gill, this dualist conversion, enshrined in and protected by a 'new constitutionalism of disciplinary neoliberalism', formalizes and legitimizes the core values of global governance (1998). Colin Hay remarks that such sanctioning processes help capitalist and neoliberal hegemony to 'subordinate social and political priorities ... to perceived economic imperatives and to the ruthless efficiency of the market' (2007: 103). Combined, then, global social policy is concerned first with the sanctioned global norm of exogenous determinism of indigenous welfare, defining the matter as one of biopolitical governance by the Post-Washington Consensus of people unable or unwilling to challenge the legitimacy of such usurpation and its negative impact on human security.

A second concern identified in the global social policy literature (and elsewhere) is the double standard reflected in the process outlined above. In a nutshell, there is substantial criticism of the new constitutionalism that prohibits key welfare practices in the insecured, underdeveloped world, by secured, developed states that benefited critically from the prescription of the very same policies in earlier years. It is no secret that, in the USA and much of Europe, public investment underpinned the early provision of state infrastructure in water and sanitation, and, later, welfare policies designed to protect the most vulnerable, especially in harsh environments (Jordan 2006; Deacon 2005b; Cichon and Hagemejer 2007). In Europe, it is axiomatic that the UK developed economically on the back of public sector investment in water provision and sanitation before the Second World War, and in welfare support afterwards. For Duffield, such 'developed life' evolved from 'regimes of social insurance and bureaucratic protection historically associated with industrial capitalism and the growth of welfare states' presently maintained by 'a range of public welfare bureaucracies, benefit entitlements and safety nets covering birth, housing, family support, education, health, employment protection and pensions' (2008: 150; Deacon et al. 1997; Wood and Gough 2006). In the USA, F. D. Roosevelt instigated, in times of economic desperation, the New Deal reforms, and water and sanitation infrastructure was state sponsored.

It remains the case that, in the secured world, the state has instigated large-scale provision of public goods such as water and sanitation, essential to health and growth, based on the experiences of Europe and North America. This is the norm. Most water and sanitation systems originated in, and are often still the subject of, public provision, or may be financed through a combination of privatization and state provision. Where privatization has been involved, it has been after the state has already created a comprehensive and effective infrastructure accessible to most of its population (Hall and Lobina 2008). Privatization has been undertaken normally after the colossal infrastructural investment costs have been borne already by state provision through taxation and borrowing on international markets. The private sector is unwilling to set tariffs sympathetically for very poor people and to cross-subsidize cost recovery where people cannot afford connection and supply, so the start-up costs are sunk in state history and public taxes.

The reverse of this experience, however, is advocated for the developing world by those in the developed world who project neoliberal values. Neoliberal governance and the Post-Washington Consensus determine, through the application of soft power (conditionality), that public infrastructure provision is tendered to the private sector, and where it exists already, that the market completes provision. The private sector has shown itself (above) unwilling to subsidize costs for clean water and/or sanitation for the poorest, and unwilling to extend or build networks where cost returns are likely to be low or absent, such as in the vast rural reaches of sub-Saharan Africa and South Asia, where they are vital for life itself.

In short, global governance dictates specific national policies in developing countries that are quite at odds with successful (and for the most part ongoing) state social practices in Europe and North America. Duffield observes that such policy reflects 'an international security architecture that both separates and reproduces the life-chance divide between the developed and underdeveloped worlds'. He refers to the developed and underdeveloped worlds as 'insured' and 'non-insured', since in the former, populations are mostly insured against life contingencies, and in the latter, they are rarely so privileged (2008: 149; Konkolewsky 2007). There is no question that the very different development approaches have the effect of ensuring decelerated development and enduring exposure to both shock and structure.

Whether the poverty that attends supranational neoliberalism is 're-discovered as a recruiting ground for the moving feast of strategic threats that liberal order is constantly menaced by' (Duffield 2008: 148), or whether it is a consequence of other structures, the global social policy literature, which I shall examine further below, is very closely related to the critical IPE material that debates causes of and responses to systemic global underdevelopment. Furthermore, both have pushed the evolution of counter-hegemonic arguments related to the efficacy of neoliberalism as it relates to vulnerable and poor people. While the former exposes the consequences of neoliberal policy regarding inequality in quite general terms, the latter is concerned more specifically with ameliorating the consequences of structural inequality derived from the imbalances created by neoliberal hegemony. Both disciplines, of critical IPE and global social policy, meet in the concept of 'embedded liberalism' as a critique of the Post-Washington Consensus on the private–public divide. Embedded liberalism represents a 'halfway house' between national state provision and international markets. John Ruggie advanced a model of economic organization and principle that involved the elevation to the international level of predominant national welfare policies, which mostly combine the mixed economics of market and state provision in the overall economy (1982; 2003). Presently, the social counterforce states use at the national level to manage neoliberal deficiencies is denied at the international level by neoliberal fiat. This differential is mirrored in the anomaly whereby Western institutions actively reject and block the policies they used in their own development strategies.

Global social policy, then, is concerned with challenging the direction in which neoliberal ideology takes social policy, towards a model of provision based on the capacity remaining after the state has been withdrawn and the market has declined on the grounds of poor cost recovery. This is known as residual social policy (Mishra 2002). While some scholars of globalization and neoliberalism believe that reform of these matters is both impossible and undesirable, others take the view that ameliorative and compensatory mechanisms acting upon neoliberalism can smooth some of its roughest edges. It is from this second perspective – that change is possible without dramatic, revolutionary and long-term transformation – that I pursue arguments from global social policy scholarship that address the failures of biopolitical governance in recognizing, accepting and addressing the avoidable social pathology of under-five mortality. By social pathology, I refer to the study and diagnosis of the social causes of disease and illness, which include the forms and rationale of economic and political rules that disburse or deny known, available treatment of lethal but preventable and/or curable diseases. The importance of social pathology reflects how the landscape of the biopolitical has changed with modernity, since presently, 'the physician and the scientist move in the no-man's land into which at one point the sovereign alone could penetrate' (Agamben 1998: 159).

WHAT KIND OF SOCIAL PROVISION? FOR WHOM?

There are two key ontologies of social provision evident in the literature. The first we have noted briefly already. According to Paul Spicker, this residual approach 'refers in the main to services offered as a safety net, for those who have no other kind of provision available' (2005: 345). It is 'residual' both because it deals with those who are left over when institutional welfare is omitted, and because those agencies that respond with provision are the residue after state and market potential has been exhausted. A second ontology sees social policy as an institutional principle: as part of the complex and multifaceted engine of global economic development, an essential element of growth upon which neoliberalism depends. These ontologies compete for position; after the Second World War, the latter was ascendant; more recently, the idea that social provision should be residual and sustained through mostly informal voluntarism or philanthropy has gained legitimacy (Deacon 2005a: 20; Yeates 2001). The difference is between seeing 'social policy as a safety net [and] a conception of active social policy as a powerful instrument for development working in tandem with economic policy' (Mkandawire 2004: 40). For both, however, in an environment characterized by needs exceeding the willingness to satisfy them, the questions of focus and application are central, whether a developmental or residual philosophy predominates, and whether a universal or more specific focus is favoured.

Presently, both approaches coexist uneasily; uneasily, because there are double standards involved that maintain asymmetries of development and insecurity. In Europe, and to a lesser extent in the USA, there are various types of social protection ideologies at work. Some are mixed roughly equally while others are biased towards greater subsidized protection (Europe) or less (the USA). Nor is the experience uniform in the global South; some regimes are broadly socially protective while others are unable to raise taxes to fund the most basic of needs. The debates revolve around universality and specificity; and between social or private funding, with the usual midpoints and extremes associated with any matter of human behaviour. Some are concerned with the geographical extent of provision, either across a nation or around the world. Others are concerned with the means by which groups or nations generate provision, proposing means ranging from states, to markets, to multi-sector state-public-market provision, to models that reject all routine provision and assume that responsibility should reasonably rest with private actors from global philanthropists to local monks (Deacon 2005b; Grugel and Piper 2007). The International Labour Organization (ILO), for example, argues that 'the ultimate aim is to build a generalized national social security system in order to guarantee to all a secure income and access to health care at a level corresponding to the economic capacity and political will of the country' (Reynaud 2002: 4). In conjunction with the ILO, Cichon and Hagemejer identify a universally applicable model of basic provision which they call a 'global social security floor'. They consider that a social security deficit involving lack of access to child benefits, schooling, basic pensions, basic social assistance for poor but active people and adequate healthcare should be universally compensated (2007: 184). It would draw from tax revenues and a wide range of private provision to supply generalized healthcare and education, as well as 'basic social assistance … that helps to overcome abject poverty for those able to work' but who might otherwise be prevented from securing enough to survive, and would also cover pensions and disability payments (ibid.: 183). This model can, it is argued, be funded by states themselves, with some transitional help. It is an ambitious objective, tied to existing international legislation that already stipulates much of this provision as a legal requirement, but it is not short of critics.

Lendvai and Stubbs, for example, claim this universal imagining of global social policy is centred on the global North, and argue that such an approach 'displaces' by suborning local perspectives into the global; 'disciplines' by projecting dominant knowledge; and 'depoliticizes' through the application of technical projects and methods (2007). Wood and Gough also reject universalism 'from the radical Right (unregulated market capitalism) or the radical Left (basic income) or the reformist Center (participation and good governance)' and focus instead on 'the particular circumstances of a country or region's welfare regime' (2006: 1697). Their analytical focus is on comparing situations across regions by characterizing provision in terms of state or market providers; informal social systems such as common social patronage; or where such a regime is absent to the extent that insecurity is routine and social protection is of a residual form. Provision may range from full and incremental welfare support, common in some European states, and including benefits from maternity leave to pension provision, to minimal, residual, extra-state, extra-market, voluntary support, with a variety of concepts of entitlement in between (Hall and Midgley 2006: 1; Yeates 2005). But, like other approaches to social provision, it does not allow for prioritization from a contingency perspective, and it does not address specifically those who have least, struggling in places where there is least likelihood of generating reliable and consistent protection.

Jean Dreze and Amartya Sen, however, imagined such a prioritization and categorization in terms of the concepts of protection and promotion (1989). The former confronted more deadly contingencies while the latter sought to elevate those not immediately threatened by dangerous threats. This ranking and prioritization approach also appears in the work of K. P. Kannan, who proposes Basic Social Security (BSS), akin to Dreze and Sen's protection, and Contingent Social Security (CSS), likened with promotion. For Kannan, they are necessarily mutually interwoven, but BSS is specifically concerned with those 'who are not in a position to access a minimum of resources to meet their economic and social requirements for a dignified life in society' (2007: 21). This marks a departure from the scholarly inquiry into universal approaches (Deacon) and rationing mechanisms of political responsibility, institutionalism and residuality (Wood and Gough), and is distinct from inquiry into establishing a common social floor, even at a national, rather than a global, level (Cichon and Hagemejer). Furthermore, Kannan suggests, it is 'a foundational requirement, in the sense that the commonly accepted notion of social security for meeting contingencies ... will not make any sense in its absence'. Kannan argues that this model of social security evolution was 'also the priority in the history of evolution of social security policies and arrangements in the West, where ... basic human deprivations have been taken care of for a large majority of the population' (ibid.: 21). Criticisms of non-transferability from Atkinson and Hills et al. (1991) are dismissed on the grounds that there have been substantial gains since decolonization and there are working models already *in situ*. Kannan substantiates this approach further by pointing to the number of humans living at the edge of survival on less than one dollar per day, but this again returns us to the familiar problem of individualism and human security and the problem of which of those 1.2 billion people to focus on or prioritize for Basic Social Security. Nevertheless, it is from these perspectives, of European precedent and mass contingency, that Kannan urges an extension of both basic and contingency needs provision and, in the case of the former, proposes that this should be applied universally. Although Kannan suggests that, within this approach, people could 'self-select', he also proposes a 'social floor', again returning us to the human security conundrum of scale, identity and coherence (2007: 23).

Much of the global social policy literature, then, responds to departure from a tradition that has grown from the European and North American experience of industrialization and development to provide means of protecting the weakest (disability support and legislation, for example) and providing essential foundations for promotion and development (healthcare and education, water and sanitation). The received and collective wisdom upon which such notions were based is threatened both in the developed and the developing worlds by a particular trend in biopolitical governance that increasingly authorizes a residualist approach to social provision, but with far greater ramifications for human security in the developing world, where vulnerability is routinely high. These conditions reflect the 'logic' of global competitiveness enshrined in the most basic neoliberal growth assumptions of biopolitical global governance. For the developed world, levels of civil resistance are almost sufficient to challenge such a position. In the poorest parts of the developing world, and in many areas within wealthy countries in the global South, the ability to prevent the elevation of the narrow residualist model favoured in neoliberal thinking is far harder to resist. Indeed, for many, the battle is already over, and for millions more who will die for the lack of affordable and accessible oral rehydration salts, for example, the battle is already lost. If it is the conclusion of critical IPE that privatization of water and sanitation is ineffective and unaffordable for the poorest, then it is the conclusion of global social policy scholars that there is inadequate coverage in any of the proposed models to protect, let alone promote, the biopolitical security needs of millions. Furthermore, there is only limited opportunity in countries unable to raise or generate sufficient taxes for social protection to cover the vast range of contingencies that threaten or extinguish millions of lives annually. The remaining approach, once global governance has deleted the option for state provision, and once the market has withdrawn because people without money cannot pay for marketized goods and services and because there is limited profit for transnational corporations, is the residualist principle, whereby spartan resources supplied from formal and informal voluntarism and charity confront the same problem of who gets what, first.

Global social policy scholarship fails to reach agreement on the best means of compensating for the human security consequences of biopolitical global governance, despite the wealth of evidence developed from the experience of the West that shows the importance and value of state provision, both for basic human security and for long-term national development. This distinction, resulting in the safest people in the minority world being secured while the least safe in the majority world are insecured, reflects the paradoxical axiom of the 'do what we say, not what we do' discourse of global governance. In the short and medium term, while honourable and worthy debate continues in the ILO and among respectable scholars, no agreement has been reached on even a level of basic needs provision, or on what this might mean, or where it might be applied. Without any such concordance, no policy reaches the people who die unnecessarily or are 'merely' marginalized in any number of ways as a consequence of global governance preferences; and the idea of global social policy is unable to create a viable response to the U5MR, even though a number of approaches have come close. A lack of agreement on the basics hampers the notion; and a lack of space in global governance discourses hamstrings the provision of a life-saving social lifeline for the poorest in the world. Thus, despite global social policy clearly challenging the efficacy and propriety of neoliberalism in terms of the concept of social care, biopolitical global governance undermines an otherwise internationally institutionalized ideology of care for vulnerable people. For this reason, although it has much merit, I suggest that global social policy is unable to challenge the scale and immediacy of the U5MR – the most visible and open running sore of the calculated mismanagement of life.

CONCLUSION

What may we reasonably surmise from these considerations? First, counter-hegemonic inquiry and argument demonstrate that 'best practice' effective in European development and applied almost universally across the developed world, and demonstrated to secure biopolitical and national development and growth, is deliberately and specifically prohibited by fiat of global governance. This raises awkward questions regarding what 'constitutes defensible human life' (Coward 2006: 67). The process of Northern inclusion and Southern exclusion occurs despite the evidence showing the large-scale failure of privatization; despite the growing reluctance of TNCs to engage in public water provision; and despite the incontrovertible fact that people without money cannot pay market prices for anything at all. It is sometimes hard to avoid the racial implications of this conclusion. Policies of biopolitical governance proven to work in white Europe after the Second World War are deliberately and consciously prohibited for people of colour in the developing world, by mainly white people in the developed world. Indeed, it seems that 'best practice' in Europe and North America is not considered appropriate for the developing world. The latest example of such double standards surfaces with regard to the global economic crisis that struck Europe and North America, where nationalization and state bail-outs of the private sector were the response to fiscal challenge which, when economic crises happen in Africa and Asia, prompt Western financial institutions to demand further austerity and privatization. Thus, what worked and works for Europe and North America in the pre-industrial, industrial and post-industrial eras is prohibited by the mainly European and North American elite of the Post-Washington Consensus, the World Bank and the IMF for people and governments in the global South. Global governance must face some serious questions about race and power, even while many are asking the question of gender.

Second, the victims who make up the global U5MR die avoidably, every year, partly because global governance authorizes the rationing of natural resources in Southern countries for the profit of Northern transnationals. Privatizing water and water services puts them beyond the reach of many of the poorest people in the world, commodifies resources that are a biopolitical necessity for the successful production and repro-duction of life, and transfers the commodified value of those resources to powerful metropolitan elites who perpetuate the Post-Washington Consensus. This process finds clear expression for the under-fives: medical epidemiology establishes immediate and proximal causation, and verifiable social pathology reveals institutional and policy causation. Ewa Charkiewicz perhaps goes too far when she writes that 'hidden behind the caring face of biopolitics is its double, the control of life by means of dispensation of death' (2005: 80). But global governance decisively and openly excludes and prevents strategies and policies proven to protect life, creating biopoverty from which death stems. This argument should not be confused with necropolitics, or 'the subjugation of life to the power of death', usually discussed in relation to sovereign warfare. But it does suggest that the 'power to expose to death' (Mbembe 2003: 11) by consequence of chosen action, and by omission of action when warning evidence is demonstrable, is an unintended, but nevertheless contingent, outcome of contemporary global governance. Part of the means by which this process is perpetuated is through moral indifference and the denial of lethal outcome that in turn perpetuates the hegemony of global governance. Simon Pemberton writes that

> Undeniably, the nation states of the developed world possess the ability to intervene in [global governance] processes and ultimately the harm they cause. They could demand a different set of economic policies. Yet they have for the past 30 years supported the loans and structural adjustment packages of the IMF and the World Bank for the benefit of the developed world [and] global capital, all at a huge cost to their populations. (2004: 72–3; Chossudovsky 1997; Townsend and Gordon 2002)

The stark evidence of the failure of these policies is both enough to warrant structural intervention to challenge their perpetuation, and a clear example of the biopolitical nature of global governance. Peter Singer makes it clearer, however. He suggests that, if we were to see a child in the middle of a busy road at risk of being knocked down and killed by a car, we would intervene. The deaths of millions of children from dirty water are every bit as predictable and preventable as the car crash; for Singer, this sanctions intervention. That child mortality is so clearly biopolitical and preventable makes intervention logical, practical and necessary.

A final conclusion we might make is that the U5M cohort provides us with a grouping around which human security policy might coalesce. In the neo-Foucauldian sense, the U5M body of human beings is a transnational population group with shared characteristics (age, physiological vulnerability, underdeveloped immune systems, lack of clean water). In addition, the ease with which a common solution may be applied (provision of clean water and sanitation in areas where the death rate is highest) makes such a policy workable. The *UN Millennium Report* declares that 'no single measure would do more to reduce disease and save lives in the developing world' than clean water and sanitation provision (Annan 2000: 61). Such interventions would not have to be geographically extensive, since 'half the need for urban sewerage connections is concentrated in 3 countries: China, India and Indonesia; and 90% of the global need for urban sewerage is in just 24 countries' (Hall and Lobina 2008: 4). The U5M grouping is an identifiable transnational population sharing the same problem that is manageable with the same solutions. The most obvious approach is a Marshall Plan strategy aimed at flooding those countries with cash for water. This would be reckless and pointless. Instead, human security policy in this domain may be generated from some of the core values and beliefs of global governance, with a few minor adjustments and a change in emphasis.

5 | SOCIAL RECONSTRUCTION AND WORLD BANK POLICY

It is clear that water and sanitation provision would directly enhance human security for millions. The question seems to revolve around how best to direct this resource. In the first instance, water is normally available where humans are, otherwise they do not stay there. It is often not clean, however, and not near by. Often, sanitation is not fully understood, and the means for disposing of human waste are often inadequate to the task of avoiding fatal disease transmission. Water must therefore be accessed more easily and must be cleaned; and fecal and other matter removed from direct human contact if human security is to be improved. Presently, in very poor communities where the U5MR is high and reducible, the state and municipal authorities normally provide only incomplete services; and, where this is to be started or improved, new state provision is forbidden by neoliberal prescription in favour of private sector enterprise. Market-induced provision has until recently been dominated by TNCs and is normally to be found in metropolitan areas, where water prices are routinely disproportionately high, and where the profits are normally expropriated abroad, in a form of capital flight. Furthermore, TNCs have shown reluctance to engage with water provision beyond major conurbations and seek substantial subsidies before considering a role. Public funding is ruled out by neoliberal determinism, and TNCs are withdrawing.

One serious consequence of this dilemma is the creation of bio-poverty. I have noted this concept earlier, but elaborate to remind and reinforce. It is biopoverty, or the calculated prohibition of physiological necessities – water, nutrition, vaccines – without which civilians die en masse. Biopoverty stands at the nexus of the biologically essentially and the institutionally prohibited. It is structural and deliberated – calculated – in character, since it is socially constructed and mobilized by social and institutional rules that determine the in/accessibility of otherwise available life-preserving resources. For brevity, it may be considered the mismanagement of physiological necessity. I have identified the absence of water as one such element of biopoverty, but others exist, ranging from absence of immunization drugs, inadequate health provision for safe childbirthing, and excision of available vaccines for curable and/ or preventable communicable diseases. For the basic needs of human security to be served, and for biopoverty to be reduced, requires an alternative approach. Since the World Bank governs development as an instrument of neoliberal global governance, and since it has the reach required to cover multiple sub-state populations at risk of death, it is to the orientation of Bank policy that this chapter turns. I discuss the prospects of enforced reform in line with the human right to water, before moving on to consider more immediately impactful reform. The first may be considered a restraining exercise of a legal nature, after the fact, that would involve complex and inevitably time-consuming processes of legal change in making international governmental organizations (IGOs) like the Bank legal duty-bearers with the same obligations as states. The second may be thought of as an adjustment exercise of a political nature, before the fact, which would involve the renegotiation of the Bank's economic policies by the member states responsible for its mandate and remit. This does not infer that the Bank is the only financial actor capable of supporting water and humans; but it is a reasonable place to start because of its self-appointed role as a development body and because of the extent and scope of its influence over very poor developing countries wielded by lending conditionalities.

LEGAL INFLUENCE ON WORLD BANK POLICY

Thinking on international law and change in IR is divided into two broad camps, each of which is subdivided into numerous intellectual factions. One says the world cannot be 'corrected' by legal intervention because the system is based on underlying biological inevitabilities and the negative element to human nature, which is immutable and incontestable. The other maintains that the international system is socially constructed and reconstructed over time, and therefore change is perfectly feasible. I start with the first of these two propositions by looking at the way existing laws codifying certain universal human rights are adhered to in an international system dominated by assumptions and beliefs pertaining to traditional ways of behaving.

Certain human rights are considered universal, if not practised or applied universally. The Universal Declaration of Human Rights (UDHR) states that 'everyone has the right to life, liberty and security of person' (Article 3); while the International Covenant on Civil and Political Rights states that 'every human being has the inherent right to life'. It is 'recognized that all United Nations member states have a legal obligation to respect human rights under the United Nations Charter and under general international law' (Armstrong et al. 2007: 152). Furthermore, 'in spite of its non-binding legal status, the Universal Declaration of Human Rights has had considerable normative impact [such that] many of its provisions are now binding through customary law' (ibid.: 156). The right to biological life at a minimum is enshrined in many other substantial legal treaties, including the US Declaration of Independence and, more latterly, in the European Convention on Human Rights (1950).

More specifically, and in relation to children under five, the UN Convention on the Rights of the Child (1989) recognizes the specific need for protection of the child 'by reason of his [sic] physical and mental immaturity' requiring that 'States' Parties recognize that every child has the inherent right to life'. Numerous other covenants are quite specific about the special requirements to protect children, which are distinct from the protection of adults (Smith 2007). States bear great responsibilities regarding children within their boundaries. Ensuring that these responsibilities are met, however, increasingly takes second place to the sustenance and protection of neoliberalism. The assumption increasingly is that the market will provide the means to the attainment of various key rights. Upendra Baxi writes that:

> The paradigm of the Universal Declaration of Human Rights is being steadily supplanted by a trade-related, market-friendly … paradigm [which] reverses the notion that universal human rights are designed for the dignity and well-being of human beings and insists, instead, upon the promotion and protection of the collective rights of global capital in ways that 'justify' corporate well-being and dignity over that of human persons. (1998: 163–4)

The Post-Washington Consensus affirms the view that market forces 'will enhance human welfare precisely by promoting the economic goals prescribed in their constituting documents' (Anghie 2000: 247). Neoliberal propaganda diverts responsibility for continued poverty and mortality in the developing world by claiming it is 'the poor' who have failed capitalism, rather than the other way round. For example, the World Bank claims that developing countries that do not comply with the diktats of neoliberalism – even though those diktats sometimes marginalize further the poorest and most vulnerable people in a population – will not experience growth, leading to 'the poor suffering the most severe consequences'. Even while dictating policies that marginalize the poorest, the Bank argues that it is the responsibility of states 'to ensure that the needs of the poor are not neglected' while simultaneously prohibiting state subsidies in preference for marketization of public services such as water provision (World Bank 1998: 8). It is Catch-22. To further the literary analogy, we may compare these contradictions to Orwellian 'doublethink', wherein aspects of globalization and global governance conjoined in neoliberalism might also cause or aggravate some of the very problems it is claimed they resolve, while this outcome is denied adiaphorically. Antony Anghie comments that 'the Bank is firmly committed to globalization; [in its view,] rather than causing poverty, globalization alleviates it' (2000: 260). While this oversimplifies the relationship between neoliberalism and growth, it clearly makes the point that the Bank is monotheist in this respect. There is one dominant view, which is that the consequences of globalization are the responsibility of developing countries. This oversimplifies the more complex and broader picture, wherein the Bank removes or prohibits those countries' capacity to cope with the negative consequences of globalization. The provision of water, enshrined in human rights legislation, is considered in terms of economics and assumed best delivered by the market, but the market inevitably will not provide for those who cannot pay. Without state provision, which is prohibited by the Post-Washington Consensus, the human right to water and the legal doctrine and statutes in which this is enshrined is rendered moot.

This is because, for the most part, international governmental organizations like the World Bank cannot be called to account in international law. Anghie notes that:

> While human rights discourse outlines a set of legal principles that further justice within states, no such principles have been formulated in international law to achieve substantive justice between states … Thus, the most blatant perpetration of international economic inequalities and injustices continues to elude any sanction by international law. (ibid.: 273)

According to Anghie, the World Bank is not subject to international human rights legislation, nor does it have to be bound by the UN Security Council's otherwise binding edicts (ibid.: 266). Systems of appeal exist; but these provide only ad hoc means to redress individual claims regarding specific policies in specific places at specific times. This means that substantial change is required if World Bank behaviour, or that of the IMF and the WTO for that matter, is to be legally restrained. International law itself does not need to be changed; existing rules and norms in well-respected declarations and charters are already in place to restrain state behaviour. The problem, instead, is one of generating IGO compliance with existing legislation (Clapham 1993; Darrow 2003; Alston 2005).

Although this may provisionally appear to offer room for manoeuvre, the desirability and possibility of such change in international law is widely disputed. Traditional thinking in IR has been hostile to law as transformative, preferring to see it as the means by which the status quo is preserved. Anne-Marie Slaughter-Burley encapsulated this notion when she wrote that realists

> Believed in the polarity of law and power, opposing one to the other as the respective emblems of the domestic versus the international realm, normative aspiration versus positive description, cooperation versus conflict, soft versus hard, idealist versus realist ... Law ... had no place in this world. (1993: 207)

Armstrong et al. conclude that in this tradition 'legal scholarship is about figuring out what law is as opposed to what it should be' (2007: 77; Onuma 2003). For legal positivists, the issue is interpretation of existing law; and for political realists, the areas of concern for law are:

> Why states devote so much attention to constructing legalized institutions that are bound to have so little effect and why states accept as credible, pledges to obey legal rules that could effectively bind them to act in ways that might be antithetical to their interests. (Goldstein et al. 2000: 391)

This perspective reflects the famous realist truism that international law is merely a 'tenuous net of breakable obligations' (Hoffman 1956) that reflect the power asymmetries inherent in anarchic order whereby 'legal rules emanate from dominant powers and represent their interests [and] bind the weaker members of the system [in which] stronger powers ... bear the cost of enforcement' (ibid.: 391). From such a perspective, change is not considered epistemologically or ontologically relevant beyond the state as agent since, in the realist worldview, 'legal change is not possible in the absence of state consent' (Armstrong et al. 2007: 111). Change is not likely and, for many, nor is it desirable in the fatalistic worldview of realism, because the explicit normative assumptions involved provide 'delusional justification for policies that are inconsistent with the realities of interest and power' (Goldstein et al. 2000: 392). It is stasis rather than transformation.

In contrast with such conclusions, other approaches address 'the role of international legal norms in shaping state behaviour [and] on the power of process and institutions to transform the self-perceptions of participants, and thus to reshape their calculation of interest' (Slaughter-Burley 1993: 222). From this perspective, international law can be 'reinvented' by 'international lawyers ... promoting better law [for] a world public order that would advance human dignity' (ibid.: 210). Evolving legal norms embed in international relations the primacy of changing ideas in a dynamic and unpredictable social environment. Or, according to Anne-Marie Slaughter et al., legal norms 'play a constitutive role in the formation of actors' identities and interests in the structure of the international system' and can thus direct the evolution of the human-political world (1998: 382). Armstrong et al. argue that conventional legal constructivism offers four contributions to an understanding of change in international relations. First, it accepts and embraces normativity. Second, it provides a more elaborate conceptualization of political and legal structure as fluid and flexible. Third, it sees actors other than states as able to introduce and have embedded new norms to which states respond positively (in some cases). Fourth, international law operates at a deeply constitutive level and shapes 'how states and other actors see themselves, their social situations and the possibilities of action' (2007: 104–5). This ontology challenges traditional realist perspectives in IR on change and its limitations, to suggest that international law shapes not just routine interactions between states and a multiplicity of actors, but also deeply held beliefs and values that are generated socially and historically.

Thus, on the one hand, norms are deeply socialized and institutionalized and therefore very hard to break. But, on the other, there is no shortage of evidence to show that change in some aspects of international relations occurs not only at the behest of consenting states or international legal process, but also in response to ideas and their primacy, exemplified most recently by the interventions of norms entrepreneurs (to which I turn in the following chapter). In addition, it has been noted that sudden external shocks (such as genocide) can cause changes to occur to both international law and international relations (Diehl et al. 2003). Opinion on change may be divided, but the evidence is not. The trend is towards, not away from, cooperation with international law and participation in normative changes in what Judith Goldstein et al. call the 'legalization of world politics' (Goldstein et al. 2000; Slaughter-Burley 1993).

While this suggests that the entrenched view is being substantially challenged, it makes little difference to the pernicious ontological divide and deadlock that hold back change; we may not expect progress on this matter in a short or even medium time span while scholars debate the epistemological veracity of their attachment, and it is in this seemingly unbridgeable gulf that opportunities to undermine biopoverty and enhance the human security of millions of children are lost. Anghie summarizes the obstacles to change thus:

> The task of creating an international economic law system that promotes international justice appears formidable. It is not simply questions of entrenched power that need to be addressed, but the whole question of articulating a vision of international justice that can critically examine the basic idea that the international order consists of sovereign states, and that the poverty and hardship experienced by a people is completely attributable to the inadequacies of the state ... [This ignores the ways in which] globalization appears to enhance the powers of transnational economic actors ... whose activities cannot be easily regulated by the state, or even by international law. (2000: 275)

Because the question of achieving even the most basic human security is complicated by intricate mechanisms of denial and of ontological and epistemological dogma, it is unlikely that this will change quickly enough to protect the millions that die avoidably for lack of accountability of IFI policy before either democratic governance or the international rule of law. Therefore, I now turn to potentially faster means of redressing this wholly soluble problem; a departure from the moral expectation that IGOs might respect legally enshrined international human rights in the implementation of their economic policies, towards a reconsideration of some of the policies that undermine human security in the first instance, which international law cannot presently engage with.

POLITICAL INFLUENCE ON WORLD BANK POLICY

Much is written about the need to democratize the World Bank, and it is implied that the result would be greater participation in Bank processes. There are three reasons I do not treat such a notion here. First, it is likely to be a lengthy process unlikely to result in substantial change. But second, and more relevant, democratization, like democracy, does not undermine immediate and deadly threats to human security. It creates a framework for thinking about rights, but such rights as the right to life, as I have demonstrated, mean little if key international institutions are not held to account for their absence. There will be little or no immediate or useful impact at all on people whose basic need is water, or any other problem of biopoverty, or of development beyond the $2 per day Rubicon. This is not to say the Bank should not be democratized;

but it is to say that democratizing the Bank will not reduce biopoverty or enhance human security for those most in need of such changes in any reasonable time frame. A third reason why I do not engage further with democratizing the Bank is that, even if the World Bank or other such large, powerful neoliberal body is institutionally democratized and its functions made more transparent, accountable and better audited, this process does not address, or challenge, the purpose of those functions, which is to extend the values, practices and misperceived outcomes of universal cosmopolitan neoliberalism globally. It puts the cart before the horse, as far as everyday lives are concerned: people need water, or some other physiological necessities presently denied to people en masse, before they need democracy; democracy does not bring human security, nor do anywhere near as many people die from a lack of democracy as die from a lack of clean water. As a development institution, the Bank could facilitate that physiological necessity, and then democratize if such change is sought by its key stakeholders. This is a question of placing everyday lives before dogmatic devotion to ideology.

Instead of engaging with this debate, and in favour of accelerating positive human security outcomes, I turn to a discussion of conditions under which an international organisation like the World Bank's policy might change politically speaking, specifically regarding a move away from a top-down, TNC emphasis towards a bottom-up indigenous approach. Insofar as the mainstream IR literature examines international institutions, it mostly does so from a functionalist perspective. That is, it is more concerned with the workings of international institutions and how these can best be refined to improve the positions of actors whose task is to manage international relations in an anarchic and ontologic- ally unchangeable environment (Keohane and Nye 2001; Martin and Simmons 1998; Kratochwil and Ruggie 1986). The imperative for such international bodies has escalated with globalization, both to accelerate international interconnectivity and to offset its downsides. The positiv- ist literature in this domain is impressive indeed, and divided along numerous fault lines. What may be taken from this literature in broad terms regarding the relations between states and IGOs like the IMF, the UN and the World Bank is that states determine IGO purpose and policy, to a greater or lesser degree, in order to express and protect the most powerful states' interests. They may also act as a brake on state behaviour in limited circumstances. But, in this literature, they are not to be considered as autonomous actors in the international system, in line with the notion of states as the pre-eminent and primary actors in inter- national relations which have created international public institutions as the servant of state. According to this line of inquiry, since the state and its priorities revolve around a mainly realist understanding of a 'regrettably' anarchic world, we may expect IGO values and behaviours to reflect such assumptions and therefore perpetuate extant systemic inadequacies, asymmetries and inequalities (Kegley 1995; Armstrong et al. 2004). The emphasis is more on the maintenance and management of extant power balances and hegemony coupled with a lesser degree of mutual gains through limited cooperation that depends on the extension of the state via a range of compliant and dependent IGOs. The emphasis in realist study, then, is on how best to manage a bad situation from a technocratic approach. To paraphrase David Kennedy, this reflects 'the replacement of political choices by technical options', a concern later echoed by Professor Michael Sandel in the Reith Lectures, and constitutes an argument that claims that there is little beyond technical management that can – or should – be done in international relations (1999: 52; Hout and Robison 2009).

In contrast with this view, it is argued that IGO behaviour is sometimes independent, but can also be changed by leading states or coalitions of states. Furthermore, such change is more likely the less radical it is and the more incentives are deployed to persuade IGO staff to co-operate. Social constructivists have challenged the notion that IGOs are solely tools of state, to suggest that they are also autonomous or semi-autonomous actors carving out their own distinctive niches, preserved in part by their domination of specialist knowledge in a process that helps maintain political distance from state influence. Michael Barnett and Martha Finnemore, for example, have shown that international organizations (IOs) 'do much more than simply execute international agreements between states. They make authoritative decisions that reach every corner of the globe and affect areas as public as governmental spending and as private as reproductive rights' (2004: 1). Taking this approach, they argue, 'helps explain the power they exercise in world politics, their propensity toward dysfunctional, even pathological, behaviour, and the way they change over time' (ibid.: 2–3). Furthermore, IOs are capable of 'taking on new missions, mandates, and responsibilities in ways not imagined by their founders' (ibid.: 3). The authors conclude from a range of studies of private and public international organizations in a number of settings that IOs routinely act quite autonomously of their state creators, citing (among others) the examples of World Bank and IMF rejection of state demands to consider social and economic externalities in international public policy (ibid.: 158–60). Their work determined that, over the longer run, IOs tend to act independently where they feel able to and where they feel they have moral and technical authority and capacity (ibid.: 159–60). This is important, because it means that IOs are not solely subject to the limited fiat of states, something that has both positive and negative consequences for the notion of change in the international system, as we shall see below.

Another substantial contribution from recent constructivist thought has been the multidisciplinary merging of methodologies applied to IGO analysis, which has amplified greatly our understanding of how IGO operations are maintained or changed. Daniel Nielson, Michael Tierney and Catherine Weaver (2006) construct a bridge between the two very different intellectual approaches of IR and constructivism by deploying a rationalist principal–agent (PA) approach to relations between states and IOs; and between IGO elites and their staff. They then consider their findings from this approach in a sociological/constructivist context. This has advanced our understanding because it has overcome an intellectual prohibition that separated the two approaches as dissociative. The rationalist–constructivist divide, as it has been called, implied that constructivism was not rational and rationalism was not the concern of constructivists (Finnemore and Sikkink 1998: 907). The insinuation has been that a rationalist–constructivist dialogue is oxymoronic, when in fact the two schools can be wed quite reasonably; it is clear that there is overlap across the disciplines, and that neither is epistemologically exclusive. The PA model maintains that an agent's behaviour can be controlled by a principal through oversight mechanisms of accountability (Weaver 2007; Nielson et al. 2006). This can be considered on two levels. First, an organizational elite may be the principal and the IGO would be the corresponding agent. Second, a state might be a principal, while an IGO would represent its agent. In the first case, it is suggested that 'organizational behaviour shifts chiefly when material incentives for the employee are altered': staff can be persuaded through positive and negative treatment to accept change (ibid.: 111).

This work was taken farther to elaborate on the principal–agent relationship and to discuss changes to the organizational culture of the World Bank from within (Nielson et al. 2006; Weaver and Leiteritz 2005). This approach conjoins rationalism and constructivism in discussing change in an underlying ethos or ideology. The essence of the authors' argument is that change can be engineered so long as internal consent is maintained, either by not diverging too much from the original ethos or by restructuring employee incentives and rewards (or both). Change, then, 'will succeed chiefly where the resulting behaviours and organizational outcomes are measurable (and thus information is more symmetric and deviant behaviour is easily identifiable), and where the proposed reforms are adjacent to existing norms (i.e. they fit within the existing culture)' (Nielson et al. 2006: 110). In short, and reflecting the earlier work of Martha Finnemore and Kathryn Sikkink (1998), 'gaps between principals' preferences and agent behaviour will shrink to the degree that new norms and ideas are adjacent to the prevailing culture' (Nielson et al. 2006: 113). The authors conclude that

> Organizational culture matters and ... it can be changed most effectively where persuasive argument finds points of convergence with existing organizational norms ... Organizational leaders may change the personnel and organizational structures as well as design measurable career incentives in order to enable and encourage the organization's staff members to learn and internalize new norms and values – that is, to change the organizational culture. (ibid.: 114)

The authors elaborate on numerous incentivization strategies and motivational frameworks which could be expanded upon with reference to the vast literature on business management, but in essence, change will more likely occur if it is incremental, and if staff are rewarded for accepting the terms and conditions of change. These approaches can be characterized as focusing on changes from within which enjoy at least some degree of internal consent, either in terms of elites designating and designing shifts that influence organizational culture, including ideology and working practices, or in terms of consensual acceptance at lower levels of the legitimacy and remunerative rewards of such shifts (ibid.; Weaver and Leiteritz 2005; Weaver and Park 2007). They are based on the assumption that the leadership of an IGO inaugurates change in response to and in agreement with principals' preferences, and on the assumption that any proposed change does not constitute a substantial departure from existing practices and key values of the organization.

In the second case, the same analytical approach can be applied to relations between states and IOs, where the state is the principal and the IGO is the agent. This literature is concerned with the management of process; it addresses the means and mechanisms that are used to limit IGOs' autonomy while maintaining their internal cohesion and cooperation. It suggests that although autonomy may arise through lack of oversight or interest on the part of states, states also have a number of means that allow them to rein in autonomous behaviour. Nielson and Tierney maintain that where member states act effectively in concert with other states and reduce the decision-making 'distance' between the principal and the agent (state and IGO), then they may select and appoint key personnel, introduce a variety of oversight mechanisms and create new contracts with appropriate rewards and punishments for achievement and failure (2003: 246; Weaver 2007). States as principals may also collaborate to maintain control and limit the autonomy of their IGO agents. Nielson and Tierney hypothesize that 'the probability [of control] will rise as the preferences of multiple principals converge or as the preferences of members within a collective principal converge' (2003: 252). Considering the inverse of this relationship, Weaver argues that agent slippage – that is, the difference between what a principal desires and what an agent does – is more likely as cohesion between principals declines. Weaver argues that 'preference differences [between principals] may produce agency slack if one or more Principals thwart the efforts of other Principals to employ control mechanisms to monitor or direct agent behaviour' (2007: 496). A different example of principal hetero-geneity involves the ability of a hegemon to delimit the terms of an agent's activities, as the USA has done through its domination of the World Bank by means of excluding other states from the Bank's presidency.

From a combination of principal–agent and constructivist approaches to organizational behaviour, then, we may discern that internal IGO behaviour can be changed as long as the changes are not substantial and do not create an employee backlash; and that deeper change is possible regarding mission and mandate, as long as there is no threat to an overarching and all-powerful hegemonic principal, and as long as there is broad agreement among enough of the principals that author-ize an IGO's *raison d'être*. This conclusion clearly differs substantially from the mainstream IR literature, which is limited by inquiry into the continued propulsion of an asymmetric status quo. In contrast, a constructivist and rationalist merger between sociological organizational and principal–agent theories

> suggests that we should expect IO policies and operational behaviour to closely reflect the preferences of the most proximate and powerful member states when principal preferences are relatively homogenous, when information asymmetries are small, and when principals are able to overcome their own collective action problems and effectively use their various control mechanisms to shape IO behaviour. (ibid.: 497–8)

Clearly, the World Bank's capacity to project with authority via condi-tionality the hegemonic practices of neoliberalism when it is opposed by some states leads us to view Barnett and Finnemore's concern that some autonomy leads to dysfunctionalism with some sympathy. But the Bank was formed by fiat of state, and its mandate and practices are maintained by political influence via its board of governors. Skogly notes that this is common practice, commenting that such 'organizations are set up by governments, and these governments constitute their decision-making bodies' (1999: 244). Similarly, Anghie remarks that IFIs are 'no more than the creation of states' (2000: 271). In the case of the World Bank, the board of governors, which is constituted of sovereign state membership, is a direct channel through which states can and do exercise influence over Bank policies via the executive directors, to whom responsibility for routine Bank management is delegated. The Bank derives from and is subject to its state sponsors; but it also demonstrates the capacity for 'quasi-autonomy' (Vetterlein 2007: 514), especially from states that challenge the authority or practice of its defining neoliberal ideology. This ideology permeates the workings of the Bank from top to bottom (Nielson et al. 2006: 109).

THINKING ABOUT CHANGE

We are now in a better position to identify conditions amenable to changing policy in IGOs generally and, more specifically, within the World Bank. The Bank has repeatedly demonstrated both responsiveness to and autonomy from external fiat at different times over different matters. It has responded in principal–agent fashion to state influence via the board of governors' indirect authority over the management of the Bank, and to organizational changes from leadership initiatives within the organization (Nielson and Tierney 2003); but it enforces the hegemonic Post-Washington Consensus in the developing world against the preferences of states in both the North and South and against mass civil society preferences in both hemispheres. It exerts authority over some of its members, but is subject to the authority of economic hegemony that derives from a minority of particularly powerful states and their belief in the validity of neoliberalism. In short, it is theoretically subject to challenge and change, but has shown considerable invulnerability to demands for ideational transformation while tolerating minimalist reform that does little to undermine its underlying credo. The lack of ideological distinction between the Washington and Post-Washington Consensus illustrates this invulnerability, while dissent is subverted in the use of Poverty Reduction Strategy Papers (PRSPs), which present the illusion of meaningful change. How, then, might meaningful and substantial change be prompted presently?

One approach might be to extend the thinking and conclusions of the rationalist-constructivist PA approach all the way from the internal to the external, from state through IGO elite to policy. Briefly put, states can dictate what the Bank does, and the Bank can tell its employees to do it. We have seen that states influence IGOs, and IGO elites influence their employees; the obvious next step would be to join this process up, so that the state might bear upon the IGO leadership, and the IGO leadership might then enforce institutional policy change. We have observed the authority of the state-run board of governors (sometimes pushed by NGOs) to influence the Bank's board of executives, and noted the ability, if not propensity at all times, of states to coalesce to rein in the Bank. This relationship is enshrined in the Bank's founding documents. The articles of the International Development Association (IDA), which is the arm of the World Bank and the World Bank Group that deals directly with the poorest states in the world, declare that 'all the powers of the Association shall be vested in the Board of Governors'. The board of governors is made up from the 185 national representatives of state, and is responsible for shaping, maintaining or changing the Bank's modus operandi, which is sufficiently vague as to be widely interpretable. This process is delegated to the executive directors, who are responsible for translating the designs of state into the mandate and policies of the Bank; the executive directors 'shall be responsible for the conduct of the general operations of the Association, and for this purpose shall exercise all the powers given to them by this Agreement or delegated to them by the Board of Governors'. This is significant, because it reminds us that states have the right to construct and reconstruct the Bank's mandate. This is

> to promote economic development, increase productivity and thus raise standards of living in the less-developed areas of the world included within the Association's membership, in particular by providing finance to meet their important developmental requirements on terms which are more flexible and bear less heavily on the balance of payments than those of conventional loans, thereby furthering the developmental objectives of the International Bank for Reconstruction and Development ... and supplementing its activities. (IDA 2009)

It seems reasonable to suggest that increasing interstate coherence will positively influence control of the Bank; we have also noted the influence of balances of power within the member states of the Bank, along with alliances. The most powerful alliance has involved the USA and Japan and, to a lesser extent, Europe. Furthermore, even were US preferences still to hold sway among the principals of the World Bank (the states from which its mandate is constituted), Weaver maintains that balances of power can evolve to challenge a hegemon's interests. She argues that 'a consensus between Japan and Europe is sufficient to effectively balance or counter US preferences, and the Bank may be theoretically effective in "shirking" the demands of the United States if it is able to play off these key differences between its most proximate (powerful) principals' (2007: 497).

But other factors in changing the balance of power of principals are at play, and Weaver's reference to Europe and Japan has a specific dimension in respect of fundamental challenges to World Bank practices and ideology, since both are advocates and practitioners of a foreign policy involving human security (Kaldor et al. 2007; Edstrom 2003); and both understand development as being more substantial than an economic imperative measured in dollars. In this context, numerous northern member states have shown discomfort regarding the Post-Washington Consensus, which dictates the present, extremist variant of neoliberalism, and consider it to be excessive for development and contributory to a range of human and geopolitical insecurity. Wider still, in the South, there has long been resentment at the enforced neoliberal conditionality that accompanies Bank lending. It is not difficult, then, to see a convergence of interests among a substantial number of principals of the World Bank in reining it in. Common among an expanding cohort of Bank principals, then, is a shared and more homogenous acceptance of the need for an alternative to a fundamentalist version of neoliberal universalism.

There are other aspects of the principal–agent relationship at work between states and the World Bank. According to Catherine Weaver and Susan Park, there is an expanding panoply of criticism of the Bank's elite that reached an apogee over the Wolfowitz affair, in which the former head of the World Bank was forced from office because of his inappropriate appointment of his partner amid allegations of corruption. In the wake of Wolfowitz's negotiated resignation, Weaver and Park maintain:

> Donor and borrower States alike are disillusioned [and] International Development Association replenishments may be increasingly hard to ensure as donors seek other outlets for their aid funds or use the power of the purse to push their often conflicting agendas. Borrower demand for Bank loans is also an increasingly uncertain variable, due to the availability of ... new sources of relatively 'string-free' bilateral

aid from countries like China and Venezuela. Furthermore, NGO watchdog and advocacy groups have gained significant traction in their campaigns and have used recent events to push for dramatic changes to the presidential selection process and the representation and voting rules on the Bank's Executive Board of Directors ... The Bank will most certainly be under even greater pressure to engage in major reform. (2007: 461)

Events in 2008 lent grist to this mill and demonstrated the social reconstruction of traditionally off-limits and key elements of the Bank's practices. Two substantial milestones were recently passed, one of which will be considered here as an example of unilateral state initiative for change, coupled with multi-state convergence on a substantial matter that has been set in stone since the Second World War. This involves the US claim on the World Bank's presidency. Although sources are still in an early stage of development, the official minutes of government committee meetings in London appear to confirm the notion that state principals, unilaterally and through a convergence of state interests, exerted sufficient pressure on the World Bank to lead to the change in the tradition of the Bank having a US president. Although Paul Cammack (2004) is critical of the British Department for International Development's (DfID) submersion in and acceptance of key tenets of neoliberalism and its international institutions, it appears that some elements of this influential body worked within the system to effect some degree of change. DfID reflected on publicly available data in response to a request under the Freedom of Information (FoI) Act for information on its role in the changing of the Bank's rules for its presidency. They stated that 'the UK ha[d] raised [this] issue consistently over many years in public statements and private conversations' (FoI 2009). The UK Secretary of State for International Development stated in uncorrected parliamentary minutes (which are unlikely to change in substance) that the UK successfully exerted influence on the World Bank by way of its position on the Bank's board of governors, and that it played a substantial role in transforming the unwritten convention that seats a European in the IMF presidency and a US citizen at the helm of the World Bank (Hansard 2008; IDC 2008; FoI 2009).

In addition, the World Bank's record of these matters, at Item 9, states that future presidential selection processes 'will be merit-based and transparent with nominations open to all board members and transparent board consideration of all candidates', and will likely be confirmed in a committee meeting scheduled for April 2009 (World Bank 2008). The

UK Secretary of State went on to comment that 'this has never been set out as explicitly before, and the gentleman's agreement [that put an American citizen permanently at the top of the World Bank] is an agreement which no longer stands in the minds of the committee who were present in Washington' (Hansard 2008). It was noted at earlier meetings, however, that European monopoly of the IMF managing directorship would have to be ceded, in a quid pro quo exchange (IDC 2008: 7). This was achieved in part through pressure applied by the UK's executive representative at the Bank. Influence was exerted via London's contribution to the replenishment of the IDA15, or the fifteenth round of topping up the Bank's credit, nation by nation. The UK's Bank representative wrote in private correspondence that 'given the size of the UK's contribution, we clearly have a legitimate claim to promote improved governance in addition'. In addition, however, she noted that 'we use all possible sources of influence to work with Board colleagues and Bank staff to promote better governance' (Moorehead 2008). A response generated through the FoI Act added nuance to this consideration. It stated that the degree of

> leverage is difficult to quantify. The UK's contribution to IDA 15 has increased our voting weight in the IDA Board. It has not increased our shareholding and voting power in the IBRD Board where decisions related to Bank governance are taken. There is a perception among some people that by becoming the largest contributor to IDA 15 our leverage in all Bank decision-making has increased. That is a moot point and not something that we would be able to quantify. (FoI 2009)

Quite clearly, however, the board of governors has been able to influence Bank policy on very substantive matters.

The extent of support for the new directive was made clear by the same UK representative, who stated for the House of Commons record that 'in their statements ... a meritocratic selection of the president [was supported by] the G24, France, Argentina, Bahrain, Brazil, Guatemala, Thailand, China, the Nordic [countries], India, Belgium, Saudi Arabia, Morocco and Côte d'Ivoire', overcoming resistance from Japan and the USA (Hansard 2008; IDC 2008; FoI 2009). This reflects early expectations in London that British leadership in this effort would require that the UK 'not only articulate a vision for reform of the World Bank but ... must pursue this with vigour, building alliances with borrower countries and with other like-minded donors in and outside the European Union' (IDC 2008: 5). It also reflects an expansion of British oversight operatives within the Bank, a development strongly urged as a means of expanding influence on the ground over the Bank (IDC 2008: 5, 23). The British government notes, however, that although there has been substantial change already, this does not mean to say that all aspects of reform have been accepted by the Bank's full board, and the implication in the record is that other reforms, such as parity of shareholder voting, will require an enduring and incremental approach if they are to succeed. A prime reason identified for this is the problem that 'donors are unlikely to wish to cede large amounts of power' (ibid.: 7). There is strong evidence, however, that there has been enough of a convergence of multistate coherence regarding the desire to change the leadership conditions at the Bank, and that this has been effected by means of principal influence on agency elite. Furthermore, the president of the World Bank, Robert Zoellick, confirmed the British leadership capacity in this process when he commented that 'the UK would be at the top of a list' of 'delegations with institutional influence' (ibid.: 53).

This, and other, reform challenges should not be considered un-critically. The recent expansion of executive seats at the Bank, from twenty-four to twenty-five by way of adding a further African position, although part of the British government's ambitions for change, does not substantially dilute the European power bloc at the board, with its eight seats in total. Nor does it change significantly the asymmetrical ratio of influence of the five key members/largest donors (France, Germany, Japan, the UK and the USA), a point ironically demonstrated in the success of the British reform efforts, which relied in part on their contributions to the IDA's replenishment process (ibid.: 20). And the move towards parity of voting as a principle at the Bank, whereby developing countries would have equal say with their developed-country counterparts regarding development policies, and which would impede substantially the internal intellectual culture and development assumptions of the Bank, may still be a long way away. But, overall, a substantial and enduring plank of elite Bank practice has been formally terminated, corroborating the proposition that a principal can influence not just an agent, but a limited number of principals can influence an agent with very powerful, vested and long-held interests. In addition, internal politics in the USA have sometimes moved away from neoliberal lending conditions regarding public sector provision in Bank policy; Weaver points out that the USA 'is not always fully capable of imposing its interests on the [Bank] at will' (2007: 501). We may reasonably imagine at this stage that an expanding number of states as principals, coupled with a diminution of US hegemony, are likely to facilitate the reshaping of the Bank's operational mandate and practices through their owner-ship of the Bank's board of governors. As Michel Camdessus reminds us from the perspective of having managed the IMF, the Bank and the IMF 'are often portrayed as unaccountable technocracies. They are, of course, responsible and accountable to their member states. The problem is not that institutions are not accountable but that they are not perceived as accountable' (2001: 369).

This problem is not specific to the Bank, but also to the states its executive represents. The request for research material made under the FoI Act in the UK revealed that 'there is further evidence relating to the World Bank's acceptance of non-US citizens as President' of the Bank. The British government concluded, however, that 'the balance of public interest in this case favours withholding the information' (FoI 2009). Within the present realist regime of international rela-tions, which has always been characterized by clandestine relationships and surreptitious diplomacy that promotes a culture of secrecy, this is perhaps understandable. It illustrates, however, the nature of the practices charged with maintaining international stability, which use closed, secretive techniques defended by claims of 'public interest', disclosure of which is decided by public bodies. These opaque behaviours sculpt the character of international relations, of mainly male networks of secretive relationships that construct the persistent and unstable hierarchies and rivalries that in turn construct the anarchy defended by the people who have manufactured it. The protection of the secret relations that define the international political system also ensures that the wider global public is less able to pursue research into the means by which this system may be changed, by concealing or restricting access to the evidence revealing how such change happens. This also stands in marked contrast, in the case of DfID and many other public bodies around the world, to the rhetoric upholding transparency and openness standards in public life.

We may reasonably affirm, from the restricted evidence, that the UK and others changed a significant plank of World Bank policy, a notion that supports the constructivist literature outlined above. For the purpose of considering change yet further, we may consider how, once the state has directed the Bank to behave in a particular way, the Bank can then implement this in its own internal practices, rather than such change being resisted or sabotaged internal counterculture. The literature identifies three persistent internal behaviours that might stymie change: the disbursement imperative; the Washington-centric approval culture; and the internal intellectual hegemony of Bank economic research agendas and assumptions. The disbursement culture involves rewards and punishments for meeting or missing lending targets, a problem aggravated by the cold war, when criteria for lending were also based on acquiring and/or maintaining the ideological support of the state borrower. Approval culture refers to the propensity for lending to be based on promoting lending for lending's sake, rather than for more objective reasons, and stems from the recognition that budgets must be emptied if they are to be replenished (Devesh et al. 1997; Miller-Adams 1999). That is, if the Bank fails to spend what its sponsors give it, there is reason to fear that subsequent budgets will be smaller and, given that traditionally Washington has been the largest individual donor, it is referred to as Washington-centric. This problem is common in liberal economics characterized by recurrent budget practices in the private and public sectors alike.

These two cultures are aggravated by the internal intellectual ethos of the Bank, which is characterized by 'an absence of ideological pluralism' (Mehta 2001; Williams and Young 1994). This means that research leadership is dominated by the cult of neoliberal economics, and challengers to this rational-objective empirical tradition remain marginalized inside the Bank, despite their legitimacy beyond its corridors (Broad 2006; Rao and Woolcock 2007; Helleiner 2001). Furthermore, where neoliberal approaches demonstrably fail, there is evidence that the Bank refuses to accept that some of its economic models fail to explain unpredicted outcomes (Banerjee et al. 2006). The characteristics of Bank practices in this respect will be immediately recognizable: preference for 'one-size-fits-all' approaches; an emphasis on practices that can be quantitatively measured and assessed; and an emphasis on tying quantifiable inputs to quantitatively described objectives. Weaver argues that the need to lend for lending's sake (the disbursement culture) in part assures that projects could be easily shaped and implemented, with reference to the conventions of the 'dismal science'. She writes that this leads staff to:

> Design projects that show the number of specific things to be accomplished, such as numbers of students enrolled in a school-building project, with targeted outcomes that attempt to correlate such outputs with the organization's goals, such as overall reduction in illiteracy rates. This significantly biases Bank projects towards development activities that can produce certain kinds of results, while steering them away from activities that may not produce immediate tangible results ... [In this process,] considerable weight is given to

economic and technical factors that are easy to identify and measure, whereas complex political and social risk assessment that involves 'soft' qualitative indicators are usually neglected or distrusted as 'unscientific'. (2007: 507)

This reflects the desire to believe that economics is a neutral and natural science, a view profoundly challenged beyond the Bank, and this belief system is visible in the type of economists recruited to the Bank and its assumptions that blind faith in an impartial market will result in some form of equitable development at some distant point in a future that the Bank holds the authority to define. In short, there are substantial drivers for internal staff behaviour antithetical to imperatives for substantial change, despite numerous attempts to change Bank practices and organizational culture in the past. This should be carefully considered, given that there is broad agreement in recent scholarship that maintains that the greater the substance of change proposed for the Bank, the less the likelihood of it occurring (above).

We arrive, then, at a position whereby mandate/policy-challenging external inputs into World Bank policy broadly (via state mandates and changing presidencies) are demonstrably feasible and result in change; and there is evidence to suggest such transformations are already under way. We also know that external pressures for change may confront internal incentives for stasis. The literature identifies a number of strategies for coping with internal intransigence under the rubric of incentivization and/or punishment. It suggests that Bank staff, like the employees of most wage-labour organizations, are susceptible to a range of remunerative incentives and punishments, as well as other adjustments to their working conditions, such as the company perks familiar to the private sector, and this is a means of reining in aberrant and autonomous IGO behaviour that Bank management can deploy (Nielson and Tierney 2003; Weaver and Leiteritz 2005). We also know, however, that this is less likely to be effective, the greater the variation from the neoliberal ideological convention that saturates the Bank. The nature of proposed changes does not, however, demand the replacement of the underlying ideology, or even a challenge to the concepts it relies on. Nor does it seek a radically revised outcome. It does, however, seek an inversion of the application of neoliberal conduct in the provision of clean water and sanitation, from top down to bottom up, while adopting aspects of top-down influence. I will discuss this strategy next, before turning to the range of ways in which the kind of Bank employee dissent (noted above) might be managed.

MOBILIZING LOCAL CAPACITY

It is sometimes assumed that people in conditions of extreme poverty and underdevelopment are powerless. Sometimes this is the case. But it would be wrong to generalize this way. People in all kinds of ghastly situations display ordinary and extraordinary agency in determining outcomes for their own lives and their own development. There may be limits, however, to what such people can achieve that come from their external environment, which they are unable to change easily. The following response to child mortality through water and sanitation provision derives from the hybrid joining of bottom-up indigenous agency with top-down ideation. It is transversal, traversing the relationship forged between autonomous needs and development, and the structural landscape in which they exist. This approach recognizes the untapped potential of indigenous capacity while recognizing the limits imposed on this by exogenous inhibitors in the form of hegemonic global governance values determining the bounds of the possible. In short, while people possess the ability and will to change their own lives, the extent to which this may happen is also constrained by external factors over which they do not exercise significant control. In a sense, it is not dissimilar to the experience whereby someone has an outstanding business idea but the bank approached for a start-up loan refuses to lend the money needed to get the idea going and to generate income and growth. The person applying for the loan may have everything needed to make the idea fly; but is structurally inhibited by the external environment that s/he cannot control – over which s/he has no power. A clear and well-publicized example may help. Many women in the Cities of London and New York may have the intention and the capability to lead large corporate bodies, but the notorious 'glass ceiling' of masculine, patriarchal obstructionism is a structural inhibitor to the will and the skill to do the jobs, disabling rather than enabling, over which many women have little control – even where technocratic legislation favours equality, since behavioural resistance may bypass technical innovation.

In various post-conflict and development places, this situation, of internal will and capacity restrained by external structure and inhibitors, prevents local people from overcoming penury. They are often able and willing to take on basic reconstruction tasks at the community level, but lack money to finance fundamental requirements. Capacity is often available or may indeed be built; but it may not be actionable. That is, people may have the capacity to enact aspects of post-conflict recovery and development, and resources may be near by; but the two are immobilized by external inhibitors such as lack of cash or market preferences that favour an approach that nullifies the potential of local capacity. For example, neoliberal growth-development approaches focus on top-down development with substantial donor determinism in the provision of 'development' in whatever forms that may take. Money to finance development is often streamed from multilateral actors like the World Bank or provided bilaterally, from state to state. It is assessed in terms of development agendas, and examined for compliance with liberal accountability practices. In this approach, TNCs bid for funds and contracts from wealthy international donors. In this situation, competitive tendering by experienced and powerful TNC bidders to international providers and donors will likely beat local bids from extremely poor people in peaceful or post-conflict spaces who are normally inexperienced in the process (assuming such tenders are invited or accepted). This robs local capacity of start-up provision and associated benefits and diminishes indigenous welfare and recovery. People do not even get a foot on the ladder before global corporations drive development based on external agendas often agreed not with local people but with unrepresentative and sometimes unelected national elites (Waldman 2008). The net effect is to extract the benefits of internal development to external actors, while marginalizing key insider knowledge and expertise and undermining the capacity for growth and development.

Local capacity is to some extent excluded from the means by which its ambitions and objectives may be realized. The process of development is indeed 'big business' and involves global institutions communicating neoliberal ideas for the management of hundreds of millions of human lives. There is an obvious net imbalance visible if one imagines what would happen if local people were given money by large bodies to implement their own needs, decided by those people, in the area of biopoverty. In other words, what if the external environment were enabling, rather than exclusive, of matters such as water and sanitation provision in areas of high and reducible infant mortality? It is often the case in places where human security and development are radically compromised that intent and ability are available but even basic physical resources are out of financial reach. Noting this dilemma, recent literature from the United Nations Development Programme (UNDP) has outlined a development approach emphasizing internal capacity nourished with external financial support, such that ability and intent are mobilized by the removal of barriers to their realization. The report was primarily concerned with post-conflict recovery, but its findings are equally applicable in areas of extreme social distress where economic deprivation and poverty have created conditions that are closely analogous with post-conflict, 'pre-development conditions'. Conditions of severe poverty are further comparable with post-conflict scenarios, since in both there is normally a severely depleted, or non-existent, physical infrastructure, including non-existent or badly damaged water supplies; questions of legitimacy and continuity in elite and local leadership; and severely disaggregated resources in general.

The UNDP report resonates with the literature on constructive post-conflict entrepreneurialism when it discusses the idea of 'indigenous drivers of economic recovery', which it classifies as 'the efforts and initiatives of local communities, individuals, households and enterprises that stimulate and impel economic activity after war' (Ohiorhenuan and Stewart 2008: 49). The notion is not complex. After war and/or in peacetime penury, there are almost always local people who know what communities need for recovery and/or development and who have the basic skills for low-technology rebuilding (one notable exception being Cambodia after Pol Pot, whose policies involved deliberately and indirectly destroying human capital). But in most places, people have the will and capability to rebuild essential foundations of their worlds; they normally lack that which has fiscal cost attached.

The UNDP report suggests that public development projects:

> Should use local capacities and inputs rather than imported ones in order to stimulate the economy in addition to providing work … Contracts tendered to local organizations, associations and firms can help build local skills and knowledge and can also foster local enterprise capacities. Activities amenable to this approach include irrigation projects with a focus on smallholder farmers, water, sanitation and solid waste management in urban and rural areas, feeder roads and rural access infrastructure, and the reconstruction or rehabilitation of public buildings. (ibid.: 75)

It concludes that 'economic recovery [or development] is quicker and more sustainable when it supports and builds on indigenous drivers because local actors are the best placed and have the strongest long-term incentive to engage in activities conducive to sustained economic recovery' (ibid.: 89). The UNDP is not alone. Increasingly, entrepreneurialism is advanced as a means for generating development and recovery. Baumol (1990), Baumol et al. (2007) and Naude (2008) point to the importance of local entrepreneurialism and social responsibilities, although they are quite firm that such local industry should follow the standard neoliberal ethos of openness to competition and accountability, as well as recognizing that it can be destructive as well as creative (Baumol et al. 2007).

But this can only be effective where external process, institutions and ideas do not control the extent to which local agency can otherwise be realized. That is, local initiatives and ventures must not be inhibited by external and/or structural factors.

The World Bank has pre-empted this approach, with some notable successes. In Bosnia and Herzegovina, the Bank funded two Local Initiatives Projects (LIPs) after the war of 1992–95 which 'aimed to provide financial resources to people wanting to start their own small businesses and to take an active part in rebuilding their livelihoods instead of depending on state social welfare funds' or, presumably, doing without (Ohiorhenuan and Stewart 2008: 85; Bojicic-Dzelilovic and Causevic 2008). The Bank is also increasingly aware, at the very least rhetorically, that supporting women works for development, and it does not take a giant leap of the imagination to unite men, women and grant-making in terms of, for example, water and sanitation provision. A conceptually similar project in Ethiopia in 2000 lent \$7 million to women in the Women's Development Initiative Project (WDIP) and found that 'it is possible to empower poor, illiterate women socially and economically through small-scale and group-based micro-business initiatives' (World Bank 2007a: 18). While there should be no prizes for this conclusion, it is surprising that a project found by the Bank to be 'highly successful in achieving its development objectives' should not be considered worthy of further expansion, which was the Bank's conclusion (ibid.: 12). Importantly, it is evidence that the Bank has evoked tactical lending (local enterprise) already, even if the performance of the state stakeholder, rather than the beneficiaries, was a problem (ibid.: 16). The potential is clear: local indigenous capacity linked to external funding determined by local biopoverty needs, rather than externally driven development agendas that outsource development to TNCs and extract financial benefits to offshore banks while untreated biopoverty kills tens of millions annually, is an obvious way forward for human security. Beyond the World Bank, the UNDP is engaged in public and private sector projects that supply micro-finance and grants to entrepreneurial youths of all backgrounds. One example is the provision of showering facilities in urban slums in Sierra Leone (UNDAF 2007).

We may note a distinction, then, between intention, capability and control which will be familiar to scholars of agency (Barnes 1999). In most societies, there exist both intent and ability to improve immediate conditions, but achieving such an outcome may be prevented by structural factors that immobilize extant capacity and will. The following section outlines an approach that could overcome this situation, aimed at immediate human security where avoidable mortality rates are highest.

A HUMAN SECURITY, SECTOR-WIDE APPROACH (SWAP)

Rather than a top-down, skewed-impact transnational private sector neoliberal approach to water and sanitation projects that delivers high end-user prices to a limited audience and which extracts substantial profit to foreign multinationals, instead, a transnational, or transversal, bottom-up indigenous private sector approach to child mortality could be evolved. This approach could mobilize externally funded local entrepreneurialism aimed at providing low-cost or free water and sanitation focused around the areas worst affected by child mortality. This would be financed by a coordinating body whose rationale lay in those people's needs, rather than the needs of their budget providers and neoliberal economic analysts.

The essence of this revised approach to child mortality is the bio-poverty conceptualization, the centring of water security and the emphasis on capacity-mobilizing by ensuring that external barriers are reduced and new support is evolved. While many organizations have introduced numerous individual approaches to child mortality, it is also the case that this has not brought down the rate substantially. This is not in any way to demean the work of UNICEF, Oxfam, CARE, Save the Children and many others. It is instead to argue that a SWAp emphasizing indigenously driven and externally funded water projects aimed at the key cause of child mortality would likely accelerate, coordinate and broaden the impact.

Conventionally, water and sanitation provision is divided between states, multi- and bilateral donors and other larger organizations, which feed in from the top down with only a modicum of bottom-up determinism. A report by Slaymaker and Newborne claims that:

> Sources of funding to the water and sanitation sector are typically diverse and poorly coordinated and flows into the sector are often extremely difficult to quantify precisely. The sector remains donor driven and dominated by major projects which are mostly funded externally. Many of these projects remain 'off-budget' or 'off-plan', or both, reflecting a continued lack of donor agreement on policy and funding priorities both between and within sectors. Consequently national governments struggle to control and account for funds flowing into the sector. (2004: 5; Fernandez 2009)

The act of securing humans from biopoverty is in this sense

commandeered, when agency and capacity at local levels are under-estimated or ignored in favour of large-scale projects involving multiple foreign stakeholders coordinated or misdirected through institutionally weak government and governance. This reflects the concern of development specialists with the illusion of 'participation', frequently in projects that originate externally, in line with external beliefs and agendas. Like democratization in developing countries, the use of nomenclature and terminology goes far in concealing the extent to which the terms hold meaning: multipartyism and 'free and fair' elections lend the impression of democratization in some developing countries' elites, but behind that vernacular often lies neo-patrimonialism and persistent informal bio-political resilience. Similarly, the application of terms like 'stakeholder' and 'participatory projects' in 'development' may belie the extent to which meaningful discussion has taken place in a development setting, and in some cases participatory consultation may be undertaken, and then ignored, if it does not reinforce development dogma. Participation may then in fact be a fraudulent representation of the partial involve-ment of people in the needs of the development community, where development is the extension and impression upon the Other of the Right way of evolving, in a paternalistic process whereby one group of people are 'developed' into something they were not before by another group of people who control knowledge and priorities. Rafael Carmen warns that participation as an external methodology and ontology may be little more than 'a vehicle, a feel-good enhancer or a cost-cutting device [or] a means towards an end such as fitting projects to people or empowering people in the "we must help them" or "we must enable them" mode' (1996: 51). Such people remain 'objects of change [rather than being] in control of that change' (ibid.: 123). They are excluded from, or marginalized in, the processes by which provision of 'their' needs is arrived at by external forces that claim authority along with technical and ideological superiority.

One major problem from this perspective is that the wealth of know-ledge shaped locally and locally focused is ignored in the process of determining what people might need and how it might arrive with them. Michael Edwards comments that paternalistic, top-down development approaches of this ilk devalue 'indigenous knowledge (which grows out of the direct experience of poor people) in the search for solutions' instead of using 'local knowledge to explore local solutions to local problems'. Edwards argues that 'indigenous knowledge' could be 'used as the basis of a successful development policy' (1989: 118). It is the case that the people who best know what they need are often least influential in determining the means by which such provision is established. The human and material resources needed for water and sanitation provision are often not absent and may not necessarily need to be 'built' or expanded dramatically, or with substantial foreign intervention. Agency is certainly present in such circumstances but it may be immobilized, disrupted or in some other way inhibited by structures and disconnects that can be overcome by developing small-scale local investment. People sometimes need, for example, money for resources or the logistical means of moving resources physically, but normally these resources are present in some form or can be fetched from near by for cash. Furthermore, the knowledge necessary for this mobilization is often well understood at the local level and, where it is not, there is room for consultancy contributions by external specialists.

What very poor people in very poor communities often lack is the means to buy, rent or otherwise access, and then maintain, basic rebuilding equipment, like earth-movers and diggers, trucks and cranes, and, as often as not, low-technology equipment like wheelbarrows, spades and ladders, or commodities like cement. Local initiatives are wide ranging, when people have the opportunity and support to self-mobilize, and basic projects often have substantial benefit. Building toilets near schools and villages, educating in basic hygiene, sinking boreholes, repairing existing facilities, connecting cheap plastic pipelines, building paths and roads to accelerate connectivity are all relatively modest exercises that often have quite sudden and disproportionate returns. Rather than the years of investment associated with TNC activities for minimal internal benefits, indigenous provision has brought, and will likely continue to bring, almost immediate reduction in foul water ingestion and intestinal diseases, while sanitation cleansing is similarly quickly determinative of health and mortality. It seems reasonable to look for ways this approach could be evolved and accelerated. In order to do this, cash and expertise are necessary where they are absent. To establish and provide for this need, I propose an interface concept or conduit system known as a Global Water Bank.

The Global Water Bank interfaces could be located in the twenty-four worst-affected parts of the world with the highest child mortality rates (Hall and Lobina 2008), and connect indigenously determined water and sanitation demand to exogenously subordinate supply of funding and expertise to ensure efficient matches between what is needed and what is produced. In this approach, needs are identified by the people with the needs in Community-Based Organizations (CBOs). CBOs would be comprised of representatives of local people and organizations that fully include women where they bear the brunt of water provision. Provision would be focused on those needs, rather than being arrived at on the basis of, for example, the proportion of a developed country's GDP that it allocates to aid and development; or on fickle policies that amount to periodic whims that change each time donor governments hold elections at home; or on the degree to which a given humanitarian NGO might be favoured by public funding based on random campaigns in unaffected developed societies.

These needs would then be transmitted to donors like the World Bank, with its development role and its range of expertise, by the locally arrayed water banks. Clearly, no multilateral or bilateral donor would likely be willing or able to organize and coordinate thousands of grants and loans to thousands more individuals in hundreds of provinces in dozens of countries. Instead, the water bank interface finesses and communicates local demand to the panoply of global public and private donors, reducing duplication of supply and of bureaucratic planning in multifarious approaches that avoidably generate high-cost jobs for people in high-profile institutions and developed countries, which inevitably subtracts from the sum total of available cash (Fernandez 2009; Slaymaker and Newborne 2004). The water banks would provide a range of services generated from this demand-led, focused provision, including low-key in-country consultancy, relatively modest unconditional grant-making and lending aimed at existing local capacity and capabilities, higher-end funding for distant resources, such as heavy earth-movers rentable from neighbouring provinces or countries, and communication facilitation for local private sector needs, such as radios and cell phones. Donors would fund, through the Global Water Bank centres, local and regional construction companies, pay for experts to train and retrain community engineers and car mechanics to maintain boreholes, and fund educators to demonstrate the efficacy of water treatment. One example might be to employ people to take basic microscopes, routinely found in children's play sets in Western countries, to communities unaware of basic hygiene rules and show the microbes in motion in their drinking water, and compare this to their absence in clean water. The emphasis is on micro-credits and grants for local people to self-mobilize, deploy their capabilities and connect with resources that lie beyond their immediate purview, to support the expansion of private sector provision of local water needs in areas worst affected by high infant mortality rates by sustaining emerging water-oriented business communities, and resource mobilization from distant parties, where necessary.

Some form of evaluation to satisfy donors and evaluate the effectiveness of the project would be required. The emphasis on bottom-up entrepreneurialism set in CBOs with local accounting can be extended to the evaluation strategy by applying and adapting the idea of most significant change (MSC), which assesses project impact from the perspective of the intended beneficiaries. In this respect, the simple test of whether the proposed interventions are working is if the U5MR drops, ascertainable epidemiologically and demographically. This departs from the MSC, which does not normally use an indicator as such, and instead relies more on people's stories, reflecting an 'everyday lives' philosophy more attuned to bottom-up improvement than top-down accounting. The qualitative, subjective methodology underscored by MSC could, however, readily be applied to the downstream impacts of water and sanitation provision that are measurable by people's stories, the core MSC methodology. For example, the stories of girl children freed from water-bearing and able to take up school could be a measure of the success of such a programme. Using this method provides ample evidence that donor funds are being properly spent. Built into this system could be an acceptance of the constructive role of Common Social Patronage (Chapter 4), where monies spent informally securing the cooperation of significant local actors are legitimized by their enshrining in more formal contracts for basic reporting and organizational tasks that would contribute to the implementation of the water and sanitation projects (Fernandez 2009). Furthermore, should the U5MR not decline, such contracts would not be extended. Given the scale of public-elite corruption increasingly common in Western democracies and aid institutions, where nobody benefits other than the thief, pragmatic formalizing of informal procedures, without which the interventions might not be as successful, and where the child mortality rate drops, should not present a dilemma for donors.

Conceptually speaking, this strategy can be applied across regions, since substantial proportions of the U5MR are a product of similar resource absences. Tactically thinking, different approaches in specific places would require particular localized responses to be undertaken within the wider strategic imperative of water and sanitation provision. Greater emphasis financially and tactically could be placed on under-exploited and already existing World Bank operations, such as the Local Initiatives Project (LIP), which provides 'financial resources to people wanting to start their own small businesses and to take an active role in rebuilding their livelihoods instead of depending on state social welfare funds', which are often non-existent (Ohiorhenuan and Stewart 2008: 85). This approach also presents a middle path between free market advocacy, and those, such as Julien Barbara, who argue for the developmental state, as a response to the failure of state recovery via market mechanisms (2008). And it offers an approach that overcomes the different conceptions of what is and is not an impediment to human well-being as it is understood by those whose lives are always structured and often ended by water inaccessibility. According to Edward Carr, this 'poverties' approach 'does not necessarily signal the death of large-scale efforts to alleviate [water] poverty, nor does it require the abandonment of development itself. Instead, [it] forces us to seriously re-think development [and human security] goals and our means of achieving them' (2008: 727).

Such an approach needs inevitably to consider field delivery, since there is a long tradition of unintended consequences in development, as elsewhere (Allen et al. 1991; Easterly 2006; Anderson 1999). Health and development are no exceptions to this, so we should anticipate that there are likely to be localized problems attached to this process. Often, challenges to a seemingly thoughtful approach arise in the context of identity politics: what aids one community may alienate another, even when there are often common interests such as improving child survival rates, beneficial to all. As with all alien interventions, local personal relationships have to be considered, and there is a broad and evolving development literature that considers this. In short, however, the best-laid plans can sometimes reignite conflict where it had been dampened, or can create conflict where none existed before. Part of the reason for this is insensitivity to or unawareness of compelling indigenous interpersonal relationships, processes with which anthropologists are routinely familiar. Natalie Grove and Anthony Zwi recommend a developmental approach that integrates health and peace-building via a mechanism that considers their impact on the local domain of developmental projects affecting health. They maintain that a cultural 'filter' might 'bring principles of conflict sensitivity into the health arena'. They suggest this would provide 'a range of prompts about how health workers in [a] community are perceived, the extent to which they have been aligned with different parties to [a] conflict' and so on (2008: 75).

The likelihood of this approach working in conditions of war, or where there are territorial disputes about water sources, is lower than in a post-conflict environment; and even there, there may be substantial challenges. The U5MR is the Foucauldian national population group, imagined internationally, which gives the human security concept a group of humans around which effective policy can coalesce, and which would almost certainly be very attractive to bilateral donors' home constituencies, especially since it would be relatively cheap and demonstrably effective. Causation is obvious and the cure technically fairly simple and achievable, but is dependent on political will, the absence of which is an exogenous inhibitor to indigenous development. Local agency and capacity take charge, overcoming an increasingly common critique of intervention, and are well motivated to deliver reductions in the child mortality rate and improvements in human security; and the method is transversal, across and within countries and continents.

GENERATING BANK COMPLIANCE

The World Bank has a key role to play in this. It is the largest development body in terms of hegemony, resources and expertise, with global representation and influence. It is an icon of the Post-Washington Consensus and a key institution and instrument of neoliberal belief and practice, and it exercises control over sovereign polities and policies through conditionality. In the acts of lending or suspending finances to developing countries, it also influences transnational private sector investment. If the Bank were to repeal its ideological embargoes, where they exist, on subsidized or free state provision of water and sanitation, and if it were to direct resources at regionally distributed water banks unconditionally, it would set an example and sanction a practice around which many other bodies might coalesce, while signalling an end to restrictive practices that contribute to the maintenance of the U5MR. The scale of funding that the Bank could release into what is in essence a community-based exercise in entrepreneurialism would quickly facilitate the creation of water banks in key areas; and its sanctioning of such an approach would almost certainly be followed by other multilateral donors. It would also be an opportunity to reconnect the Bank to people and restore its badly damaged reputation. It would in this sense become a norms entrepreneur itself, almost certainly capable of tipping norms and leading cascades of norms change. We have seen (above) how the Bank elite can be persuaded to change in broad terms. I turn now to ways in which internal resistance at lower levels in the World Bank may be managed.

We have seen in the previous chapter that the World Bank, like many other IGOs, can become at least semi-autonomous from its state sponsors, and resist changes requested of it, even as it is under the authority of its member states. One obvious criticism of the approach outlined above is that the operation could be sabotaged if Bank employees charged with designing water programmes were resistant to the principle, perhaps favouring top-down, trickle-down developmentality. How might Bank management, once persuaded by the board of governors to adopt an approach akin to the one outlined above, ensure that resistant employees cooperate? After all, such an approach marks a departure from the direction of the Bank's deeply inculcated, socialized and internalized privatization practices (although not from its underlying ideology). At least three strategies for preventing and/or managing internal dissent, manifested through non-cooperation and asymmetric information management (concealing Bank operations from Bank elites and states), become apparent. The first involves intensifying incentives for cooperation with a new mandate and re-educating existing Bank staff regarding the failure of orthodox quantitative neoliberal economics to move beyond the essential tension of very poor people not being able to pay money for water. This would require substantial internal adjustments and would most likely result in a tranche of natural wastage, as well as the reshaping of internal values and practices, or organizational culture. There is no shortage of development specialists, water experts and social economists able and willing to fill such positions with the intention of redirecting development strategies. Indeed, there would likely be great interest in filling these posts and helping reshape a badly flawed institution.

But manipulating incentives is only one approach. A second approach may be termed 'shock therapy', since the language will be familiar to Bank employees, and involves a substantial restructuring of Bank employees' conditions in line with their commitment to altered approaches to development and developmentality. That is, those unwilling to consider development economics in terms of children's essential life needs can be sacked, if they are unwilling to conform with new lending and grant-making frameworks that prioritize water and sanitation provision. This is not an unreasonable approach, nor is it without precedent in management approaches. It is quite routine for new leadership bodies in other neoliberal enterprises that bring emboldened visions to their work to replace recalcitrant colleagues; this is only the same medicine as the Bank advocates with structural adjustment. Harsh as it may seem, it is not as harsh for Bank employees as it is for those whose lives are blighted or ended as a result of financial policies unsympathetic to and incomprehensive of a very basic biological relationship between water and life for millions of people.

A third approach might involve incentivizing Bank employees by rewarding lending that is sensitive to human needs in water provision and sanitation. This can be considered a negotiating approach, whereby internal resistance to change is managed out to a point where cooperation with a new norm is achieved without sacrificing those who challenge it. Elgstrom suggests that constructivist literature is long on emulation and short on the need to negotiate change among resistant actors in order for norms to diffuse within organizations (2000). A response to this challenge might involve incentivization. Those employees most able to create inventive solutions to life-ending biopoverty could be rewarded with any number of incentives from shares to corner offices for lending strategies attuned not just to the immediate needs of water and sanitation provision (for example), but also for projects that have a 'trickle-up' effect, and impact on the social consequences of limited water provision. For example, Bank staff who design loans or grants finances that reduce and end the penury of (mostly women and girls) carrying water from distant sources could be rewarded for their role in the expansion of development opportunities for women that accompany such changes, such as higher school enrolment of girls. The Bank could especially incentivize those employees who mobilize grant-making to women and women's groups, since women do most water-carrying, understand household requirements well and, because of this knowledge and responsibility, will be better placed to reorganize water access. Bank staff should also be required to live in the field in such circumstances, and be rewarded with an appropriate and scaled-back per diem. A revised per diem scale would mollify increasing public awareness of and concern at public sector expenses, while also reflecting local living costs and experiences. It would remain above local living costs, and grant-makers, and analysts whose research and assumptions determine grant-making, could understand better the conditions faced by water-poor people. This approach would likely be attractive to economists and analysts genuinely concerned with and committed to development for people rather than for paradigms.

The intellectual methodologies involved in such approaches would remain positivist, since they revolve around epidemiological data and incontestable physiological needs. Disbursement targets would be easy to establish, and could include most obviously percentage reductions in child mortality; but they could also be extended to increased percentages of girls in school. These could also be readily measured using positivist, scientific, quantitative systems familiar to Bank expertise and experience. Embedded anthropologists could also qualitatively record and evaluate outcomes, whereby the rationale of the intervention is judged on the extent to which it meets social needs, rather than the degree to which it meets foreign organizations' benchmarks. Embedded anthropologists, using a range of agreed and negotiated Most Significant Change indicators (above), would be concerned first with the needs of the society in which they are embedded, and then with the various criteria of the society that embeds them. This type of expert knowledge could be funded on the basis of World Bank consultancies, but using country experts with language skills and long-term experience of the culture in which they have been or become embedded. This would also offer a longer-term and more meaningful internal analysis of conditions affecting indigenous everyday lives. For example, indigenous and indigenized research could consider the social and economic benefits involved in keeping girls in school as a consequence of removing from them water provision tasks, and the opportunities incumbent on a longer education.

The neoliberal development paradigm or developmentality is unable to deliver development properly reflecting equality and respect for human life beyond Westernity and its secured domains. It does not deliver biopolitical security in the areas of vital-to-life health provision and other social objectives necessary for sustainable human development and broad human security in the developing world. It has failed to prevent the evolution of vast pan-national underclasses in its own cities. But the notion that There Is No Alternative (TINA) is one of the most dangerous aspects of neoliberalism and its discourse hegemony, because ownership of the debate by denial of other opportunities that harness human energy where it is most potent forecloses potential for other development paths that are not necessarily radically distant from neoliberalism, and which exploit some of its potential – whether one believes that neoliberalism is ultimately sustainable or not. It requires thinking beyond the permissions excluded and allowed by the dogma of TINA, in ways that will 'demonstrate the possibility of visualizing a model of development which can deliver more effectively on health and other social objectives, by thinking outside and beyond the parameters of mainstream economics and of historical precedents' (Global Health Watch 2008: 7).

CONCLUSION

In 2005, a World Bank senior vice-president declared that 'health is too important to leave it to the health people', a remark that might have been intended humorously (Musgrove 2005: 352). Its candour, however, reveals the hubris of hegemony. Leaving health to World Bank privatization ideology fails to deal with the fundamental problem of how water that costs money is paid for by people who have none, or too little. Attempts to challenge such approaches should not be seen as a utopian ideal (as if there were anything wrong, or even necessarily utopian, with

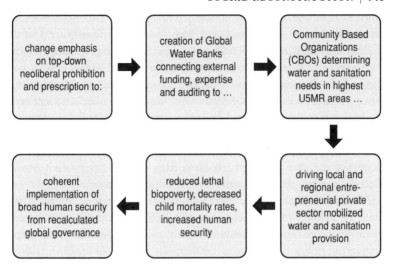

Figure 5.1 Regulating the U5MR – the potential impact of externally assisted indigenous entrepreneurialism in water and sanitation provision

seeking substantial life improvement for millions of people), but should instead be understood as a challenge to a realist-dystopian, destructive and dysfunctional form of global governance that contributes to the deaths of millions of the most vulnerable of our species. The evidence shows that water-related diseases both cause a very high proportion of the U5MR, and are also easily preventable. Furthermore, a human security approach to badly neglected levels of infant mortality can be targeted at identifiable groups of children across nations within regions whose lethal health threats share similar remedies in terms of clean water in and dirty water out. What cannot help is the application of costs to such essential provision by World Bank and neoliberal prescription for people with little or no money; and the prohibition or discouragement of public sector funding on the grounds that it might be corrupt or inefficient. Privatization in very poor countries has been shown either to fail the poorest, or to scare off international investors because of investment and development risks. It worked in the UK and Europe because private costs were sustainable without loss of life; indeed, water in the UK cannot be disconnected from private households even when bills have not been paid, since this would be in breach of the human right to water. The benefits of public or public–private provision of free clean water to the poorest are quick to manifest themselves, and externally funded local infrastructure building works would also contribute to economic growth more broadly.

This approach to the U5MR, prioritized by its conceptualization as a human security matter, is framed by the notion of global governance and national government as biopolitical in modulating life chances in a process whereby asymmetrical power in the international and national systems directs resources in ways that negatively impact directly and indirectly on human life. In their routine forms, the economic policies of the World Bank, set within the wider neoliberal paterfamilias, '[have] restricted the choices that political parties in democratic [and other] societies can adopt', aggravating, in many instances, already corrupt and self-serving local public processes that do nothing for populations at risk from the absence of essential-to-life resources (Suleiman and Waterbury 1990: 3). Since we are unable currently to agree on what constitutes human security, and since policy-makers have proven unwilling to accept a broad imagining of this concept, the approach of this work represents a midpoint between narrow and broad human security, designed to tackle the inadequacies and lethality of neoliberalism with a workable definition of human security that can be applied to people's everyday lives by drawing from the concept of biopolitics and identifying pan-national communities of people experiencing similar and reducible crises such as the U5MR. From this perspective, World Bank ideation and operations may be ruptured and retuned to the needs of the most vulnerable by way of an alternative approach to manage biopolitical inadequacy and biopoverty consequence. It is not a revolution that dismisses all aspects of the previous order, but is instead a form of transformation that retains positivist elements of human and economic accounting while rescinding and retracting dependence on and application of other aspects of the epistemology underpinning the Bank's methods. It is not rejecting the prior, but involves instead 'overlapping, interaction, and echoes' of the old and the new (Foucault 1973: 361).

6 | NORMS AND CHANGE

INTRODUCTION

If the last chapters were concerned with the kind of change needed in global governance to recalculate human security, this chapter examines how change in the international system is stimulated. In this sense, change can be understood as shifts between normalities, or norms. Norms can be understood as dominant behaviours we take for granted, see as legitimate and accept as 'the reality of life' and 'just the way things are'. They are in fact neither a singular reality nor immutable, since they change routinely over time, because where it fails spectacularly, we mostly are not exposed to this failure and the reality and brutal impact of its consequences; and their slow evolution is one reason we often do not consider them critically, notice them change or perceive them as changeable. The study of norms is not new, but until recently has been underemphasized. Social norms can be thought of as activities that we do repeatedly, without thinking about them, normally believing them to be legitimate. The fact that we do not challenge them sanctions them to the point where they develop, and are sustained by, consensual hegemony. They are dominant conventions in a given context; social practices that are supported and maintained by a wide base of concordance and acceptance. They are practices that are considered normal by a given group and, as a consequence, acceptable at any given time by that group. They are the behavioural rules and expectations we create, and they routinely mirror the rules we follow consensually with an uncritical eye. Neoliberalism, capitalism, privatization, deregulation are all norms that have evolved and been actively promoted as the best means to resolve the fundamental problem of efficient resource distribution. They enjoy, as we have seen in preceding chapters, hegemony but are in fact promoted by a relatively small elite which determines the nature of global and local economies. We accept this system because we are told there is no alternative and because we generally believe it works for the best; because where it seems to fail, we are told that it will work with time; and because we are not fully conscious of the extent and role of neoliberalism in the regulation of global lives. In this sense, 'power [in the international system] is manifest primarily through hegemonic discourses that naturalize normality' (Lipschutz 2005: 15). When the demands of this power to acquiesce to dominant and directed norms are not met by 'unruly' actors, such as those challenging globalization or social injustice, for example, Lipschutz and Rowe maintain that 'more instrumental forms of power – force, coercion, influence – appear' (2005: 15).

Norms are often divided into two categories: regulative and constitutive. Regulative refers to the means by which existing international behaviours are maintained. They 'prescribe, proscribe and order behaviour, operate like standards that specify the proper enactment of an already defined identity and establish rights and obligations' (Bjorkdahl 2002: 15). Constitutive norms, on the other hand, direct departure from regulative norms. That is, they are norms that enable variety in the choices people can make to achieve their goals. Bjorkdahl writes that 'international norms ... create permissive conditions for action [which] structure realms of possibilities and define a range of legitimate policy options that would not have been self-evident in the absence of such norms' (ibid.: 22). We may distinguish between them in terms of possible outcomes. Regulative norms dictate the limits of the possible: they are what restrict people to particular 'principles, norms and rules that prescribe and proscribe varieties of behaviour' (ibid.: 22), whereas constitutive norms allow policy-makers to conceive and respond to alternative 'principles, norms and rules' that generate different outcomes. In Bjorkdahl's words, they 'may provide the inspiration and motivation for foreign policy development and implementation' (ibid.: 23).

Christine Ingebritsen tells us that a norm in international relations can be viewed as a 'global code of appropriate behaviour' (2002: 11). From an overtly state-centric perspective, Gregory Raymond refers us to norms as 'generalised standards of conduct that delineate the scope of a state's entitlements, the extent of its obligations, and the range of its jurisdiction' (1997: 128). Similarly state-centrically, Janice Thomson refers to norms as 'normal state practices' (1993: 81); while Gary Goetz and Paul Diehl qualify this position by adding that norms remain norms because they are coercible, rather than automatically and dependably adhered to (1992). Expanding from the confines of state-centric assumptions, Peter Katzenstein writes that norms are 'collective expectations for the proper behaviour of actors with a given identity' (1996: 5). These norms are 'spontaneously evolving, as social practice; consciously promoted, as political strategies to further specific interests; deliberately negotiated, as a mechanism for conflict management; or as a combination, mixing these three types' (ibid.: 21). We may consider democracy in such terms, following Katzenstein's formula. As the cold war has morphed into the ill-defined post-cold-war world, democracy has evolved in some developing countries that were not democratic to reorganize societies, even if for many this is more by nomenclature than nature; democracy is consciously promoted in the literature, the media and by national and international organizations to refine social organization; it is negotiated through elections and post-electoral conflict; and, in the case of international peace-building, it is presented through state-building interventions as a means of settling conflict and transforming civil and elite society by means of a host of international actors from the UN to local NGOs. Looking to older examples to affirm consistency in norms changes, during the cold war a fundamental premise that had characterized international relations for a century shifted when decolonization began. Even if the cold war masked a shift from imperial to neo-imperial relations, a fundamental idea and value – that of the legitimacy of direct metropolitan domination – passed into history (Falk 2000; Crawford 1993), even if some favour its return. Farther back, the routine norm of international slavery was abolished, ending a widely maintained and practised convention in Europe, Africa, the Caribbean, the Middle East and most other parts of the world. And yet farther back in history, the international system shifted from one of absolute monarchies to the Westphalian parliamentary system of states, and the Enlightenment promoted progress towards a more even distribution of power (a process that has become distorted over time). And, returning to the present, dominant norms persist but, revealing their subjective and contested nature, are under challenge and flux. The use of landmines and cluster munitions has been outlawed by broad, if incomplete, international consensus, as part of a process that may see their use terminated *in toto*. Nuclear weapons conventions have similarly come under fire; the states possessing most nuclear weapons have agreed to contain and reduce their arsenals, even as the number of states and other actors acquiring them has expanded. An International Criminal Court exists where none existed before to try international war criminals. From almost complete marginalization, matters of gender and inequality occupy the vernacular if not the values of many major international and national actors. Yet more recently, the dominant international norm of protected tax havens like Liechtenstein and Monaco, normally invulnerable to scrutiny, was largely overturned in a matter of a few weeks in the spring of 2009. Some of these changes are problematic: they are not necessarily for the good of everyone, as the concept of equality is sidelined by the pre-eminence of the individual enshrined in the ideology of neoliberalism. But together, they constitute evidence of substantial social construction and reconstruction – norms and norms change – in the international system.

NORMS CHANGE

Change can be understood as a movement between norms, where an idea or belief, or set of ideas or beliefs, is supplanted by others to direct, shape and create new social behavioural norms. I use the word 'social' in its widest sense, to encompass all human social interaction, embracing politics, economics and 'culture'. Before proceeding to constructivist literature, I will take this opportunity to reiterate that there remains a dominant body of thought that maintains that consideration of change is based on undesirable moral subjectivity, a process to which cosmological IR objects. The hegemony of these beliefs, implanted in and restrictive of state policy, and the architectures of epistemological and ontological denial sustain the present violent dystopia of mass human insecurity, permitting only glacial progress on matters of global security that affect hundreds of millions of everyday lives with which realism appears largely unconcerned. This hegemony, and the capacity to subjectively marginalize debate and lives it does not judge fit to consider in a security sense, stymies progress because by its ontological and epistemological nature it cannot and will not change and is good only for maintaining the structural status quo. For this reason, I circumvent further consideration of the destructive discipline and move to more constructive discussion of the means of change and the potency this enables.

The literature on norms change was reinvigorated in 1998, following a hiatus of some two decades after 'the debate of the 1970s on transnational relations closed the book on the subject prematurely' (Risse-Kappen 1995: 5). In 1998, Martha Finnemore and Kathryn Sikkink published groundbreaking research that advanced the debate substantially. Their definition reflects Katzenstein's, presenting norms as 'a standard of appropriate behaviour for actors with a given identity'. While this immediately raises the spectre of subjectivity, since the view of the appropriateness of an actor's behaviour will inevitably vary depending on who is judging that actor, the fact that the definition and article refer to conformity to a given standard is key to the notion of norms as uncritically repeated behaviour on the part of an agent or community. This interpretation leads Finnemore and Sikkink to identify a 'life cycle' of norms which involves three stages. The first involves the emergence of a norm, although the matter of where ideas themselves come from is not pursued in any great depth, apropos the remit of the article. Instead, the emergence of norms is attributed to domestic norms entrepreneurs, who 'attempt to convince a critical mass of states (norms leaders) to embrace new norms' (ibid.: 895). An entrepreneur is a person who makes things happen that were not happening before. Daniel Gilman writes that a norms entrepreneur is someone:

> Who identifies and markets norms, whether for money, reputation, power, or other social capital ... A norm entrepreneur is a person who notices a pattern, identifies it as such, and somehow foists it on the public as a normative, and not merely descriptive, model or standard. Senator Joseph McCarthy, The Beatles, Madonna, and Miss Manners ... may all be seen as norm entrepreneurs. (2002: 2395)

Norms entrepreneurs, then, 'persuade others to internalize new norms' (Elgstrom 2000: 457). They are normally equipped with 'organizational platforms' from which to lobby and influence; these might be international organizations like the UN, Transnational Advocacy Networks (TANs), or national advocacy groups like Women's Aid in the UK or the 50-50 Group in Sierra Leone. These platforms often provide political elevation for transmission into the international debating arena of new proposals for change. Elgstrom notes that in the early stages, 'one major task for moral entrepreneurs is to get the norms they advocate on the agenda, to get major actors to pay attention to the issue' (ibid.: 460). From such an elevation they can be heard and listened to, allowing norms entrepreneurs to 'call attention to issues or even "create" issues by using language that names, interprets, and dramatizes them' (Finnemore and Sikkink 1998: 897). In common vernacular, this is known as 'framing the issue': identifying a matter of subjective importance and extending public consciousness of it with a goal to improving matters. An essential difference between an effective norms entrepreneur and someone who merely publicly demands change reflects the difference between making noise in a public vacuum and being listened to by those who make policy.

This may take place in conditions of hostility to, or rejection of, the new proposition. Finnemore and Sikkink refer to the example of women's suffrage, reminding us that the demand for a new norm of electoral equality faced sustained opposition from the old (and dominant) norm of political chauvinism and exclusion. I repeat this example, because women's rights scholar-entrepreneurs are still attempting to frame new gender-fair norms into a masculine and often suspicious and chauvinist series of predominant behaviours, especially in the domain of what constitutes security. Reflecting successful norms conversion in this arena, despite sustained resistance, parliamentary gender quotas are now embedded and internalized in a majority of states worldwide (Dahlerup and Freidenvall 2005; Krook 2007). The authors continue that, since a new norm is by definition different to an old norm (the distinction here being the difference between continuity and change), we may reasonably expect that the advancement of a new norm will meet entrenched resistance until a particular state or group of states adopts the norm and agrees to attempt to project it beyond their own boundaries. In a very real sense, this is the point at which the human security concept lies presently: it has been elevated by the UNDP into the international arena and is supported by a range of actors with limited influence in the international system, but further integration and adoption of the concept have been halted as a result of challenges to its conceptual coherence and practicability. If a critical mass evolves far enough – if enough states take a new proposal on board and adopt it – Finnemore and Sikkink argue that 'the norm reaches a threshold or tipping point'. Although they recognize that it is empirically hard to quantify when such a tip begins, they suggest that the threshold is roughly one-third, and note that some states have a greater weight, or international influence, than others, meaning that a purely quantitative assessment is insufficient to determine when sufficient momentum is reached to create a more substantial, cascade effect (1998: 901). This element is especially important with regard to the next section of the chapter.

The second stage invokes a different process. Whereas the emergence phase is characterized by domestic activity by norms entrepreneurs, the second stage, or 'cascade', is characterized more by an 'international or regional demonstration effect ... in which international and transnational norm influences become more important than domestic politics for effecting norm change' (ibid.: 902). If norms change begins in the domestic arena, the process is accelerated in the international setting after the tipping point is reached and the cascade takes effect. This form of international socialization is familiar to the traditional schools of international relations, and may involve 'diplomatic praise or censure, either bilateral or multilateral, which is reinforced by material sanctions and incentives' (ibid.: 902; Landolt 2004). In this more international phase, norm transmission by states may be supported by non-state actors, such as NGOs, which will apply pressure to non-conforming states or multilateral actors, or may monitor and audit compliance in reforming states (Keck and Sikkink 1999). Where this process succeeds, it is thanks to 'pressure for conformity, desire to enhance international legitimation, and the desire of state leaders to enhance their self-esteem'

(Finnemore and Sikkink 1998: 895). It may also be that states adopt norms for reasons of altruism: on the grounds, in other words, that the 'logic of appropriateness' guiding norms conventions evolves because conformers 'understand the behaviour to be good, desirable, and appropriate [reflecting] habit, duty and responsibility as well as principled belief' (ibid.: 912). These forces work in association with identity. That is, compliance is generated across a range of actors who share labels and behaviours, such as 'democratic' or 'Asian', for example. In Finnemore and Sikkink's words, 'what happens at the tipping point is that enough states and enough critical states endorse the new norm to redefine appropriate behaviour for the identity called "state" or some relevant subset of states (such as a "liberal" state or a European state)' (ibid.: 902). There is, then, a process of leadership by key states with particular interests in instigating a new norm, socializing in their slipstream enough other states to reach the political escape velocity required to create a cascade and a tipping point.

We may say that national adoption of new norms in particular states is followed by international socialization of those norms by a majority of the remainder; what follows this is a reversion to the local, wherein the new norms are accepted broadly in the international system, become 'taken-for-granted' and 'are no longer a matter of broad public debate' (ibid.: 895). This is the third stage, referred to as 'internalization'. Having been elevated across the international system at the international level, the new norm is finally inculcated into recipient state conformism. That is, as well as states having accepted a new norm, processes and actors appear to ensure that it is fully embedded in national practices. This involves, for example, codification of a new norm and its passing into formal legislation; the implementation of the new norm to agreed standards, normally managed though bureaucratic processes, perhaps; and the testing of conformity, by means of accountability and oversight activities (surveillance, monitoring and auditing). Eventually, this process 'makes conformance with the norm almost automatic' (ibid.: 904). This perspective must be carefully qualified, since it is a state which accepts the validity of an internationally migrating norm; but states are also reactive to their populations, especially, theoretically, in democracies. The literature also suggests that the norm that has travelled must be 'salient' to the host society into which it is inserted by its political elite. For example, although the British government has acquiesced to a number of norms transfers from European legislation, from the shape of bananas to the limits to a motorcycle's top speed, members of British society have caused the government to rescind its adoption of some trans-European norms. Cortell and David argue that there must exist in the recipient nation not just elite will, but also 'a durable set of attitudes toward the norm's legitimacy' (2000: 69).

Finnemore and Sikkink discuss factors most likely to influence norms adoption, addressing state status in the international system. It is suggested that states are more susceptible to adopting norms when adoption would enhance their position among their peers. And, in that hierarchical and competitive peer system, it is the more prominent states whose norms are most likely to be adopted, while a third factor concerns the extent to which the inherent 'intrinsic quality' of a norm determines its adoption. Thus, 'clear and specific' norms are more likely to travel than norms that are 'ambiguous and complex' (Bailey 2008); and norms that relate to intrinsically 'good' behaviours are more likely to earn compliance (Finnemore and Sikkink 1998: 907). Universalism, individualism and values adjacent to current hegemonic practices are more likely to generate concordance than a norm characterized intrinsically by something found in practice less acceptably and less commonly, such as dictatorship, or communism. Other conditions may also make norms more or less prone to adoption. For example, Margaret Keck and Kathryn Sikkink propose that norms which are related to preventing bodily harm of innocent or vulnerable people are especially prone to adoption (1998). Finnemore and Sikkink concur, proposing that this hypothesis 'explains why norm campaigns around slavery and women's suffrage [have] succeeded'. They further suggest that the vulnerability thesis might be evidenced by the manner in which anti-smoking campaigns have applied arguments regarding 'the effects [of smoking] on vulnerable or innocent bystanders of second-hand smoke' (1998: 907). This thesis does not hold up, however, when applied to campaigns to end female genital mutilation (FGM). Jeffrey Legro suggests that such rejection reflects a lack of contextual legitimacy in a given culture, a claim that could embrace the culture of patriarchy and control of women's independent behaviour (1997). Despite a range of campaigns that have clearly focused on the vulnerability of women to having their sexual organs brutally mutilated and excised, the practice remains socially condoned and enforced in parts of Africa, the Middle East and Asia. The thesis that human dignity is substantially transcultural may hold, but only until it meets a more powerful transcultural antithesis such as global patriarchy. Patriarchal structures, practices and values are hegemonic globally, and routinely and daily result in human dignity as it is commonly understood being marginalized and subsumed to its diktats; extreme poverty, sex trafficking, infanticide and slavery are all related directly and indirectly to patriarchy and its economic neoliberal progeny (Roberts 2008a; Bhattacharrya 2005; Griffin 2007). This is partly because both are characterized, authorized and legitimized by competitiveness, hierarchies of inequality condoning domination and exploitation generally, masculinity and hyper-masculinity legitimating direct and indirect violence against men and women, and the relegation and repression of women globally.

The evidence shows that change happens under certain conditions when certain social forces are at work. We may reasonably conclude that the nature of the international system is not biologically fixed but socially determined by human ideas and the social mechanisms and institutions we deploy to advance and implement them. The norms literature suggests that ideas that shape the world are social in construction and subject to reconstruction under certain circumstances. Finnemore and Sikkink advance a model whereby a new norm takes root in one state and is ultimately evolved into an international norm across many others. Various conditions must apply for this to happen, but there is empirical evidence to demonstrate that there is substance to the argument (Keck and Sikkink 1998; Risse et al. 1999).

To this end, I propose a strategy, or an approach, for achieving the objectives identified in the preceding chapter. These were twofold. First, in order to make biopolitical global governance less lethal and dysfunctional for millions of infants, the World Bank can desist from prohibiting states to which it lends from providing water and sanitation for free for people with no money. Second, the Bank can work with indigenous and regional private sectors where the U5MR is highest to develop accessible provision of clean water and sanitation for those unable to afford it, with the goal of reducing deaths from easily preventable illnesses. What is being proposed as a new norm is a different take on privatization, which would involve ending one World Bank neoliberal emphasis and starting another. The details were developed in the preceding chapter; briefly, I propose that the Bank can facilitate grants and credits to small-scale private sector actors in and around the worst-affected locales and regions for capacity mobilization, building and construction materials and equipment and basic locally sustainable education programmes to create water supply and sanitation for those unable to afford it or access it. It was noted in the previous chapter that there would derive from this a substantially disproportionate trickle-up effect, whereby low-cost inputs would yield high-value, high-volume outputs; such an approach constitutes sound investment practice.

This change in perspective on privatization, which does not eschew

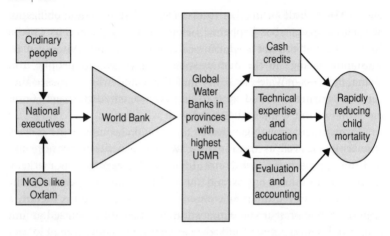

Figure 6.1 Schematic outlining paths of pressure invoked by norms entrepreneurs and the 'downstream' effect on global governance, biopolitical management and human security

the principle but instead makes it more localized and less subject to asymmetric advantages in international relations that benefit transnational corporations, becomes the Stage 1 objective of domestic norms entrepreneurs in any number of states, where people are aware of the ease and cheapness with which the U5MR can be reduced. It is particularly applicable in the UK, from where the most recent norms change at the Bank were directed, but it can be evolved more widely. The strategy is laid out in diagram form below, and proposes that a combination of public norms entrepreneurs and Transnational Advocacy Networks can convince the UK and other governments that such a plan is reasonable and within their capacity. Once governments are persuaded of the legitimacy and efficacy of the proposal and of the high likelihood of success, based on scientific evidence and argument and buoyed by recent experiences, state elites may act through the board of governors to guide the Bank's board of executives to revise privatization emphases and approaches in line with water and sanitation provision, drawing from Bank funding for indigenous and regional capacity mobilization coupled with appropriate expertise injections from local, regional and international actors.

Given that it requires little or no additional funding, either from the public in any given country or from their associated governments, this would be a readily endorsable populist policy reflecting a much-needed and morally minded attempt to end or dramatically reduce the U5MR at little or no cost to taxpayer and state. The mobilization of such campaigns has happened before; there are numerous existing NGOs and public figures who have demonstrated the ability to make substantial change in the human security of vulnerable people, from Diana, Princess of Wales, to any of the other actors who have used their elite status to mobilize audiences to support a favoured campaign. Given the scope of the U5MR; the speed with which effects are visible; the employment and growth generation that would accompany the projects themselves, as well as the rapidly realizable benefits to mass health, such an approach is tenable and durable. This approach is markedly different from others, however, because, unlike most operations of this type, it does not require public money beyond the usual tax regime. It requires public pressure on elite institutions, perhaps mobilized around high-profile entrepreneurs' and advocacy networks' commitment to care. The UK could have a leadership role in this process, given that its role in changing the World Bank presidency suggests it may be a critical state; one with particular influence in a particular institution. This constitutes Stage 1 of Finnemore and Sikkink's three-phase model.

There seems good reason to expect that the second stage, involving a tipping point, is also practicable, given the insubstantial conceptual change required; the adjacency of the new norm to existing privatization norms; the inherent quality of the project; its inexpensiveness and its clarity and specificity; the observable and quantifiable returns; the legitimacy accorded a state among its own population for leading such a demonstrably and inherently 'good' project; the status among international peers accorded to such a moral project requiring so little material input; and the creditable research indicating quite precisely the means of preventing and reducing high U5MR rates and the vast and extant knowledge base and experience in providing preventive interventions.

In addition, and perhaps more importantly than some of the others, the strategy outlined above may be especially prone to succeed because of its obvious connection with vulnerability and innocence. There can be no humans more vulnerable than infants, and death from diarrhoea, on the scale that it occurs, represents a profound assault on the bodies of extremely poor children. In addition, there is reason to believe that norms relating to such matters are more likely to be adopted if there is a short causal chain; medical epidemiology confirms this. Furthermore, while sceptics might proclaim the World Bank to be impervious to external manipulation of its norms, this is not necessarily nor likely to be the case. In addition to recent leadership norms changes, Susan Park has demonstrated that the World Bank 'consumes' norms from

Transnational Advocacy Networks as well as diffuses them by virtue of its location in relation to neoliberal hegemony (2005; Keck and Sikkink 1999). While this is both interesting and encouraging, however, it may be of less importance in this case, since the point of pressure at the Bank is the board of executives, accessed via the state-populated board of governors. The record (above) also shows that under forty states mobilized alongside the UK to achieve the recent shift in the Bank's rules for its presidency, implying a tipping point lower than the one-third normally considered relevant. Nor was a state cascade required. The new Bank presidency norm is now being internalized at the Bank and around the international system as a consequence.

CONCLUSION

Norms can be thought of as routine functions that organize our daily and global existence and priorities. They originate from human thinking, idealistic or realistic, utopian or dystopian; they reflect our beliefs and morality; and they are inevitably subjective and value laden. Presently, the norms of global governance consciously prioritize certain subjective values and beliefs above others. They actively neglect the staggering under-five mortality rate; consciously, because decision-makers in structures of national and global governance are both fully aware of the scale of the U5MR, and of the ease of its diminution. They choose, however, to direct their attention and resources to other matters, none of which compares in terms of the number of humans – the tens of millions – who die unnecessarily and preventably. This is not to make a moral judgement or to direct blame and culpability; it is to advance an alternative security agenda based on humans rather than states. Recent research published in the foreign policy analysis sector tested, and confirmed, the belief that 'principled and causal beliefs' may change significant aspects of international relations (Hook 2008). Developing this conclusion further, Kevin Esterling identifies the importance of credibility in such an evolution, arguing that 'the extent to which beliefs matter depends critically on the evidence indicating that the beliefs are plausible' (2004: 7). According to these literatures, global norms, or the international status quo derived from dominant ideas, can be changed if creditable research indicates the idea will work.

It is not a question of the 'restructuring of the entire system of values which forms the basis of our civilization today', proposed by Michel Camdessus – itself not necessarily a bad idea (2001: 363). The proposed adjustments navigate a path between dystopian stasis and utopian transformation that is at once plausible and populist, a less comprehensive but consequentially more achievable and impactful challenge to the dogmatic adherence to ideas whose time, current crises and past failures suggest, has come. The norms literature allows us to think about how the Bank's policies and its directive capacity – its ability to make things happen – can be changed. Recent evidence suggests the Bank is subject to many diverse pressures for change, and that a key access route to Bank policy is to be found in the board of executives, since states can manipulate policy via their ownership of the board of governors. And the literature suggests such new norms are feasible; indeed, this particular task seems more likely than not to work, since it satisfies a substantial majority of the criteria indicating whether norms change may be anticipated. Rather than discrediting such efforts by labelling them utopian, the empirical evidence seems strongly to support the notion that reshaped norms focused on the most vulnerable children in the developing world will give them the same chance their counterparts in the developed world enjoy.

CONCLUSION

The human security concept is in a quandary. From a broad and progressive imagining of how humans everywhere could be treated well, the concept has been reduced in potency and marginalized in practice by a seemingly irreconcilable dispute over its legitimacy as a security notion and its coherence as a meaningful contributor to everyday human lives. Discourse, where debate has extended beyond theory, has become stultified and trapped in academia, unrecognized by a majority of those concerned with the global human condition in the places worst impacted by human insecurity. It has been rendered unintelligible by definitional disagreements, disparaged as a means by which interventionary liberal imperialism is sanctioned, and vilified as a disguise for security and assimilation interests in the global North. Failure to engage with matters of power in the international system has exposed its proponents to criticisms of naivety, while states that have adopted it have dwindled. Within the discipline most concerned with questions of international security, the subject has been sidelined and stymied, rejected and resented as an illegitimate interloper in the affairs of state. Some have even suggested it should be dropped entirely and energy directed at instigating alternative approaches to reinvigorate a process whose value has been marginalized and undermined.

But beyond the physical and intellectual boundaries of mainstream state-centric security studies, there is a substantial and broad counter-hegemonic recognition of the need for something akin to human security. Human security means placing humans at the beginning of the security equation, where global and national policy-makers determine what government and governance policies to prioritize and how to implement them. Such a process could begin by considering the very large numbers of humans dying avoidably, and would include an honest assessment of the causes of those deaths including, where relevant, the role of global governance in regulating human life outcomes globally. From this perspective, that 'something' is needed to counter the consequences of an economic Darwinism that subsumes the process of human development to the chimera of unfree markets and invisible hands, intellectually legitimized by the facile fantasy that the world is an objective entity constituted of objective facts understood by objective observers. It is not; perhaps if it were, there would not be this debate, or indeed any other.

Where the idea of human security has fallen in the past, however, an intellectual 'double movement' picks up the idea, unencumbered by the silo thinking of much liberal security literature, proposing a wide range of compensatory mechanisms and practices aimed at securing the insecured. In 2010, perhaps more than ever, the notion of human security, understood in terms of the damage being done to millions of people by the implosion of unregulated capitalism, in turn exposing the rapacious practices of a brutal and unfair market, is necessary. But state policy responses have largely been limited to the confines of liberal thought, a paradigm consigned by Enlightenment limits and ideological dogma to the narrow imaginings of the liberal half-peace, blinded by its own hubris to the potential of post-liberal potential. Systemic cause and effect, and liberal roles in perpetuating structured violence, remains neither recognized nor confronted by those who primarily dictate human outcomes globally. Resistance has proved largely futile to date.

The counter-hegemonic discourse has failed to advance the human security concept to a point where substantial improvements are made to the vulnerable, everyday lives of those people whose human security is compromised or ignored by those who determine what security is, who may define it and with whom it is concerned. Much outstanding work has been done to build on existing frameworks of provision, from human rights advocacy to social security networks and international development discourses. There is debate and there is policy; but debate is mainly unproductive in real terms, and policy is narrow and inconsistent. Both may be progressive but they have not generated the escape velocity required to turn a profound idea into a significant reality for a meaningful proportion of the most vulnerable people in the world – in which the concept's origins lie. The breadth of that idea has partly been its downfall, whether from the fatalistic perspective of dystopian realism or from the unfortunate if unsurprising incoherence of more sanguine commentary.

A middle way exists: a connection between, on the one hand, realism and liberalism, which maintain that the concept of human security is normative, undesirable for this reason and has no place in the world of what security is, and, on the other, constructivists, who maintain that security is indeed based on ideas and consequentially must necessarily and inevitably facilitate normative imaginings of what security could be.

This way connects the positivism demanded by realism and that provided by medical science with constructivist research on norms regeneration; another 'bridge' between rationalist and constructivist worldviews. Where the data are scientifically and objectively ascertainable and verifiable in positivist fashion, the epistemological concerns of realism can be catered for. This in turn enhances the potential for policy coherence where causation is identified by scientific process. And, where mainstream security has objected to the human security concept on the grounds that there is no way to identify and prioritize one particular group over another for treatment, elevating to the transnational Foucault's discussion of populations as biopolitically regulated with shared contingencies and characteristics creates groupings around which human security policy can coalesce. The populations exhibiting similar characteristics are sub-state and transnational. Coupling this with the identification, again by scientific means, of human beings most at risk based on preceding levels of avoidable mortality facilitates a far broader and coherent identification of sub-state transnational human security groupings facing similar, and preventable, contingencies.

Such transversal populations experiencing similar life-ending but preventable contingencies in this case are children under the age of five, whom scientific research proves die avoidably from biological causes that can quickly and readily be reduced through the provision of clean water intake and effective sanitation – social processes that have long underpinned, and been provided by, a majority of states in the global North. But it is not limited to the U5MR. The same approach can be applied where scientific methodologies can rank target grouping, nationally or transnationally, by level of severity and prioritize those facing the greatest human security threat of all, which is death. Examples of such subject-security groupings, which must have ascertainable and preventable cause, include communicable diseases, for example, mortality from which also runs to the millions annually. And, in most cases, these diseases are cheaply preventable and costs can be sustained by the World Bank by applying the same mechanisms of persuasion for reform via norms entrepreneurialism.

The essence of this approach lies in a state governor-directed, World-Bank-executive-sustained shift from a top-down transnationally exploitative form of neoliberal commerce to an externally and unconditionally supported bottom-up community entrepreneurialism. This frees autonomous determinism from exogenous inhibitors, accelerating local human security provision and invigorating a fundamental element of development processes enjoyed in Europe for up to a century already.

This would substantiate the concept of 'stakeholders', since the people who would determine the means of clean water provision and sanitation would be the main beneficiaries of this course of action. A key requirement for launching this process is norms change, in an international system understood by a majority of people as mostly fixed. But norms change is ever more apparent, and the World Bank's change of seating rules is but one example. Substantial norms are not merely being challenged more routinely, partly in response to neoliberal dysfunctionalism and the myths upon which it rests. They are changing as this work is written, indicating a trend. The once unassailable sovereignties of tax-haven states like Liechtenstein and Switzerland that have long harboured immeasurable tax revenues hidden by powerful multinationals from their own governments and people now find themselves facing censure by key leaders in the Western world in an astonishingly rapid turnaround of events and practices. Weapons once privileged by state-centric thinking, which have been with us for decades and which were seen as beyond public purview, are now routinely, if imperfectly, consigned to recycling by social pressure on political elites. Even cluster munitions, which escaped the landmines ban, are increasingly falling prey to changes in norms and values. This range of means by which change occurs is not yet fully understood; but it is most certainly happening, and ordinary people clearly have an extraordinary role to play, perhaps now more than ever. The evidence of socially driven transformation in the international system stands as a signal both that once unimaginable change is now within the remit of everyday people and that some of the most fundamental claims of those whose conservative but influential thinking has in the past defined the limits of how we may think have been severely misguided. It is now entirely reasonable to believe that substantial change in various aspects of the international system is both likely and desirable. Indeed, amid the pain of recession, there is substantial reason for a broader optimism, whereby the evolution of human security is ever more tied to a wide range of human agency.

The implication of this evidence-based realization has the potential for substantial impact on millions of everyday lives, of real human beings whose physiologically essential conditions can be radically advanced by simple changes in existing external policies that mobilize existing capacity. But beyond this, the biopolitics of the biopoverty approach to human security outlined here affirms the structural nature of the problem and the institutional mis/management that projects the underpinning neoliberal ideation. Foucauldian biopolitics allows us to see government, and global governance, as far more than merely Weberian, technocratic bureaucracy, to reveal the rationale and mechanisms of power at both levels. In so doing, the human security biopoverty approach reveals three conditions of hegemonic neoliberalism. The first is that global governance is inevitably as biopolitical as national government. Human security is regulated, to different extents and in different places, by the biopolitical choices and preferences of neoliberal global governance. Supranational global governance is able to influence particular social policies around the world, with greater susceptibility to extreme neoliberal prescription in the global South than in the global North, since there is greater susceptibility to and dependence on IFI lending in the South than in the North. In the respect, neoliberal global governance is responsible for the calculated management and mismanagement of the life and death opportunities of billions of people globally. It enables hundreds of millions by equipping them with the health, education, tools and skills to engage its mechanisms, while disabling billions more by proscribing and prohibiting the means of engagement with that same machinery. Biopolitical global governance disrupts locally legitimized biopolitical resilience without compensating for the loss caused by disruption and prescription. The biopolitics of global governance hold sway indirectly and directly over mass life and death; over human security broadly.

A second characteristic of global governance recognizable from this approach reflects the way that biopolitical power is projected, by means of capillary distribution. Where Foucault referred us to the capillary power of the state, extending from and through multiple points to manage populations, the same idea describes global governance. Ideational hegemony in multiple arenas directs the rules and practices of governance through innumerable nodal bodies such as public IFIs. These in turn flash the instructions to subgroups and affiliates such as TNCs, but that power is also extended to the state level and below, in both developed and developing worlds, including liberal human rights bodies and development NGOs. The capacity of that power to disseminate itself differs from place to place in a relationship that reflects the relative capacity to reject external hegemonic rules without suffering internal destabilization and disruption. From vulnerable and susceptible states, the ideational hegemony implicit and explicit in neoliberal global governance is conducted through state institutions and practices to and through civil society, to determine the life outcomes of hundreds of millions of people. But to suggest that this capillary biopolitical determinism is a one-way process would be to misunderstand or ignore the reverse process, of capillary biopolitical resilience, displayed in the everyday responses of some of the poorest people in the world, who manipulate and redirect biopoverty and other resources in ways unfamiliar to liberal distributional processes and illegitimate in terms of liberal values, which, liberal or not, are in part responsible for mass avoidable mortality. For hundreds of millions of people at the margins of global governance and human security, common social patronage is every bit as biopolitical as the form of global governance that disrupts it, to which it presently responds, and which long predates the arrival of neoliberalism. As Merlingen remarks, 'the docility of the governed is never assured ... resistance is woven into the very fabric of power' (2006: 190).

A third characteristic of global governance affirmed by this biopolitical and biopoverty approach to human security is its blatant asymmetry of power: blatant in its operation and blatant in the ways in which this asymmetry is empirically ignored (international institutions maintain a level playing field and are neutral themselves), epistemologically denied (markets are objective and free while normative change is unlikely and undesirable), and ontologically legitimized (There Is No Alternative to neoliberal hegemony). Global governance scholarship's primary perception of its subject matter in terms of technocratic 'solutions' to institutional problems allows it to ignore the notion of neoliberal ideological power and to deny the relationship between centre-cause and peripheral-effect that asymmetric power necessarily and unavoidably describes. This is a profoundly unbalanced position to take, which disallows engagement with the role of its own subject matter in the calculated mismanagement of human security globally. Global governance is ideationally hegemonic and brooks no critical opposition to the failed and destructive value-laden beliefs from which it is socially constructed. It is not a neutral system for the mutual benefit of all but a powerful force for projecting neoliberal hegemony, sustaining dominance, subverting and co-opting resistance and assimilating difference with indifference. Global governance creates and reinforces international asymmetries of opportunity, privilege, wealth, development and human security, while dictating on what terms these concepts can be discussed, in which locations, by whom, and to what end. Human security thereby becomes a function of asymmetrical, biopolitical, global governance: a systemically delineated outcome that defines and sculpts levels and locations of human security and human insecurity around the world. Understanding this asymmetry in Foucauldian terms, however, 'emphasizes [both] the likelihood of resistance and the reversibility of power relations' self-evident in their social construction (ibid.: 190).

This aspect of human security has not received the intellectual attention needed to make more sense of the concept or its corollary, human insecurity; the two cannot be thought of distinctly since both are products of power and its use and abuse. This book has been a response to the problem of tradition and subjective normality as encoders of hierarchies and power that maintain differential rates of human security in different parts of the world. It also stems from the adiaphoric denial by mainstream security institutions of the role of socially constructed power in the international system, its inevitable asymmetries, and their lethal but preventable impact on millions of lives, at the very same time as those same institutions refuse to negotiate the space in which such matters are rigorously discussed. We are still not 'doing' international relations 'as if humans mattered', and this is a compelling comment on the hubris and arrogance of those who limit the terms of the debate; it is also a comment on the distance they are from the social reality of the world they have constructed and which they perpetuate. Ultimately, it is an attempt to render human security practicable by taking it beyond the narrowest imaginations that have been submerged in the mainstream, and it is a challenge to liberal claims to civilizational achievement and the hubris uncritically associated with such monotheist jingoism and liberal ideological narcissism.

BIBLIOGRAPHY

Abouharb, M. R. and D. Cingranelli (2008) 'A human rights-based approach to economic development', in *Human Rights and Structural Adjustment*, Cambridge: Cambridge University Press, pp. 227–39.

Abueva, J. (1966) 'The contribution of nepotism, spoils, and graft to political development', *East-West Center Review*, 3: 45–54.

Ackerly, B., M. Stern and J. True (2006) *Feminist Methodologies for International Relations*, Cambridge: Cambridge University Press.

Agamben, G. (1998) *Homo Sacer: Sovereign Power and Bare Life*, Stanford, CA: Stanford University Press.

Agenor, P.-R. and B. Moreno-Dodson (2006) 'Public infrastructure and growth: new channels and policy implications', Policy Research Working Paper WPS 4064, Washington, DC: World Bank.

Albert, M. and P. Lencon (2008) 'Introduction to the forum: Foucault and international political sociology', *International Political Sociology*, 3(2): 265–77.

Aldridge, A. (2005) *The Market*, London: Polity.

Allen, B., G. Thompson and D. Porter (1991) *Development in Practice: Paved with good intentions*, London: Routledge.

Alston, C. (2005) *Non-State Actors and Human Rights*, Oxford: Oxford University Press.

Anderson, M. (1999) *Do No Harm: How Aid Can Support Peace – or War*, Boulder, CO: Lynne Rienner.

Anghie, A. (2000) 'Time present and time past: globalization, international financial institutions and the Third World', *New York University Journal of International Law and Politics*, 32: 243–90.

Annamradju, S., B. Calaguas and E. Gutierrez (2001) *Financing Water and Sanitation: Key issues in increasing resources to the sector*, Oxford: WaterAid.

Annan, K. (2000) *We the Peoples: The Role of the United Nations in the 21st Century*, UN Millennium Report, New York: United Nations.

Anonymous (2001) *Discrimination against Men in the UK*, UK Men's Movement, www.ukmm.org.uk/issues/dam.htm, accessed 4 January 2009.

Armstrong, D., T. Farrell and H. Lambert (2007) *International Law and International Relations*, Cambridge: Cambridge University Press.

Armstrong, D., L. Lloyd and J. Redmond (2004) *International Organisation in World Politics*, Basingstoke: Palgrave Macmillan.

Atkinson, A. and J. Hills (1991) 'Social security in developed countries: are there lessons for developing countries?', in E. Ahmad, J. Dreze, J. Hills and A. Sen, *Social Security in Developing Countries*, Oxford: Clarendon Press.

Bailey, J. (2008) 'Arrested development: the fight to end commercial whaling as a case of failed norm change', *European Journal of International Relations*, 14(2): 289–318.

Banerjee, A., A. Deaton, N. Lustig and K. Rogoff (2006) *An Evaluation of World Bank Research 1998–2005*, Washington, DC: World Bank.

Barbara, J. (2008) 'Rethinking neo-liberal state building: building post-conflict development states', *Development in Practice*, 18(3): 307–18.

Barnes, B. (1999) *Understanding Agency: Social Theory and Responsible Action*, London: Sage.

Barnett, M. and R. Duvall (2005) 'Power in global governance', in M. Barnett and R. Duvall, *Power in Global Governance*, Cambridge: Cambridge University Press, pp. 1–32.

— (2006) 'Power in international politics', *International Organization*, 59: 39–75.

Barnett, M. and M. Finnemore (2004) *Rules for the World: International Organizations in Global Politics*, Ithaca, NY: Cornell University Press.

Barratt-Brown, M. (1993) *Fair Trade: Reform and Realities in the International Trading System*, London: Zed Books.

Bastian, S. (2004) 'Human rights and human security: an emancipatory political project', *Conflict, Security and Development*, 4(3): 411–18.

Bauman, Z. (1998) *Work, Consumption and the New Poor*, Buckingham: Open University Press.

Baumol, W. (1990) 'Entrepreneurship: productive, unproductive, and destructive', *Journal of Political Economy*, 98(5): 893–921.

Baumol, W., R. E. Litan and C. J. Schramm (2007) *Good Capitalism, Bad Capitalism and the Economics of Growth and Prosperity*, New Haven, CT: Yale University Press.

Baxi, U. (1998) 'Voices of suffering and the future of human rights', *Transnational Law and Contemporary problems*, 125(8): 125–70.

Baylis, J., S. Smith and P. Owens (2008) *The Globalization of World Politics: An introduction to international relations*, Cambridge: Cambridge University Press.

BBC (2009) Reith Lectures, London: Radio 4.

Bellamy, A. and M. McDonald (2002) 'The utility of human security: which humans? What security? A reply to Thomas and Tow', *Security Dialogue*, 33(3): 373–7.

Bello, W. (1989) *Brave New Third World. Strategies for Surviving in the Global Economy*, San Francisco, CA: Food First Books.

Benstein, S. and L. W. Pauly (2007) *Global Liberlaism and Political Order: Toward a New Grand Compromise?*, Albany: State University of New York Press.

Berenskoetter, F. (2007) 'Thinking about power', in F. Berenskoetter and M. Williams, *Power in World Politics*, London: Routledge, pp. 1–23.

Berenskoetter, F. and M. Williams (2007) *Power in World Politics*, London: Routledge.

Beyer, C. (2008) *Violent Globalisms: Conflict in Response to Empire*, Aldershot: Ashgate.

Bhaskar, R. (2008) *Understanding Peace and Security*, London: Routledge.

Bhattacharrya, G. (2005) *Traffick: The Illicit Movement of People and Things*, London: Pluto.

Bieler, A. and A. D. Morton (2008) 'The deficits of discourse in IPE: turning base metal into gold?', *International Studies Quarterly*, 52: 103–28.

Bjorkdahl, A. (2002) 'Norms in International Relations: some conceptual and methodological reflections', *Cambridge Review of International Affairs*, 15(1): 9–23.

Black, R. (2003) 'Where and why are 10 million children dying every year?', *The Lancet*, 361(9376): 2226–34.

Blanchard, E. (2003) 'Gender, International Relations, and the development of feminist security theory', *Signs: Journal of Women in Culture and Society*, 28(4): 1289–312.

Bloom, D. and D. Canning (2004) 'The health and wealth of Africa', *World Economics*, 5(2): 57–81.

— (2007) *The Growth Commission*, www.growthcommission.org/ storage/cgdev/documents/bloom_ canning_on_health.pdf, accessed 6 June 2008.

Bloom, D., D. Canning and J. P. Sevilla (2001) *The Effect of Health on Economic Growth: Theory and Evidence*, Cambridge, MA: National Bureau of Economic Research.

— (2004) 'The effect of health on economic growth: a production function approach', *World Development*, 32(1): 1–13.

Bloom, D., D. Canning, B. Graham and J. Sevilla (2002) 'Improving health: a key to halving global poverty by 2015', in M. Agosin, D. E. Bloom, G. Chapelier and J. Saigal, *Solving the Riddle of Globalization and Development*, London: Routledge, pp. 104–23.

Bojicic-Dzelilovic, V. and F. Causevic (2008) 'Microfinance in post-conflict economic recovery: lessons from Bosnia and Herzegovina', Bureau for Crisis Prevention and Recovery Background Paper, New York: UNDP.

Booth, K. (2005) *Critical Security Studies and World Politics*, Boulder, CO: Lynne Rienner.

Booth, K. and J. Wheeler (2008) *The Security Dilemma: Fear, Co-operation and Trust in World Politics*, Basingstoke: Palgrave Macmillan.

Box, S. (1983) *Power, Crime and Mystification*, London: Tavistock.

Broad, R. (2006) 'Research, knowledge and "paradigm maintenance": the political economy of research within the World Bank's development economics vice-presidency', *Review of International Political Economy*, 13(3): 387–419.

Brown, C. (2009) 'Structural realism, classical realism and human nature', *International Relations*, 23(2): 257–70.

Buchanan, A. and M. Decamp (2007) 'Responsibility for global health', in R. Cook and C. G. Ngwena, *Health and Human Rights*, London: Ashgate, pp. 506–23.

Buzan, B., O. Waever and J. de Wilde (1998) *Security: A New Framework for Analysis*, Boulder, CO: Lynne Rienner.

Cahill, K. (1993) *A Framework for Survival: Health, Human Rights and Humanitarian Assistance in Conflicts and Disasters*, New York: Council on Foreign Relations.

Calaguas, B. and M. O'Connell (2000) 'Poverty Reduction Strategy Papers and water: failing the poor?', WaterAid Discussion Paper, www.partnershipsforwater. net/psp/tc/TC_Tools/002F_

PRSP%20failing%20poor.pdf, accessed 2 April 2009.

Camdessus, M. (2001) 'The IMF at the beginning of the twenty-first century: can we establish a humanized globalization?', *Global Governance*, 7: 363–70.

— (2003) *Financing Water for All: Report of the World Panel on Financing Water Infrastructure*, Kyoto: World Water Council.

Cammack, P. (2004) 'What the World Bank means by poverty reduction, and why it matters', *New Political Economy*, 9(2): 189–211.

— (2008) 'Poverty policy and the politics of competitiveness', in P. Kennet, *Governance, Globalization and Public Policy*, Cheltenham: Edward Elgar, pp. 131–50.

Caplan, R. (2004) 'Partner or patron? International civil administration and local capacity-building', *International Peacekeeping*, 11(2): 229–47.

Carin, B., R. Higgott, J. Scholte, G. Smith and D. Stone (2006) 'Global governance: looking ahead 2006–2010', *Global Governance*, 1(6).

Carmen, R. (1996) *Autonomous Development: Humanizing the Landscape: An Excursion into Radical Thinking and Practice*, London: Zed Books.

Carr, E. (2008) 'Rethinking poverty alleviation: a "poverties" approach', *Development in Practice*, 18(6): 726–34.

Chandler, D. (2008a) 'Human Security II: waiting for the tail to wag the dog, a rejoinder to Ambrosetti, Owen and Wibben', *Security Dialogue*, 39(4): 463–9.

— (2008b) 'Human security: the dog that didn't bark', *Security Dialogue*, 39(4): 427–38.

Chang, H.-J. (2002) *Kicking Away the Ladder: Policies and Institutions for Economic Development in Historical Perspective*, London: Anthem Press.

Charkiewicz, E. (2005) 'Corporations, the UN and neo-liberal bio-politics', *Development*, 48(1): 75–83.

Chen, L. and V. Narasimhan (2003) 'Human security and global health', *Journal of Human Development*, 4(2): 181–90.

Chen, S. and M. Ravallion (2008) 'The developing world is poorer than we thought, but no less successful in the fight against poverty', Policy Research Working Paper 4703, Washington, DC: World Bank.

Chesterman, S. (2004) *You the People: The United Nations, Transitional Administration and Statebuilding*, Oxford: Oxford University Press.

Chossudovsky, M. (1997) *The Globalization of Poverty: Impacts of IMF and World Bank Reforms*, Goa: Other India Press.

Cichon, M. and K. Hagemejer (2007) 'Changing the development policy paradigm: investing in a social security floor for all', *International Social Security Review*, 60(2/3): 169–96.

Clapham, A. (1993) *Human Rights in the Private Sphere*, Oxford: Clarendon Press.

Clements, D., D. Nshimirimanda and A. Gasasira (2008) 'Using immunization delivery strategies to accelerate progress in Africa towards achieving the Millennium Development Goals', *Vaccine*, pp. 1926–33.

Cohen, S. (2008) *States of Denial: Knowing about atrocities and suffering*, Cambridge: Polity.

Commission on Global Governance

(1995) *Our Global Neighbourhood*, Oxford: Oxford University Press.

Connell, R. (2000) *The Men and the Boys*, Cambridge: Polity.

Cornia, G. (2001) 'Social funds in stabilization and adjustment: a critique', *Development and Change*, 32(1): 1–32.

Cortell, A. and J. David (2000) 'Understanding the domestic impact of international norms: a research agenda', *International Studies Review*, 2(1): 65–87.

Coward, M. (2006) 'Securing the global (bio)political economy: "empire", poststructuralism and political economy', in M. de Goede, *International Political Economy and Poststructural Politics*, London: Palgrave, pp. 60–76.

Cox, R. (1983) 'Gramsci, hegemony and International Relations: an essay in method', *Millennium: Journal of International Studies*, 12(2): 162–75.

— (1987) *Production, Power and World Order: Social Forces in the Making of History*, New York: Columbia University Press.

— (1993) 'Gramsci, hegemony and International Relations', in S. Gill, *Gramsci, Historical Materialism and International Relations*, Cambridge: Cambridge University Press.

— (1995) 'Critical political economy', in B. Hettne, *International Political Economy: Understanding Global Disorder*, London: Zed Books.

— (1997) 'Democracy in hard times: economic globalization and the limits to liberal democracy', in A. McGrew (ed.), *The Transformation of Democracy*, Cambridge: Polity.

— (2005) 'Global perestroika', in R. Wilkinson, *The Global Govern-* ance Reader, London: Routledge, pp. 140–55.

Cox, R. and M. G. Schechter (2002) *The Political Economy of a Plural World: Critical Reflections on Power, Morals and Civilization*, London: Routledge.

Craig, D. and D. Porter (2006) *Development beyond Neoliberalism: Governance, Poverty Reduction and Political Economy*, London: Routledge.

Crawford, N. (1993) 'Decolonization as an international norm: the evolution of practices, arguments, and beliefs', in L. Reed and C. Kaysen, *Emerging Norms of Justified Intervention*, Cambridge, MA: Committee on International Security Studies.

— (2009) 'Human nature and world politics: rethinking "man"', *International Relations*, 23(2): 271–88.

Crow, B. and M. Thorpe (1992) *Survival and Change in the Third World*, Cambridge: Polity.

Dahlerup, D. and L. Freidenvall (2005) 'Quotas as a fast track to equal political representation for women', *International Feminist Journal of Politics*, 7(1): 26–48.

Darrow, M. (2003) *Between Light and Shadow: the World Bank, the International Monetary Fund and International Human Rights*, Oxford: Hart.

Davies, R. and J. Dart (2005) *The 'Most Significant Change' (MSC) Technique*, www.mande.co.uk/docs/MSCGuide.pdf, accessed 12 April 2009.

Deacon, B. (1997) *Global Social Policy: International organizations and the future of welfare*, London: Sage.

— (2000) *Globalization and Social Policy: The threat to equitable welfare*, Geneva: United Nations Research Institute for Social Development.

— (2004) *The Politics of Global Social Policy*, Geneva: United Nations Research Institute for Social Development.

— (2005a) 'From "safety nets" back to "universal social provision"', *Global Social Policy*, 5(1): 19–28.

— (2005b) 'The governance and politics of global social policy', *Social Policy & Society*, 4(4): 437–45.

Deacon, R., M. Hulse and P. Stubbs (1997) *Global Social Policy: International organizations and the future of welfare*, London: Sage.

Deraniyagala, S. (2005) 'Neoliberalism in international trade: sound economics or a question of faith?', in A. Saad-Filho and D. Johnston, *Neoliberalism: A Critical Reader*, London: Pluto.

Devesh, K., J. P. Lewis and R. C. Webb (1997) *The World Bank: Its First Half Century*, vol. 2, Washington, DC: Brookings Institution.

Dharmadhikary, S. (2005) *Unravelling Bhakra: Assessing the Temple of Resurgent India*, Badwani: Manthan Adhyayan Kendra.

Diehl, P. (1997) *The Politics of Global Governance: International Organizations in an Interdependent World*, Boulder, CO: Lynne Rienner.

Diehl, P., C. Ku and D. Zamora (2003) 'The dynamics of international law: the interaction of normative and operating systems', *International Organization*, 57: 43–75.

Dillon, M. (2008) 'Underwriting security', *Security Dialogue*, 39(2/3): 309–32.

Dillon, M. and L. Lobo-Guerrero (2008) 'Biopolitics of security in the 21st century: an introduction', *Review of International Studies*, 34: 265–92.

Dillon, M. and J. Reid (2001) 'Global liberal governance: biopolitics, security and war', *Millennium: Journal of International Studies*, 30(1): 41–66.

Dingwerth, K. and P. Pattberg (2006) 'Global governance as a perspective on world politics', *Global Governance*, 12: 185–203.

Dogan, M. and D. Pelassy (1990) *How to Compare Nations: Strategies in Comparative Politics*, New Jersey: Chatham House.

Doig, A. (1984) *Corruption and Misconduct in Contemporary British Politics*, Harmondsworth: Penguin.

Drache, D. (2001) 'The fundamentals of our time', in D. Drache, *The Market of the Public Domain: Global governance and the asymmetry of power*, London: Routledge, pp. 1–34.

Dreze, J. and A. Sen (1989) *Hunger and Public Action*, Oxford: Oxford University Press.

Duffield, M. (2001) *Global Governance and the New Wars: The Merging of Development and Security*, London: Zed Books.

— (2005a) 'Human security: development, containment and re-territorialization', in C. Browning and P. Cornish, *The Globalization of Security*, ISP/NSC Briefing Paper 05/02, London: Chatham House.

— (2005b) *Human Security: Linking development and security in an age of terror*, Bonn: EADI.

— (2008) 'Global civil war: the non-insured, international containment and post-interventionary society', *Journal of Refugee Studies*, 21(2): 145–65.

Dunne, T. and B. Schmidt (2008) 'Realism', in J. Bayliss, S. Smith and P. Owens, *The Globalization of World Politics: An introduction to international relations*, Oxford: Oxford University Press, pp. 90–107.

Dwivedi, G. and S. Dharmadhikary (2006) *Water: Private, Limited: Issues in Privatisation, Corporatisation and Commercialisation of the Water Sector in India*, Badwani: Manthan Adhyayan Kendra.

Eade, D. (1997) 'Preface', in *Development in Practice Reader*, Oxford: Oxford University Press.

Easterly, W. (2006) *The White Man's Burden: Why the West's efforts to aid the rest have done so much ill and so little good*, Oxford: Oxford University Press.

Edstrom, B. (2003) 'Japan's foreign policy and human security', *Japan Forum*, 15(2): 209–25.

Edwards, M. (1989) 'The irrelevance of Development Studies', *Third World Quarterly*, 11: 116–35.

Eisenstadt, S. and S. Roniger (1982) 'Patron–client relations as a model of structuring social exchange', *Comparative Studies in Society and History*, 22(1): 42–77.

Elgstrom, O. (2000) 'Norms negotiations: the construction of new norms regarding gender and development in EU foreign aid policy', *Journal of European Public Policy*, 7(3): 457–76.

Elson, R. (1997) *The End of the Peasantry in Southeast Asia: A Social and Economic History of Peasant Livelihood, 1800–1990s*, London: Macmillan.

Enloe, C. (2000) *Bananas, Beaches and Bases: Making Feminist Sense of International Politics*, California: University of California Press.

Esterling, K. (2004) *The Political Economy of Expertise*, Ann Arbor: University of Michigan Press.

Evans, P. (2000) 'Fighting marginalization with transnational networks: counter-hegemonic globalization', *Contemporary Society*, 29(1): 230–41.

Evans, T. (2002) 'A human right to health?', *Third World Quarterly*, 23(2): 197–215.

Falk, R. (2000) 'Humane governance for the world: reviving the quest', *Review of International Political Economy*, 7(2): 317–34.

Fernandez, Dr G., MD (humanitarian intervention specialist in Somalia, Darfur and Iraq) (2009) Skype interview, Geneva–UK, 11 April.

Fields, Belden A. (2003) *Rethinking Human Rights for the New Millennium*, London: Palgrave Macmillan.

Fine, B., C. Lapavitsas and J. Pincus (2001) *Development Policy in the Twenty-first Century: Beyond the Post-Washington Consensus*, London: Routledge.

Finnemore, M. and K. Sikkink (1998) 'International norm dynamics and political change', *International Organization*, 52(4): 887–917.

FoI (Freedom of Information request) (2009), F2009-021, by private correspondence, 12 February.

Foucault, M. (1973) *The Order of Things*, New York: Vintage.

— (1979) *The History of Sexuality: An introduction*, London: Allen Lane.

— (2003) *Society Must Be Defended: Lectures at the Collège de France 1975–1976*, London: Penguin.

— (2007) *Security, Territory, Population: Lectures at the Collège de France 1977–1978*, Basingstoke: Palgrave.

Frankman, M. (1997) 'No global war? a role for democratic federalism', *Journal of World-Systems Research*, 3(2): 321–38.

Fraser, N. (1989) *Unruly Practices: Power, Discourse and Gender in Contemporary Social Theory*, Minneapolis: University of Minnesota Press.

Freedman, L. (1998) 'International security: changing targets', *Foreign Policy*, Spring, pp. 48–64.

Freyberg-Inan, A. (2006) 'Transition economies', in R. Stubbs and G. Underhill, *Political Economy and the Changing Global Order*, Oxford: Oxford University Press, pp. 419–30.

Fuchs, D. A. (2002) 'Globalization and global governnace: discourses on political order at the turn of the century', in D. Fuchs and F. Kratochwil, *Transformative Change and World Order: Reflections on Theory and Practice*, Munster: LIT Verlag.

Gable, L. (2007) 'The proliferation of human rights in global health governance', *Journal of Law, Medicine and Ethics*, 35(4): 534–44.

Gaventa, J. (2007) 'Levels, spaces and forms of power', in F. Berenskoetter and M. Williams, *Power in World Politics*, London: Routledge, pp. 205–24.

George, S. (1989) *A Fate Worse than Debt*, London: Penguin.

George, S. and F. Sabelli (1994) *Faith and Credit: the World Bank's Secular Empire*, London: Penguin.

Gerring, J. (1999) 'What makes a concept good? A criterial framework for understanding concept formation in the social sciences', *Polity*, 31(3): 357–93.

Gilby, N. (2008) 'Corruption and the arms trade: the United Kingdom's Ministry of Defence and the bribe culture', *The Economics of Peace and Security*, (3)1.

Gill, S. (1995) 'Globalisation, market civilisation, and disciplinary neoliberalism', *Millennium: Journal of International Studies*, 23(3): 399–423.

— (1998) 'New constitutionalism, democratisation and global political economy', *Global Change, Peace & Security*, 10(1): 23–38.

Gill, S. and D. Law (1993) 'Global hegemony and the structural power of capital', in S. Gill, *Gramsci, Historical Materialism and International Relations*, Cambridge: Cambridge University Press, pp. 93–126.

Gillespie, D. (2003) 'Knowledge into action for child survival', *The Lancet*, 362: 323–7.

Gills, B. (2007) *The Clash of Globalizations: 'Empire' or 'Cosmopolis'?*, London: Routledge.

Gilman, D. (2002) 'Of fruitcakes and patriot games', *Georgetown Law Review*, pp. 2387–412.

Gilpin, R. (2000) *The Challenge of Global Capitalism: The world economy in the 21st century*, Princeton, NJ: Princeton University Press.

Gilroy, P. (2002) 'Toward a critique of consumer imperialism', *Public Culture*, 14(3): 589–91.

Glasius, M. and M. Kaldor (2005) *A Human Security Doctrine for Europe*, London: Routledge.

Glinavos, I. (2007) Book review, *Development and Change*, 38(4): 764–5.

Global Health Watch (2008) *Global Health Watch 2: An Alternative World Health Report*, London: Zed Books.

Goetz, G. and P. Diehl (1992)

'Towards a theory of international norms: some conceptual and measurement issues', *Journal of Conflict Resolution*, 36: 634–64.

Goldstein, J. L., M. Kahler, R. O. Keohane and A.-M. Slaughter (2000) 'Legalization and world politics international organization', 54(3): 385–99.

Gordenker, L. and T. G. Weiss (1996) 'Pluralizing global governance: analytical approaches and dimensions', in L. Gordenker and T. G. Weiss, *NGOs, the UN and Global Governance*, Boulder, CO: Westview.

Gordon, D. (2007) 'Poverty, death and disease', in P. Hillyard, C. Pantazis, S. Tombs and D. Gordon, *Beyond Criminology: Taking harms seriously*, London: Pluto, pp. 251–66.

Grant, J. (1993) 'Jump-starting development', *Foreign Policy*, 91: 124–37.

Grayson, K. (2008) 'Human security as power/knowledge: the biopolitics of a definitional debate', *Cambridge Review of International Affairs*, 21(3): 383–401.

Greig, A., D. Hulme and M. Turner (2007) *Challenging Global Inequality: Development Theory and Practice in the 21st Century*, London: Palgrave Macmillan.

Griffin, P. (2007) 'Sexing the economy in a neo-liberal world order: neo-liberal discourse and the (re) production of heteronormative heterosexuality', *British Journal of Politics and International Relations*, 9(2): 220–38.

Grove, N. and A. B. Zwi (2008) 'Beyond the log frame: a new tool for examining health and peace-building initiatives', *Development in Practice*, 18(1): 66–81.

Gruber, L. (2000) *Ruling the World: Power, politics and the rise of supranational institutons*, Princeton, NJ: Princeton University Press.

Grugel, J. and N. Piper (2007) *Critical Perpsectives on Global Governance*, London: Routledge.

Gutlove, P. and G. Thompson (2003) 'Human security: expanding the scope of public health', *Medicine, Conflict and Survival*, 19: 17–34.

Halabi, Y. (2004) 'The expansion of global governance into the Third World: altruism, realism or constructivism?', *International Studies Review*, 6: 21–48.

Hall, A. and J. Midgley (2006) *Social Policy for Development*, London: Sage.

Hall, D. (1999) 'Privatisation, multi-nationals, and corruption', *Development in Practice*, 9(5): 539–56.

— (2003) *Financing Water for the World: An alternative to guaranteed profits*, London: Public Services International.

— (2004) *Water Finance – a discussion note*, London: Public Services International.

Hall, D. and E. Lobina (2006) *Water as a Public Service*, London: Public Services International.

— (2008) *Sewerage Works*, London: Public Services International.

Hamlin, C. and S. Sheard (1998) 'Revolutions in public health: 1848, and 1998', *British Medical Journal*, 317: 587–91.

Hansard (2008), 12 November, www.parliament.the-stationery-office.com/pa/cm200708/cmselect/cmintdev/uc1195/uc119502.htm, accessed 12 February 2009.

Hardt, M. and A. Negri (2000) *Empire*, London: Harvard University Press.

— (2004) *Multitude: War and*

democracy in the age of empire, New York: Penguin.

Harrington, M. (1992) 'What exactly is wrong with the Liberal State as an agent of change?', in V. S. Peterson, *Gendered States: Feminist (Re)Visions of International Relations Theory*, Boulder, CO: Lynne Rienner.

Harrison, E. (2007) 'Corruption', *Development in Practice*, 17(4/5): 672.

Harvey, D. (2007) 'Neoliberalism as creative destruction', *Annals of the American Academy of Political and Social Science*, 610(21): 21–44.

Hathaway, O. (2002) 'Do human rights treaties make a difference?', *Yale Law Journal*, 1870: 1935–2034.

Hawkins, V. (2008) *Stealth Conflicts: How the World's Worst Violence Is Ignored*, Aldershot: Ashgate.

Hay, C. (2007) 'The normalizing role of rationalist assumptions on the institutional embedding of neoliberalism', in R. Vij, *Globalization and Welfare: A critical reader*, London: Palgrave, pp. 88–105.

Health, C. O. (2001) *Macroeconomics and Health: Investing in Health for Economic Development*, Geneva: World Health Organization.

Held, D. (2004) *Global Covenant: The Social Democratic Alternative to the Washington Consensus*, Cambridge: Polity.

— (2008) 'At the global crossroads: the end of the Washington Consensus and the rise of global social democracy?', in *The Global Politics of Globalization*, London: Routledge, pp. 95–112.

Held, D. and A. McGrew (2003) *The Global Transformations Reader*, Cambridge: Polity.

Held, V. (2006) *The Ethics of Care*, Oxford: Oxford University Press.

Helleiner, G. (2001) 'Markets, politics and globalization: can the global economy be civilized?', *Global Governance*, 7: 243–63.

Hemson, D., K. Kulindwa, H. Lein and A. Mascarenhas (2008) *Poverty and Water: Explorations of the reciprocal relationship*, London: Zed Books.

Hobsbawm, E. (1997a) *The Age of Capital, 1848–1875*, London: Weidenfeld and Nicolson.

— (1997b) *The Age of Revolution: 1789–1848*, London: Weidenfeld and Nicolson.

Hoffman, S. (1956) 'The role of international organizations: limits and possibilities', *International Organization*, 10: 357–72.

Hook, S. (2008) 'Ideas and change in US foreign aid: inventing the Millennium Challenge Corporation', *Foreign Policy Analysis*, pp. 147–67.

Hopenhayn, M. (2004) 'Global approaches, dispersed agents: comments on Deacon: the politics of global social policy change', *UNRISD*, 20/21 April.

Horkheimer, M. (1974) *Eclipse of Reason*, London: Continuum International.

Hout, W. and R. Robison (eds) (2009) *Governance and the Depoliticisation of Development*, London: Routledge.

Hudson, H. (2005) '"Doing" security as if humans matter: a feminist perspective on gender and the politics of human security', *Security Dialogue*, 36(2): 155–74.

Hurrell, A. (2005) 'Power, institutions, and the production of inequality', in M. Barnett and R. Duvall, *Power in Global Governance*, Cambridge: Cambridge University Press, pp. 33–58.

— (2007) *On Global Order: Power,*

Values and the Constitution of International Society, Oxford: Oxford University Press.

Huxley, A. (1977) *Brave New World*, London: Grafton.

IDA (International Development Association) (2009) *Articles of Agreement*, World Bank, go.World Bank.org/7XO4MV27To, accessed 23 January 2009.

IDC (International Development Committee) (2008) *DfID and the World Bank: Government Response to the Committee's Sixth Report of Session 2007–08*, House of Commons, London: The Stationery Office.

ILO (2004) *A Fair Globalization: Creating Opportunities for All*, Geneva: World Commission on the Social Dimension of Globalization.

Ingebritsen, C. (2002) 'Norms entrepreneurs: Scandinavia's role in world politics', *Conflict and Cooperation*, 37(1): 11–23.

Isbister, J. (2003) *Promises Not Kept: Poverty and the Betrayal of Third World Development*, London: Palgrave.

Jackson, R. and G. Sorenson (2007) *Introduction to International Relations: Theories and Approaches*, Oxford: Oxford University Press.

Jacobsen, K. (1998) 'Studying global governance: a behavioural approach', in C. Ku and T. G. Weiss, *Toward Understanding Global Governance: The International Law and International Relations Toolbox*, New York: Academic Council on the United Nations System, pp. 13–26.

Jenssen, C. (2001) 'Medicine against war: an historical review of the anti-war activities of physicians', in I. Taipale, *War of Health? A Reader*, Helsinki: Physicians for Social Responsibility.

Johnstone, I. (2005) 'The power of interpretive communities', in M. Barnett and R. Duvall, *Power in Global Governance*, Cambridge: Cambridge University Press, pp. 185–204.

Johnstone, P. and G. Brown (2004) 'International controls of corruption: recent responses from the USA and the UK', *Journal of Financial Crime*, (11)2: 217–48.

Jones, G. (2003) 'How many child deaths can we prevent this year?', *The Lancet*, 362(9377): 65–71.

Jordan, B. (2006) *Social Policy for the Twenty-first Century*, Cambridge: Polity.

Joseph, J. (2008) 'Hegemony and the structure-agency problem in International Relations: a scientific realist contribution', *Review of International Studies*, 34(1): 109–28.

Kaldor, M. (1999) *New and Old Wars*, Cambridge: Polity Press.

— (2007) *Human Security: Reflections on Globalization and Intervention*, Cambridge: Polity Press.

Kaldor, M., M. Martin and S. Selchow (2007) 'Human security: a new strategic narrative for Europe', *International Affairs*, 83(2): 273–88.

Kannan, K. (2007) 'Social security in a globalizing world', *International Social Security Review*, 60(2/3): 19–37.

Kapstein, E. (2005) 'Power, fairness and the global economy', in M. Barnett and R. Duvall, *Power in Global Governance*, Cambridge: Cambridge University Press, pp. 80–101.

Katzenstein, P. (1996) 'Alternative perspectives on national security', in P. Katzenstein, *The Culture of National Security: Norms and*

Identity in World Politics, New York: Columbia University Press, pp. 1–32.

Keck, M. and K. Sikkink (1998) *Activists beyond Borders: Advocacy Networks in International Politics*, Ithaca, NY: Cornell University Press.

— (1999) 'Transnational advocacy networks in international and regional politics', *International Social Science Journal*, 159: 89–102.

Kegley, C. (1995) *Controversies in International Relations Theory: Realism and the Neoliberal Challenge*, New York: St Martin's Press.

Kelsall, T. (2008) 'Going with the grain in African development?', *Development Policy Review*, 26(6): 627–55.

Kennedy, D. (1999) 'Background noise? The underlying politics of global governance', *Harvard International Review*, 21(3): 52–7.

Kenny, C. (2008) 'Corruption in water – a matter of life and death', in H. Labelle, *Global Corruption Report 2008: Corruption in the Water Sector*, New York: Transparency International, pp. 16–17.

Kentor, J. (2004) 'Quantifying hegemony in the world economy', in T. Reifer, *Globalization, Hegemony and Power: Antisystemic movements and the global system*, Boulder, CO: Paradigm, pp. 74–88.

Keohane, R. and J. Nye (2000) 'Introduction', in J. Nye and J. Donahue, *Governance in a Globalizing World*, Washington, DC: Brookings Institution, pp. 1–44.

— (2001) *Power and Interdependence*, New Jersey: Longman.

Keynes, J. (1936) *The General Theory of Employment, Interest and Money*, New York: Harcourt Brace.

Khong, Y. (2001) 'Human security:

a shotgun approach to alleviating human misery?', *Global Governance*, 7: 231–6.

Kilburn, R. and L. A. Karoly (2008) *The Economics of Early Childhood Policy: What the dismal science has to say about investing in children*, Santa Monica, CA: RAND.

Kingsbury, D. (2007) *Political Development*, London: Routledge.

Kinsella, H. (2005) 'Securing the civilian: sex and gender in the laws of war', in M. Barnett and R. Duvall, *Power in Global Governance*, Cambridge: Cambridge University Press, pp. 249–72.

Kirchner, E. and J. Sperling (2007) *Global Security Governance: Competing perceptions of security in the 21st century*, London: Routledge.

Knight, W. (2003) 'Coexisting civilizations in a plural world', *International Studies Review*, 5: 403–5.

Konkolewsky, H.-H. (2007) 'Looking forward to social security for all', *International Social Security Review*, 60(2/3): 197–200.

Kopits, G. (1993) *Towards a Cost-effective Social Security System*, Geneva: International Social Security Association.

Koskenniemi, M. (2007) *From Apology to Utopia: The Structure of International Legal Argument*, Cambridge: Cambridge University Press.

Kozul-Wright, R. and P. Rayment (2007) *The Resistible Rise of Market Fundamentalism: Rethinking development in an unbalanced world*, London: Zed Books.

Kratochwil, F. and J. G. Ruggie (1986) 'International organization: a state of the art on an art of the state', *International Organization*, 40(4): 753–75.

Krause, K. (2004) 'The key to a powerful agenda, if properly delimited', *Security Dialogue*, 35(3): 367–8.

Krook, M. (2007) 'Candidate gender quotas: a framework for analysis', *European Journal of Political Research*, 46: 367–94.

Kubiak, A. (2001) *Corruption in Everyday Experience*, Batory, www.batory.org.pl/ftp/program/przeciw-korupcji/publikacje/corrupt_everyday.pdf, accessed January 2009.

Labelle, H. (2008) *Global Corruption Report 2008: Corruption in the Water Sector*, New York: Transparency International.

Landolt, L. (2004) '(Mis)constructing the Third World? Constructivist analysis of norm diffusion', *Third World Quarterly*, 25(3): 579–91.

Lang, T. and C. Hines (1993) *The New Protectionism: Protecting the Future against Free Trade*, London: Earthscan.

Larner, W. (2006) 'Neoliberalism: policy, ideology, governmentality', in M. de Goede, *International Political Economy and Poststructural Politics*, London: Palgrave, pp. 199–218.

Larner, W. and W. Walters (eds) (2004) *Global Governmentality: Governing International Spaces*, London: Routledge.

Lawson, G. (2008) 'A realistic utopia? Nancy Fraser, cosmopolitanism and the making of a just world order', *Political Studies*, 57(5): 1–26.

Lee, E. (1996) 'Globalization and employment', *International Labour Review*, 135(5): 485–97.

Leff, N. (1964) 'Economic development through bureaucratic corruption', *American Behavioural Scientist*, 8(3): 8–14.

Legro, J. W. (1997) Which norms matter? Revisiting the failure of Internationalism', *International Organization*, 55(1): 31–63.

Lendvai, N. and P. Stubbs (2007) *Post-colonial Dialogue or His Master's Voice? Translating the periphery in GSP studies*, Florence.

Lipschutz, R. (2005) 'Global civil society and global governmentality: or, the search for politics and state amidst the capillaries of social power', in M. Barnett and R. Duvall, *Power in Global Governance*, Cambridge: Cambridge University Press, pp. 229–48.

Lipschutz, R. D. and J. K. Rowe (2005) *Globalization, Governmentality and Global Politics: Regulation for the rest of us?*, London: Routledge.

Lobina, E. and D. Hall (2003) *Problems with Private Water Concessions: A review of experience*, London: Public Services International.

Mac Ginty, R. (2008) 'Indigenous peace-making versus the liberal peace', *Cooperation and Conflict: Journal of the Nordic International Studies Association*, 43(2): 139–63.

Mack, A. (2004) 'A signifier of shared values', *Security Dialogue*, 35(3): 368–9.

— (2005) *The Human Security Report 2005: War and Peace in the 21st Century*, Oxford: Oxford University Press.

Mackenbach, J. (2007) 'Sanitation: pragmatism works', *British Medical Journal*, 334(7): 1–3.

Martin, L. and B. A. Simmons (1998) 'Theories and empirical studies of international institutions', *International Organizations*, 52(4): 729–57.

Maxwell, S. (2005) 'The Washington

Consensus is dead! Long live the meta-narrative!', ODI Working Paper 243.

Mbembe, A. (2003) 'Necropolitics', *Public Culture*, 15(1): 11–40.

McCloud, D. (1995) *Southeast Asia: Tradition and Modernity in the Contemporary World*, Boulder, CO: Westview Press.

McDonald, M. (2008) 'Securitization and the construction of security', *European Journal of International Relations*, 14(4): 563–87.

McMichael, A. (1999) 'Prisoners of the proximate: loosening the constraints on epidemiology in an age of change', *Journal of Epidemiology*, 149: 887–97.

McSweeney, B. (1999) *Security, Identity and Interests: A Sociology of International Relations*, Cambridge: Cambridge University Press.

Mehrotra, S. and E. Delamonica (2005) 'The private sector and privatization in social services: is the Washington Consensus dead?', *Global Social Policy*, 5(2): 141–73.

Mehta, L. (2001) 'Commentary: the World Bank and its emerging knowledge empire', *Human Organization*, 60(2): 189–96.

Meier, B. (2007) 'Advancing health rights in a globalized world: responding to globalization through a collective human right to health', *Global Health, Law and Ethics*, Winter, pp. 545–55.

Merlingen, M. (2006) 'Foucault and world politics: promises and challenges of extending governmentality theory to the European and beyond', *Millennium: Journal of International Studies*, 35: 181–96.

— (2008) 'Monster studies', *International Political Sociology*, 3(2): 272–4.

Meyer, E. and S. Schwartz (2000)

'Social issues as public health: promise and peril', *American Journal of Public Health*, 90(8): 1189–91.

Millen, J., A. Irwin, J. Y. Kim and J. Gershman (2000) *Dying for Growth: Global Inequality and the Health of the Poor*, Monroe, ME: Common Courage Press.

Miller-Adams, M. (1999) *The World Bank: New Agendas in a Changing World*, London: Routledge.

Mishra, R. (2002) 'Richard Titmuss and social policy', *Journal of Social Policy*, 31: 747–52.

Mkandawire, T. (2004) *Social Policy in a Development Context*, Basingstoke: Palgrave.

Moorehead, S. (2008) Email communication with author, 3 December.

Morton, A. (2007) *Unravelling Gramsci: Hegemony and passive revolution in the global economy*, London: Pluto.

Murphy, C. (2000) 'Global governance: poorly done and poorly understood', *International Affairs*, 76(4): 789–803.

Musgrove, P. (2005) 'Ideas versus money: a conversation with Jean-Louis Sarbib', *Health Affairs: the Policy Journal of the Health Sphere*, 341: W5-352.

Muzaffar, C. (1995) 'From human rights to human dignity', *Bulletin of Concerned Asian Scholars*, 27(4): 6–8.

Naude, W. (2008) 'Entrepreneurship, post-conflict', in T. Addison and T. Bruck, *Making Peace Work: The Challenges of Social and Economic Reconstruction*, London: Palgrave Macmillan, pp. 251–63.

Neild, R. (2002) *Public Corruption: The Dark Side of Social Evolution*, London: Anthem Press.

Newman, E. (2001) 'Human security

and constructivism', *International Studies Perspectives*, 2: 239–51.

Nielson, D. and J. T. Tierney (2003) 'Delegation to international organizations: agency theory and World Bank environmental reform', *International Organization*, 57: 241–76.

Nielson, D., M. J. Tierney and C. E. Weaver (2006) 'Bridging the rationalist–constructivist divide: re-engineering the culture of the World Bank', *Journal of International Relations and Development*, 9: 107–39.

Noel, A. (2006) 'The new global politics of poverty', *Global Social Policy*, 6(3): 304–33.

Novitz, T. (2008) 'International law and human rights in the context of globalization', in P. Kennett, *Governance, Globalization and Public Policy*, Cheltenham: Edward Elgar, pp. 107–30.

Nyamu-Musembi, C. and A. Cornwall (2004) *What Is the 'Rights-based Approach' All About?*, Brighton: Institute of Development Studies.

Oberleitner, G. (2005) 'Human security: a challenge to international law?', *Global Governance*, 11: 185–203.

Ogbaharya, D. G. (2008) '(Re-)building governance in post-conflict Africa: the role of the state and informal institutions', *Development in Practice*, 18(3): 395–402.

Ohiorhenuan, J. and F. Stewart (2008) *Post-Conflict Economic Recovery: Enabling Local Ingenuity*, New York: UNDP.

Onuf, N. (1989) *World of Our Making: Rules and Rule in Social Theory and International Relations*, Columbia: University of South Carolina Press.

Onuma, Y. (2003) 'International law in and with international politics: the functions of international law in international society', *European Journal of International Law*, pp. 105–39.

Orwell, G. (1950) *Nineteen Eighty-Four*, London: Penguin.

Owen, T. (2004) 'Human security – conflict, critique and consensus: colloquium remarks and a proposal for a threshold-based defintion', *Security Dialogue*, 35(3): 373–87.

Paris, R. (2001) 'Human security: paradigm shift or hot air?', *International Security*, 26(2): 87–102.

— (2004) *At War's End*, Cambridge: Cambridge University Press.

Park, S. (2005) 'Norm diffusion within international organizations: a case study of the World Bank', *Journal of International Relations and Development*, 8: 111–41.

Patomaki, H. (2008) *The Political Economy of Global Security: War, future crises and changes in global governance*, Abingdon: Routledge.

Payne, A. (2005) *The Global Politics of Unequal Development*, London: Palgrave Macmillan.

Pemberton, S. (2004) 'A theory of moral indifference: understanding the production of harm by capitalist society', in P. Hillyard, C. Pantazis, S. Tombs and D. Gordon, *Beyond Criminology: Taking Harm Seriously*, London: Pluto, pp. 67–83.

Peters, D. (2008) 'Scientific approaches to understanding and reducing poverty', *Annals of the New York Academy of Sciences*, pp. 1–34.

Peters, D., A. Garg, A. Bloom, G. Walker, W. Brieger and M. Rahman (2007) 'Scientific approaches to understanding and reducing poverty', *Annals of the New York Academy of Sciences*.

Peterson, V. S. (1992) *Gendered States: Feminist (Re)Visions of International Relations Theory*, Boulder, CO: Lynne Rienner.

Phillips, N. (2006) 'Latin America in the global political economy', in G. R. Underhill, *Political Economy and the Changing Global Order*, Oxford: Oxford University Press, pp. 332–43.

Piachaud, J. (2008) 'Global health and human security', *Medicine, Conflict and Survival*, pp. 1–4.

Pogge, T. (2002) *World Poverty and Human Rights*, Cambridge: Polity.

— (2008) *World Poverty and Human Rights*, Cambridge: Polity.

Polanyi, K. (2002) *The Great Transformation: The Political and Economic Origins of Our Time*, Boston, MA: Beacon Press.

Porta, D. and Y. Meny (1997) *Democracy and Corruption in Europe*, London: Pinter.

Preiswerk, R. (1982) 'Could we study International Relations as if people mattered?', in R. Falk, S. K. Kim and S. H. Mendlowitz, *Toward a Just World Order*, Boulder, CO: Westview, pp. 175–97.

Procacci, G. (1991) 'Social economy and the government of poverty', in G. Burchell, C. Gordon and P. Miller, *The Foucault Effect*, Chicago, IL: University of Chicago Press, pp. 151–67.

Pugh, M. (2005) 'The political economy of peacebuilding: a critical theory perspective', *International Journal of Peace Studies*, 10(2): 23–42.

Rae, H. (2008) 'Theories of state formation', in M. Griffiths, *International Relations Theory for the Twenty-first Century*, London: Routledge, pp. 123–34.

Randall, V. and P. Burnell (2005) *Politics in the Developing World*, Oxford: Oxford University Press.

Randall, V. and R. Theobald (1985) *Political Change and Underdevelopment: A Critical Introduction to Third World Politics*, London: Macmillan.

Rao, V. and M. Woolcock (2007) 'The disciplinary monopoly in development research at the World Bank', *Global Governance*, 13: 479–84.

Rapley, J. (2004) *Globalization and Inequality: Neoliberalism's Downward Spiral*, London: Lynne Rienner.

Raymond, G. (1997) 'Neutrality norms and the balance of power', *Cooperation and Conflict*, 32(2): 123–46.

RBM (2008) Roll Back Malaria, 9 April, rbm.who.int/cmc_upload/0/000/015/363/RBM Infosheet_10.htm, accessed 9 April 2008.

Reiman, J. (1979) *The Rich Get Rich, the Poor Get Prison: Ideology, class and criminal justice*, Chichester: Wiley.

Reinert, E. (2007) *How Rich Countries Got Rich ... And Why Poor Countries Stay Poor*, New York: Carroll and Graf.

Reynaud, E. (2002) *The Extension of Social Security Coverage: The approach of the International Labour Office*, Geneva: ILO.

Richmond, O. (2005) 'Understanding the liberal peace', Experts Seminar, Transformation of War Economies, University of Plymouth.

— (2008) *Peace in International Relations*, London: Routledge.

Riley, S. (1998) 'The political

economy of anti-corruption strategies in Africa', *European Journal of Development Research*, 10(1): 129–59.

Risse, T., C. Ropp and K. Sikkink (1999) *The Power of Human Rights: International Norms and Domestic Change*, New York: Cambridge University Press.

Risse-Kappen, T. (1995) 'Bringing transnational relations back in: introduction', in T. Risse-Kappen, *Bringing Transnational Relations Back In*, Cambridge: Cambridge University Press, pp. 3–33.

Ritzen, J. (2005) *A Chance for the World Bank*, London: Anthem.

Roberts, D. (2001) *Political Transition in Cambodia 1991–1999: Power, Elitism and Democracy*, London: Curzon Routledge.

— (2008a) *Human Insecurity: Global Structures of Violence*, London: Zed Books.

— (2008b) 'Hybrid polities and indigenous pluralities: advanced lessons in statebuilding', *Journal of Intervention and Statebuilding*, 2(1): 379–402.

— (2008c) 'Postconflict statebuilding and state legitimacy: from negative to positive peace?', *Development and Change*, 39(4): 537–55.

— (2008d) 'The science of human security: a response from political science', *Journal of Medicine, Conflict and Survival*, 24(1): 16–22.

— (2008e) 'The superficiality of statebuilding in Cambodia: patronage and clientelism as enduring forms of politics', in R. Paris and T. Sisk, *Postwar Statebuilding*, London: Routledge.

Rodrik, D. (2007) *One Economics, Many Recipes: Globalization, Institutions and Economic Growth*, Princeton, NJ: Princeton University Press.

Rose, N. (2007) 'The death of the social? Refiguring the territory of government', in V. Ritu, *Globalization and Welfare: A critical reader*, London: Palgrave, pp. 195–211.

Rosen, G. (1993) *A History of Public Health*, Baltimore, MD: Johns Hopkins University Press.

Rosenau, J. N. (1995) 'Governance in the twenty-first century', *Global Governance* 1(1): 13–43.

Rosenau, J. and E.-O. Czempiel (1992) *Governance without Government: Order and change in world politics*, Cambridge: Cambridge University Press.

Rowlands, J. (2008) 'Good governance and development; public administration and democratic governance: governments serving citizens; learning civil societies: shifting contexts for democratic planning and governance', Book review, *Development in Practice*, 18(6): 801–4.

Ruggie, J. (1982) 'International regimes, transactions, and change: embedded liberalism in the postwar economic order', *International Organisation*, 36(2): 379–415.

— (2001) 'global_governance.net: the global compact as learning network', *Global Governance*, 7: 371–8.

— (2003) 'Taking embedded liberalism global: the corporate connection', in D. Held, *Taming Globalization*, Cambridge: Polity, pp. 93–129.

Rupert, M. (2005) 'Class powers and the politics of global governance', in M. Barnett and R. Duvall, *Power in Global Governance*, Cambridge: Cambridge University Press, pp. 205–28.

Schmidt, S., C. Lande and L. Guasti (1977) *Friends, Followers and Factions: A Reader in Political Clientelism*, Berkeley: University of California Press.

Scholte, J. A. (2005) *Globalization: A Critical Introduction*, London: Palgrave.

Schwartz, J., S. Hahn and I. Bannon (2004) *The Private Sector's Role in the Provision of Infrastructure in Post-Conflict Countries*, Washington, DC: Public-Private Infrastructure Advisory Facility.

Sen, G. and P. Ostlin (2007) *Unequal, Unfair, Ineffective and Inefficient – Gender Inequity in Health: Why it exists and how we can change it*, Sweden: Karolinska Institutet.

Serrand, N. and J. E. Stiglitz (2008) *The Washington Consensus Reconsidered*, Oxford: Oxford University Press.

Sheehan, M. (2006) *International Security: An Analytical Survey*, Boulder, CO: Lynne Rienner.

Singer, P. (2009) *The Life You Can Save: Acting Now to End World Poverty*, London: Picador.

Sissener, T. (2001) *Research for Development and Justice*, Chr. Michelsen Institute, www.cmi.no/ publications/ file/?910 =anthropological-perspectives-on-corruption, accessed 16 January 2009.

Skogly, S. (1999) 'The position of the World Bank and the International Monetary Fund in the human rights field', in R. Hanski and M. Suksi, *An Introduction to the International Protection of Human Rights*, Turku Institute for Human Rights, pp. 231–50.

Slaughter, A.-M., A. S. Tulmello and S. Wood (1998) 'International law and international relations theory: a new generation of legal scholarship', *American Journal of International Law*, 92: 367–97.

Slaughter-Burley, A.-M. (1993) 'International law and international relations theory: a dual agenda', *American Journal of International Law*, 87: 205–39.

Slaymaker, T. and P. Newborne (2004) *Implementation of Water Supply and Sanitation Programmes under PRSPs: Synthesis of research findings from sub-Saharan Africa*, London: Overseas Development Institute and WaterAid.

Smith, A., A. Stenning and K. Willis (2008) *Social Justice and Neo-liberalism: Global Perspectives*, London: Zed Books.

Smith, R. K. M. (2007) *Textbook on International Human Rights*, Oxford: Oxford University Press.

Solomon, M. S. (2006) 'Review: power in global governance', *International Studies Review*, 8(2): 327–9.

Sorensen, G. (2006) 'Liberalism of restraint and liberalism of imposition: liberal values and world order in the new millennium', *International Relations*, 20(3): 251–72.

Sorensen, J. (2001) 'Balkanism and the new radical interventionism: a structural critique', *International Peacekeeping*, 9(1): 1–22.

Spence, M. (2008) *The Growth Report: Strategies for Sustained Growth and Inclusive Development*, London: Commission on Growth and Development.

Spicker, P. (2005) 'Targeting, residual welfare and related concepts: modes of operation in public policy', *Public Administration*, 83(2): 345–65.

Stiglitz, J. (2002) *Globalization and Its Discontents*, London: Penguin.

Stoett, P. (1999) *Human and Global Security: An Exploration of Terms*, Toronto: University of Toronto Press.

Stoker, G. (1998) 'Governance as theory: five propositions', *International Social Science Journal*, 155: 17–28.

Stoltenberg, J. (2006) 'Our children: the key to our common future', *The Lancet*, 368(9541): 1042–7.

Strange, S. (1999) 'The Westfailure System', *Review of International Studies*, 25: 345–54.

Suhrcke, M. (2006) 'The contribution of health to the economy in the European Union', *Public Health: Journal of the Royal Institute of Public Health*, 120: 994–1001.

Suleiman, E. and J. Waterbury (1990) *The Political Economy of Public Sector Reform and Privatization*, Boulder, CO: Westview.

Sylvester, C. (1994) *Feminist Theory and International Relations in a Postmodern Era*, Cambridge: Cambridge University Press.

Taback, N. and R. Coupland (2007) 'The science of human security', *Medicine, Conflict and Survival*, 23(1): 3–9.

— (2008) 'Commentary', *Medicine, Conflict and Survival*, 23(3): 23–4.

Tagliabue, J. (2002) 'As multinationals run the taps, anger rises over water for profit', *New York Times*, 26 August.

Talbot, J. (2002) 'Is the international water business really a business?', World Bank Water and Sanitation Lecture Series, Washington, DC, 13 February.

Tambiah, S. (1977) 'The galactic polity: the structure of traditional kingdoms in Southeast Asia', *Annals of the New York Academy of Sciences*.

Taylor, A. (2007) 'Governing the globalization of public health', in R. Cook and C. Ngwena, *Health and Human Rights*, London: Ashgate, pp. 525–33.

Taylor, M. (2008) 'Development economics in the wake of the Washington Consensus: from Smith to smithereens?', *International Political Science Review*, 29(5): 543–56.

Tharoor, S. (2005) 'Saving humanity from hell: the failure of the UN to make heaven on earth should not obscure its mundane achievements', *New Internationalist*, January.

Thomas, C. and M. Weber (2004) 'The politics of global health governance: whatever happened to "health for all by the year 2000"?', *Global Governance*, 10: 187–205.

Thomas, N. and W. T. Tow (2002) 'The utility of human security: sovereignty and humanitarian intervention', *Security Dialogue*, 33(2): 177–92.

Thomson, J. (1993) 'Norms in International Relations: a conceptual analysis', *International Journal of Group Tensions*, 23(1): 67–83.

Tiihonen, S. (2003) *The History of Corruption in Central Government*, Amsterdam: IOS Press.

Townsend, P. and D. Gordon (2002) *World Poverty: New policies to defeat an old enemy*, Bristol: Policy Press.

Turay, J. (2009) Interview with author, Crab Town Slum, Sierra Leone, 8 June.

UN (2006) *United Nations Human Development Report*, New York: United Nations.

UNDAF (2007) *Peace Consolidation and Accelerating Development 2008–2010*, United Nations Country Team Sierra Leone,

www.undp.org/execbrd/word/
UNDAF%20RMs/SIERRA%20
LEONE%20-%20Draft%20
UNDAF%20MATRIX.doc.

UNDP (1994) *Human Development Report*, New York: UNDP.

— (2008) *Human Development Report 2007/2008: Fighting climate change: Human solidarity in a divided world*, New York: UNDP.

UNHDR (2006) *Human Development Report 2006 – beyond scarcity: power, poverty and the global water crisis*, New York: United Nations.

UNICEF (2007) *Progress for Children: A World Fit for Children Statistical Review*, New York: UNICEF.

Van Lerberghe, W., C. Conceicao, W. van Damme and P. Ferrinho (2002) 'When staff is underpaid: dealing with individual coping strategies of health personnel', *Bulletin of the World Health Organisation*, 80(7): 581–4.

Veitch, S. (2007) *Law and Irresponsibility: On the legitimation of human suffering*, London: Routledge-Cavendish.

Vetterlein, A. (2007) 'Economic growth, poverty reduction and the role of social policies: the evolution of the World Bank's social development approach', *Global Governance*, 13(4): 513–33.

Victora, C. et al. (2003) 'Applying an equity lens to child health and mortality: more of the same is not enough', *The Lancet*, 362: 233–41.

— (2004) 'Achieving universal coverage with health interventions', *The Lancet*, 364: 1541–8.

Vij, R. (2007) *Globalization and Welfare: A critical reader*, London: Palgrave.

Wade, R. (2004) 'Is globalization reducing poverty and inequality?', *World Development*, 32(4): 567–89.

Waldman, M. (2008) *Falling Short: Aid Effectiveness in Afghanistan*, ACBAR Advocacy Series, Oxford: Oxfam.

Walker, R. (1984) *Culture, Ideology and World Order*, London: Westview.

Wallerstein, I. (1997) 'Forum 2000: concerns and hopes on the threshold of the new millennium', *Uncertainty and Creativity*, Prague.

Walton, J. and D. Seddon (1994) *Free Markets and Food Riots: The Politics of Global Adjustment*, Oxford: Blackwell.

Ward, P. (1989) 'Introduction', in P. Ward, *Corruption, Development and Inequality: Soft Touch or Hard Graft?*, London: Routledge.

Watson, A. (2008) 'Can there be a "kindered" peace?', *Ethics and International Affairs*, 22(1): 35–42.

Watson, G. (2009) 'View from the basement', *Times Higher Education Supplement*, 16 April, pp. 42–7.

Watson, M. (2007) 'IPE, neoclassical economics and everyday life: moral critique versus moral theory in critical IPE', PERC Workshop, Sheffield: University of Sheffield.

Watts, S. J. (2003) *Disease and Medicine in World History*, London: Routledge.

Weaver, C. (2007) 'The world's bank and the bank's world', *Global Governance*, 13: 493–512.

Weaver, C. and R. J. Leiteritz (2005) 'Our poverty is a world full of dreams: reforming the World Bank', *Global Governance*, 11: 369–88.

Weaver, C. and S. Park (2007) 'The role of the World Bank in poverty alleviation and human development in the twenty-first century: an introduction', *Global Governance*, 13: 461–8.

Weiss, L. (2000) 'Globalization and the myth of the powerless state', in R. Higgott and E. Elgar (eds), *The Political Economy of Globalization*, Cheltenham: Palgrave Macmillan.

Wendt, A. (1999) *Social Theory of International Politics*, Cambridge: Cambridge University Press.

— (2003) 'Why a world state is inevitable', *European Journal of International Relations*, pp. 491–542.

WHO (1995) *The World Health Report 1995: Bridging the Gaps*, Geneva: World Health Organization.

— (2007) *The World Health Report 2007: A Safer Future – Global Public Health Security in the 21st Century*, Geneva: World Health Organization.

— (2008) *World Health Organization World Health Statistics*, Geneva: World Health Organization.

Wight, C. (2006) *Agents, Structures and International Relations: Politics as Ontology*, Cambridge: Cambridge University Press.

Wilkinson, R. (2004) 'Introduction', in R. Wilkinson, *The Global Governance Reader*, London: Routledge.

Wilkinson, R. and K. Pickett (2009) *The Spirit Level: Why More Equal Societies Almost Always Do Better*, London: Allen Lane.

Williams, D. and T. Young (1994) 'Governance, the World Bank and liberal theory', *Political Studies*, XLII: 84–100.

Williams, M. (1994) *International Economic Organisations and the Third World*, London: Harvester Wheatsheaf.

Wood, G. and I. Gough (2006) 'A comparative welfare regime approach to global social policy', *World Development*, 34(10): 1696–712.

World Bank (1989) *Sub-Saharan Africa: From Crisis to Sustainable Growth*, Washington, DC: World Bank.

— (1998) *Development and Human Rights: The Role of the World Bank*, Washington, DC: World Bank.

— (2001) *World Development Report 2000–2001: Attacking Poverty*, New York: Oxford University Press.

— (2004) *World Development Report 2004*, Washington, DC: World Bank.

— (2007a) *World Development Indicators Database*, siteresources. worldbank.org/DATASTATISTICS/Resources/GNIPC.pdf, accessed 30 March 2009.

— (2007b) *Implementation and Completion and Results Report ICR134*, Washington, DC: World Bank.

— (2008) Development Committee Documentation and Statements, web.World Bank.org/WBSITE/EXTERNAL/DEVCOMMEXT/0,, menuPK:60001657~pagePK:64001141~piPK:64001176~theSitePK:277473,00.html, accessed 12 February 2009.

Yeates, N. (2001) *Globalization and Social Policy*, London: Sage.

— (2005) *Globalisation and Social Policy in a Development Context: Regional Responses*, Geneva: United Nations Research Institute for Social Development (UNRISD).

Young, T. (1994) '"A project to be realised": global liberalism and contemporary Africa', *Millennium: Journal of International Studies*, 24(3): 527–46.

Zalewski, M. (2006) 'Survival/representation', in M. de Goede, *International Political Economy and Poststructural Politics*, London: Palgrave, pp. 25–42.

Zizek, S. (2002) *Looking Awry*, Cambridge, MA: MIT Press.

INDEX

118, 121, 122, 124, 127, 128, 131, 144, 147, 150, 154, 158, 164, 165
Held, David, 50, 52, 73, 75
Held, Virginia, 52
Helleiner, Gerald, 77, 129
Hemson, David, 97
Hopenhayn, Martin, 49
Horkheimer, 79
Hout, Will, 118
Hudson, Heidi, 9
human nature, 3, 4, 10, 31, 78, 111
human security: and biopolitics/ biopower, 23, 41, 44, 45, 146, 163, 165; and biopoverty, 45, 116, 132, 134, 163, 164, 165; and child mortality, 6, 72, 109, 135, 140, 141, 145, 146, 162; and democracy, 116, 117; and denial, 80, 81; and global governance, 21, 50, 52, 54, 106, 145, 164, 165; and international law, 116; and medical science/health, 54–61, 69, 70; and norms, 156, 157, 164; and poverties approach, 140; and power, 5, 6, 13, 17, 20, 22, 24, 26, 30; and social policy, 98, 100, 105, 106; and World Bank, 116, 117, 124; as bio-life, 26, 41, 45; as neoimperial, 19; as structural violence, 12; co-option of, 18, 19, 51; definitions, 9, 15, 16, 17, 18, 25, 146, 160, 161; inclusion/ exclusion of, 9, 10, 15, 16, 17, 18, 19, 20, 21, 51; variant (broad), 1, 4, 5, 15, 16, 18, 19, 20, 21, 22, 23, 25, 30, 41, 42, 48, 51, 53, 55, 57, 58, 61, 69, 70, 144, 145, 146, 160; variant (narrow), 9, 11, 16, 18, 19, 22, 25, 146; policy incoherence, 15, 19, 20, 55, 105; rationale, 1, 4, 16, 21, 22, 160; redefining, 25, 160, 161; reification of, 22, 23, 25, 42, 44, 45, 55, 109; sector-wide approach, 135
Huxley, Aldous, 5

ideas: as determinative, 2, 3, 29, 33,
38, 115, 155; as constructs, 3; as global governance, 3, 7, 13, 20, 29, 35, 46, 48, 54, 132; as hegemonic, 32, 33, 46; as norms, 6, 20, 33, 115, 120, 150, 158; as power, 13, 20, 31, 32, 38, 48
IMF, 36, 83, 89, 96, 107, 109, 113, 117, 118, 125, 126, 128
indigenous capacity: and building, 131; and local entrepreneurship, 131, 132, 133; and mobilization, 131; and structural inhibitors, 130–2, 137; and UNDP, 132, 133; and the World Bank, 134
indirect violence, 12, 13, 14, 155
Ingebritsen, Christine, 148
International Development Association (IDA), 123, 125
international law: 111, 112, 113; and change in, 114–15; and human rights, 112, 113; and international governmental organizations, 111; and IGO impunity, 113; and international relations, 114–16; and water, 113;
international relations: and colonial/ postcolonial state, 88, 89, 92, 99, 149; and international law, 111, 114, 115; and international organizations, 9, 117, 121; and masculinity, 12; and ontology-epistemology, 7, 12, 19, 20, 30, 33, 39, 41, 46, 50, 54–6, 76, 77, 80–1, 114–16, 119, 146, 150, 161, 162, 165; and power, 12; liberal theories of, 4, 10, 11, 27, 119; and Weberian state, 37, 52, 88, 163
international security, 5, 12, 13, 16, 18; and populations, as security referent, 22, 23, 24, 25, 26, 38, 40, 43, 45, 109, 112, 140; and 'speech act', 16; as subjective, 18

Jackson, Robert, 3, 11
Johnstone, Ian, 31
Johnstone, P., 91
Jones, Gareth, 57

and global governance, 35, 36, 41;
and Post-Washington Consensus,
124; and privatization, 73, 84;
and social policy, 52, 53, 60, 101,
102, 103, 107; and World Bank,
83, 112; as an idea/belief system,
3, 7, 13, 20, 29, 35, 46, 48, 54, 74,
76, 132; as asymmetrical, 13, 20,
30, 38, 39, 41, 42, 46, 121, 146,
156, 165; as biopolitical, 38, 42; as
dystopic, 145; as hegemonic, 34,
35, 79, 81, 121, 144, 164; as social
construct, 5, 7, 81; as structurally
destructive, 26, 51, 78, 88, 89, 146;
epistemology and ontology of, 78,
80, 81; exclusion from, 63, 65, 76,
98; requirements for engagement
with, 62–7; universalism of, 4, 117
Newborne, Peter, 135
Newman, Ted, 13, 57
Nielson, Daniel, 119–22, 130
norms, meaning, 147–50; and change,
150–9; and entrepreneurs, 151,
152, 156, 157, 162; and life-cycle,
150, 151; and tipping points, 141,
152, 153, 157, 158; and cascade,
141, 152, 153, 158; and internalization, 153, 154; and examples,
124–7, 154–5
Novitz, Tonia, 82
nuclear weapons, 10, 16, 149
Nye, Joseph, 29, 117

Oberleitner, Gerd, 17, 20
Ogbaharya, Daniel, 87
Ohiorhenuan, John, 133, 134, 139
Onuma, Yasuaki, 114
Orwell, George, 5
Owen, Taylor, 21, 44, 45, 57
Oxfam, 134

Paris, Roland, 17, 18, 37
Patomaki, Heikki, 10
Pattberg, Klaus, 28
Payne, Anthony, 31, 74, 77, 81, 82
Pelassy, Dominique, 87
Pemberton, Simon, 59, 81, 108

Peterson, V. Spike, 12, 60
physiology: and biological life, 26,
97; and biopolitical resistance,
85; and biopoverty, 26, 110; and
epidemiology, 143; and human
needs, 1, 25, 26, 97; and neoliberal
illogic/dysfunctionalism, 117; and
water, 85, 109; and World Bank,
117; as defining human security, 1,
25, 110, 163
Piachaud, Jack, 55, 57
Pickett, Kate, 78
Piper, Nicola, 77, 99, 103
Pogge, Thomas, 6, 52, 60
Polanyi, Karl, 48, 49
Porta, Donatella, 90, 92
Porter, Doug, 50, 73, 76
Post-Washington Consensus: and
global social policy, 53, 99, 100,
101, 102, 107, 113; and liberal
fundamentalism, 53, 83, 86, 101,
122, 124; and World Bank,
141; as destructive, 76, 82; as
developmentality, 75, 86, 112; as
hegemonic, 83, 108, 122, 124;
definition, 73
Poverty Reduction Strategy Papers,
73, 122
Preiswerk, Roy, 9
principal-agent approach, 119, 121,
122, 124
privatization: and child mortality, 59,
67, 69, 71, 97; and corruption, 84,
87, 90, 91, 96; and education, 59;
and global governance, 74; and
growth, 84, 97; and healthcare,
59, 144; and impoverishment,
67, 85, 88–90, 97, 107, 145; and
literacy, 59; and the state, 36, 67,
73, 84, 90, 92, 97, 101; and water
and sanitation provision, 73, 81,
92, 93, 97, 100, 106, 108, 155, 156;
and women, 97; as ideational, 74,
142, 147
Procacci, Giovanna, 80
protectionism, 51, 77, 80
public service, 88, 89